The Man in the Ivory Tower

Frank Cyril James. Portrait by John Gilroy, 1956

The Man in the
Ivory Tower

F. Cyril James of McGill

STANLEY BRICE FROST

McGill-Queen's University Press
Montreal & Kingston · London · Buffalo

©McGill-Queen's University Press 1991
ISBN 0-7735-0803-1

Legal deposit first quarter 1991
Bibliothèque nationale du Québec

Printed in Canada on acid-free paper

This book has been published with the help of a grant
from the Canadian Federation for the Humanities, using
funds provided by the Social Sciences and Humanities
Research Council of Canada.

Canadian Cataloguing in Publication Data

Frost, Stanley Brice, 1913–
    The man in the ivory tower: F. Cyril James of McGill
    Includes bibliographical references.
    ISBN 0-7735-0803-1
    1. James, F. Cyril (Frank Cyril), 1903–1973.
    2. McGill University—Presidents—Biography.
    3. College presidents—Quebec (Province)—Montréal—
    Biography. I. Title.
    LE3.M217J34 1991   378.1'11   C90-090490-9

The typeface used in the text is Palatino, set by the
Instructional Communications Centre at
McGill University.

FRANK CYRIL JAMES

Political economist, scholar-leader
of a distinguished university, protagonist
of higher learning throughout the world.

Harvard citation, 15 June 1961

Contents

Preface

In 1970, I visited Dr James in his retirement home in the small country town of Amersham, in the English county of Buckingham. We reminisced about "the James era" at McGill University and, prompted by my great admiration for Dr James, and for what he had accomplished, I suggested he consider writing an autobiography.

He did not warm too readily to the idea, but admitted others had made the same suggestion. Some time later he began to collect relevant papers, press cuttings, and so on, arranging them in chronological order and interleaving his private diary notes into the typewritten journal he had kept in the 1940s. To this collection he added two large scrapbooks he had already put together that contained press cuttings, book reviews, and other memorabilia from his early student days and on into the middle '30s. Finally, he began, somewhat fitfully I imagine, to write the autobiography. He had finished five chapters, reaching into his graduate student days at Philadelphia when he died of a heart attack in May 1973.

Although I had never thought of myself as enjoying his particular friendship, he had asked me a year or two earlier if I would act as his literary executor, and I had agreed, thinking I would be concerned only with such matters as any correspondence that might arise with his publishers. But when his will was read, I was surprised to find it included a provision that his private papers be kept closed from researchers for a period of twenty years from the time of his death and that of his wife, Irene James, unless I in my capacity as literary executor permitted access to anyone who wanted to write a biography.

I had believed an autobiography written by Dr James would have been of distinguished merit; a biography of a university principal, on the other hand, however outstanding, I thought would appeal only to a limited circle of readers. My opinion was supported by others I consulted, who were in a position to make an informed judgment. So I did not pursue the matter further, nor did anyone else – apart from one tentative inquirer, who, after he had seen the mass of material involved, was not heard from again. In my own case, I was already committed to the writing of a history of McGill University; the second volume, carrying the story down to 1971 (my *terminus ad quem*) was published in 1984. But in the process of dealing with the important postwar decades I began to think that Cyril James might have been much more than simply a university principal and that there was in this man a story that should indeed be told. I began exploring the private papers for myself, with a view to writing a biography. What was begun from a certain sense of duty soon became an enthusiastic enterprise that needed no further justification than its own merit. This book is the result.

The private papers of Dr James not only showed how interesting and significant his career had been, as a contribution both to the domestic history of the United States in the years between the wars and then later to the development of Canada during World War II and the postwar decades, but also revealed the man himself as a complex and fascinating personality. One of his associates accused him of "being looked on by most people as a demi-god in an ivory tower." In public he was indeed of a style and stature to provoke such an exaggeration; but in his private diaries he did not hide his weaknesses from himself, and if a biography was to be written he did not want them to remain hidden from others. What emerges most clearly, however, is that he was a man seized of a dominating conviction – that education was the surest hope for the future of mankind. He was through and through an internationalist and, in the words of the Harvard citation, "a protagonist of higher education throughout the world."

In view of the permission given to a biographer, I have not hesitated to use both the public and the private papers freely. The autobiographical chapters were too long to serve as anything other than a most valuable source. I have, of course, also had access to the prolific material in university reports, journals, and other papers. I am greatly indebted to Robert Young of the University of Western Ontario for his study of the Committee on Reconstruction, and to Gwendoline Pilkington for her studies on the history of the National Conference of Canadian Universities (NCCU). In order to meet changing circumstances, the NCCU has from time to time modified its name (Association of Universities and Colleges of Canada, [AUCC]; National Conference of Canadian Universities and Colleges, [NCCUC]; to avoid confusion I have stayed with the form NCCU – the form used for the greater part of the James period.

A major source of James anecdotes is Edgar Andrew Collard's *The McGill You Knew; An Anthology of Memories, 1920–1960*, and I am grateful for Dr Collard's permission to quote freely from it. I owe a particular debt to Doreen Darby, Irene James' niece, for family information and especially for the privilege of reading, and being allowed to quote from, James' letters to her in the years 1952–63. Mrs Darby has also given me much personal encouragement, for which I thank her most sincerely. Patricia Bates, the daughter of James' brother Douglas, has also corresponded with me and permitted me to quote from that correspondence. Since these ladies were at different times members of the James household, their comments have particular significance.

The deposit of Dr James' papers in the university archives has been fully described by Faith Wallis for the publication *A Guide to Archival Resources at McGill University*, vols. 1–3, 1985. Volume 1, pp. 10–11, lists the records of the Principal's Office 1940–62, access to which is generally restricted. Volume 2, pp. 40–3, describes the deposit of private papers under the headings "Private and Autobiographical Records, 1905–1971," "General, ca. 1925–1952," "Research, 1870–1970" (the earlier materials relate to the history of banking in Chicago), "Teaching, 1924–1959," "Addresses, 1939–1967," "Pictorial Materials, ca. 1925–1970," and "Miscellaneous, 1900–." In addition the Rare Book Department of the McLennan Library possesses the original manuscript of *The Growth of Chicago Banks* and two drafts of James' account of his visit to the USSR in 1959. A cursory glance at Dr Wallis' detailed descriptions shows not only the variety of material in this deposit but also the fact that the papers I have used, although voluminous, are but a small part of the collection. I hope this book will alert other researchers to the rich resources waiting to be explored. The major proportion of the deposit will be accessible after May 1993, but much is already available.

I owe an immense debt to the members of the McLennan Library Reference Department and to Robert Michel and his colleagues in the university archives. Their patience, though often sorely tried, has proved inexhaustible. In that same connection I have to thank Marian Shulman, who, as research assistant, expertly identified many people and places mentioned in the diaries. I am indebted also to Roy Morrison for assistance with the changes in the purchasing power of the Canadian dollar in the middle decades of the century and to Abal Sen, cartographer to the McGill Geography

Department, for the map of James' journey criss-crossing the United States in 1936. Many individuals have contributed information, answered questions, and related anecdotes. I am grateful to them all.

The McLennan Library has generously provided me with an office, and the university has given me the facilities needed to complete the task. I deeply appreciate the encouragement of Principal David Johnston and of the director of university libraries, Eric Ormsby, and all their colleagues, among whom I must particularly mention Associate Vice-Principal Sam Kingdon. Without their confidence and help, I could not have completed what proved a much greater task than I had at first imagined. I acknowledge gratefully the interest and the skills of Véronique Schami, whose assistance in the preparation of the manuscript has proved a major contribution to the venture.

In writing this book, I have become very aware of the responsibility that lies upon the shoulders of a biographer. It is in his or her hands to determine the after-image of the subject, especially when it is unlikely that another biographer will follow to balance or correct the faults of the first. Having now lived intimately with Cyril James for five years, I have a far greater understanding of his achievements than when I knew him in person, and my former feelings of deep respect have been tempered by a sympathetic regard for a complex personality. While this book will, I hope, contribute to the recognition of a significant figure in Canadian and indeed world-wide educational history, it will also, I believe, remind those who read it of Shakespeare's great understatement, "What a piece of work is a man."

Stanley Brice Frost

CURRENCY RELATIONSHIPS

Since money expressed in Canadian, British, and American currency is often mentioned in the Cyril James story, the following table may be of help to readers.

Years	British Pound in relation to US Dollar	Canadian Dollar in relation to US Dollar	Canadian Price Index Fluctuation
1920s	$4.86 US	$0.86 US	$1.00
1930s	4.86	1.04	.80
1940s	4.03	0.90	1.00
1950s	2.80	1.05	1.50
1960s	2.80	0.92	1.80
1970s	2.40	1.00	3.00
1980s	2.20	0.80	6.50

The relationships described are only approximate since considerable fluctuations could occur within the decades or indeed within a much shorter period of time. The last column indicates that in the 1980s a Canadian consumer would have had to pay approximately $6.50 for a "basket" of goods that cost $1.00 in the 1920s.

The Man in the Ivory Tower

CHAPTER ONE

The Early Influences

Early in the morning of 4 September 1939, the transatlantic liner the *Antonia* steamed up the St Lawrence and docked at Montreal. The passengers who disembarked were in a thankful but sombre mood. At Quebec the previous day they had heard the dreaded news of the outbreak of war between Britain and Germany. This morning they had been further shocked by the report of the sinking of their sister ship, the *Athenia*, by a German submarine. Safely landed, they realized they themselves had had a narrow escape.

The passengers found themselves in a country preoccupied with wartime preparations. The official declaration by Canada had not yet been made, but already memories of 1914 were being evoked and everyone knew that the patterns of life were going to change dramatically. The atmosphere was one of uncertainty and confusion.

Among those arriving on the *Antonia* were a young professor of economics and his wife. Their home was in Philadelphia and they were returning from vacation in England. He had been invited to serve as director of the McGill School of Commerce, and with some misgivings he had agreed to do so for two years, while on extended leave from the University of Pennsylvania. He had been recruited by Principal Lewis Douglas, with the strong backing of Chancellor Edward Beatty; his task was to reform the school of commerce, which had been in poor condition for many years. The difficulty of the assignment was obviously now much increased: a Canada newly plunged into wartime preparations would not provide many opportunities for academic reconstructions.

Events at McGill moved rapidly in a way no one could have predicted. Within two months, Lewis Douglas had returned to his natural habitat in Washington, DC, and the young economics professor had been appointed to succeed him as principal of McGill.

Three weeks later, Chancellor Beatty, the dominating influence in university government for nearly two decades, became severely ill. The young professor found himself without mentors, head of a university he did not know, in a country to which he was a stranger, and with both university and country caught up in the feverish activities of war. He himself was untried: he had not previously held any major administrative office. His name was Frank Cyril James.

F. C. James was born in London, England, in 1903. In the family he was always known as Frank. His father, Frank James senior, was employed by the New River Company, one of the predecessors of the Metropolitan Water Board. His position in the company was a lowly one; at the end of thirty-six years he had risen to the rank of inspector and merited a superannuation diploma and a gold watch. The family home was humble, but the father's wages were sufficient to meet the modest needs of his wife and three boys – Frank junior, Mervyn, born three years after Frank, and Douglas, born in 1908. The family's small cottage in Stoke Newington was, in the years before World War I, in the northern fringes of London, yet with easy access to St Paul's and the city. The open countryside was within walking distance, but the weekend footsteps of father and son were more often turned toward London.

As I grew older, we went for longer walks ... Throughout his life, Dad was always enthusiastic about long walks and nowhere was he happier than in London – so that I saw and absorbed unconsciously much of the history and atmosphere of a city that was only just beginning the process of change from Dickensian times that has since been accelerated by two world wars. There were still hansom cabs and four-wheelers, and the automobiles that one encountered were still something of a modern curiosity. For twopence one could travel on top of a bus drawn by two horses from Newington Green to the Bank of England.[1]

These boyhood experiences implanted a lasting affection, so that in later life, in far-off Montreal, James built up a small collection of materials dealing with London and its history. His early years also planted other seeds, which grew into a life-long love of fine books and the enjoyment of a catholic range of literature.

At about the time I learned to read, Arthur Mee started publication of *The Children's Encyclopaedia* in fortnightly parts which (if memory serves me) cost sixpence each. Dad subscribed on my behalf. These were the first books that I owned; the instalments were studied by both of us each fortnight, as they arrived, and ultimately there were eight large volumes bound in red cloth to which I often referred.

But there are deeper memories, and the most precious of them is the hour of twilight during the autumn and winter when most of the day's work was done and the younger children were in bed. Mother and I would sit beside the fire and she would read to me until Dad came home at about half-past six. Usually she read poetry, and I could recite many of our favourite poems long before I was able to read. As I read some of them to-day, or recall a verse on some occasion that evokes it, I can still see in my mind's eye that little room with the flickering firelight reflected on the walls and the tall, handsome paraffin lamp (one of our prize possessions!) glowing above her head. I realise to-day that mother was a beautiful woman, with excellent features and a mass of coal-black hair; even at the age of five I had a feeling of something utterly lovely and secure as she sat there, reading splendid things in a quiet musical voice.

Frank senior was the son of a railway engineer who had gone off to make a fortune building railways in Brazil and died of fever in Campinas; his grandfather and his great-grandfather had been blacksmiths on Tyneside. James never referred to the fact that he and James McGill both had forebears in the smithy, though he must have noticed it. He knew that his roots were solidly spread in the working class of England. (There was also a maternal grandmother who came from Kilkenny in Ireland.) But as the references to books and poetry show, there could be in a London workman's home in the first decade of the twentieth century a meaningful awareness of beauty, literature, and culture.

As Frank James junior approached adolescence, two other influences largely took over from the home the shaping of his future. Theses were his life at school and in the church. The first resulted from that peculiarly English institution, "the eleven-plus examination." Before World War I (and indeed long afterward) children were required without warning or special preparation to write examination papers in arithmetic and English composition. Among the working classes there was little awareness of what was at stake and, for most children, none of today's parental anxiety and feverish coaching. Those children who passed the first set of exams were then set to repeat the performance, presumably with questions of increased difficulty. The few who slipped past both entrapments (the success rate in 1919 for example was 2.04 per thousand)[2] were given free places at "grammar" schools by the London Educational Authority. Grammar schools offered secondary education and the opportunity to pass the matriculation examination of London University. A college education and a university degree then became possible, and a considerable first step had been taken on the ladder of "upward social mobility." In the early decades of the century, especially for a boy from the average working-class family, these possibilities were even more significant than they are in England today.

At age five, Frank James went to elementary school and so in due time encountered the eleven-plus examination; but he was not one of the fortunate. As a result, a career as an office-boy and subsequently perhaps as a clerk was the best to which he could aspire. He had already had a taste of the life of the respectable poor for which he appeared destined. In his autobiographical chapters, James wrote:

Economically, the years from 1908–11 were probably those in which the family was most comfortable in economic terms. ... By 1911 business was once again brisk, and retail prices were rising, but the wages paid by institutional employers like the Metropolitan Water Board did not keep pace with inflation. For the decade that followed ... the family was never wholly free from financial worries ...

During the 1914–18 war, Frank James senior was in a protected occupation, but because many younger men had enlisted he had to work longer hours, and the family saw much less of him. The increased income from overtime pay was still insufficient, and James' mother responded to the government's appeal for women to release manpower from the work force by taking a job in a small-arms factory at Ponders End. This solved the financial problem for the time being but disturbed family life still further. Almost equally disruptive were the shortages of food and fuel that meant somebody, often Frank, had to spend hours lining up outside a shop or coalyard to purchase a small portion of the newly available supply. In addition Frank had a series of errand-boy jobs that took up a few hours each evening and most of the day on Saturday. The family was by no means immune from wartime inconveniences and disruptions.

Before we leave the early home, there is one matter that calls for comment. In this careful account of a family of father and mother with three boys, there is no mention of a sister. Yet a sister appears without explanation in Canada at later stages of the

James story. Possibly she did not live at home, and may have been the earlier child of either the mother or the father. She immigrated to Canada at an early age, a year or two before Frank left for the United States, and she finally settled in Vancouver. Why James should not have mentioned her can only be surmised; every family is entitled to its own secrets. But this reticence does suggest that James' account of his early home was to some extent an edited one and possibly an idealized one. In his later years he renewed bonds of sympathy with his sister. Frank James was to travel very far from his beginnings, but he never wholly lost touch with home and kindred, and as we shall see, his later family relationships accord well with his account of his earliest years.

Relegated with the majority of working-class children to remain at the primary level until he finished his schooling at age fourteen, Frank James junior had no prospects of any better way of life than that which his father had achieved. But the first of many happy accidents was about to befall him. The London Education Authority had further elaborated its grammar school scholarship plan, instituting a supplementary examination for children aged thirteen. This time James was fortunate, and he gained a place at Hackney Downs School, founded in 1874 by the Grocer's Company. He also received a bursary of £15.00 a year, which released him from his part-time employments. In the Fifth Form at age sixteen he attempted the examinations for matriculation at London University, but failed miserably. By way of explanation, he says that his brother Mervyn, then aged twelve, had died of influenza that summer and that he himself had engaged in a number of time-consuming extramural activities.

But once again a kindly fate watched over him. The university had recently decided to offer a Bachelor of Commerce degree, and a dedicated master in Hackney Downs School suggested to the boys who had failed the summer matriculation that they return to the school in September and constitute something new: A Commercial Sixth Form. The master's name was Charles Davenport.

Davvy was one of the greatest teachers I have ever encountered ... short and thin, reminiscent of a Cockney sparrow, he was almost completely bald, and the cloth cap he habitually wore was in sharp contrast to the Headmaster's top-hat. But he taught each subject methodically and with enthusiasm, working every bit as hard as his pupils, and putting the whole of his great soul into the task ... There were seven of us ... Davvy's work bore fruit on December 19th. All of us had passed Matriculation

... As an evidence of Davvy's personality it is enough to say that each of us kept in touch with him by correspondence or personal visits ... when after his retirement from H.D.S. he went to live in Monmouth, there were two occasions on which we drove to Monmouth as a group to entertain him to a celebratory dinner. The last occasion was on August 18th, 1955, two months before his death, and even now [ca. 1971], fifty years after we left H.D.S., the five survivors dine together in London once or twice a year. Davvy's memory is still alive in us.

All of those seven men had noteworthy careers, and each of them recognized his immense debt to a man who regarded the teaching profession as a vocation.

The autobiographical chapters give us a nostalgic glimpse of a teenage summer at this time, but the closing sentences suggest that already James was not a typical young holiday-maker.

From September 11th to September 17th [my schoolfriend] Tugwell and I went to Southend for a holiday – the first that either of us had spent away from our respective families. The days were occupied by long walks, with time for swimming when the tide was high but what astounds me most as I look back over the record is how far money still went in 1919 despite the wartime inflation. We each started out with three pounds. The return railway fare was six shillings and sixpence; bed and breakfast for a week cost us one pound each – yet when we returned home I still had two shillings and threepence in my pocket as well as copies of Dante's *Divine Comedy* and A.R. Wallace's *Voyage up the Amazon* which I had purchased while we were away.

James records that on entering the Sixth Form he received an increased bursary of £22.50 and forthwith bought Johnson's *Lives of the Poets*, Chambers' *Encyclopedia of English Literature* and Milton's collected poems. He adds, "Before the end of November [1919] I started writing up notes on the various theologies, heresies and forms of religion, even though these subjects had no relation to the matriculation syllabus." In this way he began to form the habit of wide-ranging reading that was to characterize him all his life.

The other major influence in James' life in wartime and postwar London was St Mary's Church, the parish church of Stoke Newington. In school, he had not been attracted by football or cricket, although he did engage in some rowing on the River Lea and as stroke-oar led his team to victory in intramural competition. Most of his leisure activities revolved around the church.

Leaving aside the quality of religious experience, which can never be explained, it is almost impossible to describe to a generation familiar with radio, television, gramophones and easy travel, the place that the Church occupied in a comparatively static community fifty years ago. St. Mary's Church, consecrated in 1895, was undoubtedly one of Gilbert Scott's masterpieces in the Gothic perpendicular style and was cathedral-like in its proportions. The oaken pews were hand-carved; the organ splendid and the organist an accomplished musician. The choir was good and the great stained glass windows a riot of colour. Here one was caught up in a sense of beauty such as one could find nowhere else in the neigh-bourhood, and there was also a sense of belonging to a community of shared ideals and common worship ... I became a sacristan and, at that time [1917] my ultimate ambition was to become either a parson or a schoolmaster.

The rector generously gave James and one of his friends free access to the church records. They were thrilled to discover that the history of the parish went back to at least 1313, when the first rector "Thomas de London" was appointed. The two boys decided to write a history of the parish, and filled a drawer with laborious long-hand copies of fascinating documents, marvelling at the staying-power of James Clyve, rector in 1531, who, although ordained a Roman Catholic priest in the earlier reign of Henry VIII, could nevertheless acquiesce in Thomas Cromwell's anti-monastic zeal during Henry's later years, turn reforming presbyter under Edward VI, revert to Roman Catholicism when Mary ascended the throne, accept the Anglican Settlement under Good Queen Bess, and die rector of Stoke Newington in 1562. They also observed the ravages of plague in 1625, when each death from the pestilence was recorded in the burial register with a red cross, sometimes two or three such interments taking place in a single day. The boys' work was a labour of love that came to naught, but it gave them a first-hand experience of the significant past; James retained a reverence for history all his life.

For a boy growing up in the church community, it was not only the sanctuary and its services that were influential. Peripheral to the worship, liturgy, and festivals were sunday school, the bible class, the Good Templars, and the Alliance of Honour.

On January 1st, 1919, I began to keep a diary, and its pages reflect my increasing variety of extracurricular activities, as well as some of my thoughts. On January 14th, 1919, I joined the Victoria Park Lodge of the International Order of Good Templars – and two weeks later was elected secretary. On February 9th, seven members of the Bible Class at St. Mary's decided to form a Stoke Newington branch of the Alliance of Honour – and once again I was elected secretary.[3]

These and similar societies, whatever their proposed formal purpose, served to provide a social life for the church members. They organized outings in summer to local beauty spots and socials in winter in the church hall; they arranged debates, discussions, and lectures. Such activities require organization, direction, and leadership, and Frank James found he had the ability to supply what was needed.

In particular, he discovered he had the gift of public address. While still in his teens, he was being invited to other churches and congregations, to give talks to their societies and organizations. On one occasion he addressed the Upper Holloway Baptist Church, where he had an audience of 350; a little later he became involved in the Harbour Light Mission, situated in a poor district behind the Children's Hospital in Great Ormond Street.

On December 22nd, 1921, I gave my first address at the Harbour Light – on *Christmas Legends*, which was the germ out of which my annual lecture [on that subject] at McGill was to develop – and during the spring and summer I gave several lectures to the Young Peoples Association of which I became a Chairman, and occasionally took the Sunday evening service and preached ... The chief advantage for me lay in the fact that I was learning to marshal ideas, to express them clearly and to gain that confidence which enables a man to get up and face an audience. I have never entirely gained it, and even today have butterflies in my stomach immediately before I start to talk.

In England, in the years before and between the wars, it was the churches that gave many future labour-leaders, politicians, and other public figures their first social opportunities and training, and it was in these activities that Frank James began to develop those powers of administration, committee diplomacy, and public address that in his mature years were to prove so effective.

It was also in these church activities that the young man first found himself in mixed society. In the Good Templars Lodge there were both older and younger members, some of them women with daughters Frank's own age. He discovered he enjoyed their company. In particular, he was attracted by a Mrs Leeper and her daughter Irene, whom he met in 1920 and with whom he shared many country excursions. Six years later, Irene Leeper was to become his wife.

After the important hurdle of London matriculation had been surmounted, Charles Davenport was not finished with James and his six fellow students. Knowing that London allowed external students to register for its degrees, he proposed that the seven boys continue in the Commercial Sixth Form and prepare for the Intermediate Examination of the London Bachelor of Commerce degree. James' school tuition fees would continue to be paid and he would receive the increased bursary of £22.50. Although he would be dependent on his parents for board, lodging, and clothes, with careful managing he could meet his other expenses. With his parents' consent he decided to remain at school and register as an external candidate for the commerce degree.

Davenport had not only coached the boys for the matriculation examination, but had also taught them how to work hard and how to manage their time. He brought them to his house for an hour before school in the morning or met them for a session at the end of the day; he also required steady application in periods of self-directed study in school and at home. James learned to budget his time with prepared schedules, and in this way he was able to continue in moderation his social activities without endangering his academic ambitions. At a club whose members came mostly from St Mary's, he played tennis, and at school he continued his interest in rowing.

Realizing the unusual determination of this group of senior boys, the headmaster at Hackney Downs School brought in lecturers with specialized competence. Consequently, at the end of the first year in the Sixth Form, James passed the B Com Intermediate Examination papers in geography, French, and economics. In the second year, even though Davenport was absent a great deal because of ill-health, James passed the remaining subjects: accounting, banking, industrial history of Britain, and world economic history. These successes meant he had completed the equivalent of the first year of the three-year Bachelor of Commerce degree. At the end of the academic year, he received the Form Prize, a splendid leather-bound *Anthology of English Prose*. The headmaster's summation of James' final school report read: "He is keen and intelligent; can always be relied on to do his best."

On the strength of his success in the university examinations, James applied in May 1921 for entry into the London School of Economics and to the London County Council for a Senior Scholarship, worth £90.00 a year. He was not successful in winning a scholarship, but this is not surprising given the fact that the *Scholarships and Training of Teachers Handbook* published by the Council for 1921–2 records that only 66 Senior County Scholarships were provided for the whole of London that year. (As part of the post-war economy measures, the number of scholarships was being drastically reduced: In 1919 the number had been 102. By 1922, it was 59.) However James was offered a one-year extension of his Intermediate Scholarship, which gave him a free place at the London School of Economics and his old bursary of £22.50. He was now eighteen, and acceptance would mean the limitations of a very tight budget and continued dependence on his parents. In later years, he came to appreciate more and more the sacrifices his parents had made for him, especially at this critical time in 1921. Ten years later, when he began to earn a respectable salary, he responded by assisting his parents to obtain a new house in a very pleasant location in the London suburb of New Southgate. His first book, published in 1930, was "affectionately dedicated to my Mother and Father."

But if money was in short supply, there was much else that made the first years in the university a memorable and pleasurable experience. The London School of Economics, commonly known by its initials LSE, was at that time still confined to the Passmore Edwards Hall in Clare Market. East of Kingsway and south of Lincoln's Inn Fields, the area was a tangle of narrow streets and filthy lanes that for centuries had been one of the worst slums of London. Dickens, with a quick eye for a lurid background, located his *Bleak House* in this notorious neighbourhood. It had been cleaned up considerably in the decade before World War I, but Janet Beveridge's story of the birth of LSE in "environs which maintained their Dickensian character"[4] was annotated by James with the comment: "Dad still thought it rather unsavoury when I went there in 1921." It was indeed a long way from Clare Market to the quadrangles and dreaming spires of Oxford, but Frank James made his way each day from Stoke Newington to LSE with a sense of great privilege and adventure. He kept a meticulous record of his experiences; one of the more lively comments concerns one of his teachers, the redoubtable Lillian Bowles.

Rather untidy in her dress, with hair awry because she was always running her fingers through it, she had a mastery of economic history and could express herself in a fashion that held an undergraduate audience spell-bound. Even today, half a century later, when I re-read the notes that I took during her lectures, I can recapture some of the excitement that she aroused in me.

Another of his teachers was Hugh Dalton, who went on to become a socialist politician and chancellor of the Exchequer, 1945–7, in the postwar Labour Government. James remembers him as "a brilliant lecturer who used few notes and expressed his rather dogmatic opinions in splendid English."

Less regularly, James also attended some courses not on his prescribed schedule, including one on politics given by Clement Attlee, the future prime minister, and others on social philosophy by Leonard Hobhouse. James also audited some lectures on the social background of education by R.H. Tawney, "with whom I was to receive an honorary degree at Birmingham in 1952." A short series of addresses by Sir Walter Raleigh on modern poetry impressed him deeply, and their influence was to remain with him all his life. Two visitors who gave him his first distant contacts with McGill were Professor Frederick Soddy, who "outlined the strange monetary theory that he was later to expand in his book on *Wealth, Virtual Wealth and Debt*," and Professor Stephen Leacock, who must have talked on an academic subject, and unremarkably at that, for James had no particular memory of it. But the young man's mind was wide open, and he was ready to learn about anything and everything. "It was a fascinating way of life and on 16th February 1922 I wrote in my diary (somewhat priggishly but with truth) 'Work occupies so much of my life that I almost love it and am jealous of its company being intruded on by social engagements'."

James was in fact revelling in his first year at university, and was crowding a great deal more than just lectures into his busy schedule. He records that most days he walked from his home in Stoke Newington to Clare Market – a five-mile journey that must have taken him well over an hour. The morning was spent in lectures, but after a light lunch he went, presumably by the underground railway, to Hammersmith for rowing practice on the Thames. He had continued his school interest in this sport by joining the LSE Boat Club and subsequently the University of London Boat Club. "The climax (or anticlimax) of my rowing career came on June 24th, 1922 at the Marlow Regatta when LSE was beaten by Henley Rowing Club in the race for the Borgnis Challenge Cup."

To obtain a degree the student must have spent three years in the college program. So although in September 1922, James sat and passed the examinations for the first part of the finals, he still faced two more years of university study. The extension of his London County Intermediate Scholarships had now terminated and he again applied for a Senior County Scholarship. This would have afforded him a free place at the LSE plus the £90.00 bursary; had he been successful he would have been, like Goldsmith's parson, "passing rich." However, the number of these scholarships had been even further reduced from the previous year and James was not among the successful. He was offered the continuation of his free place at LSE, but the lack of bursary was calamitous. He had no alternative but to seek employment.

Later, he was not able to recall why he opted for the banking world, but it proved a choice of considerable importance. It was in and around banks that he was to finance his future career and to make a name for himself in influential circles. His initial experience, however, was scarcely propitious; he was engaged as a junior clerk on probation at a salary of £87.50 – £2.50 less than the bursary he had missed.

But he was determined not to lose sight of the B Com degree. His free place at LSE was tenable in an evening program and after work he hurried across the city, from Bishopsgate to Clare Market, three or four nights a week according to his course schedule. Sometimes his work detained him long after the lecture hour had begun; sometimes he was forced to miss lectures; sometimes he left the bank with permission to return to complete his tasks after lectures were finished. He rose at six A.M. and regularly walked from home to Bishopsgate, Monday through Saturday. The weekend began when the bank released its staff at about 2:30 Saturday afternoon; the rest of the day he generally spent with Irene Leeper. Sunday was fully taken up by St Mary's, the Alliance of Honour, or the Harbour Light Mission. It was a busy and demanding schedule, but he gained an insight into the significance of banking, and he was not too tired at the end of the working day to respond to the challenges of lectures.

At this time, James' intention was to sit the remaining papers for the second part of the B Com final examinations the following summer (1923). If successful, he would have gained the academic credits necessary for the degree, but would still have another year's attendance at lectures to fulfill. In such a situation, a student was permitted to spend that third year at another university. Two of his professors suggested to James that he could take advantage of this regulation by means of a Sir Ernest Cassel's Travelling Scholarship. In October 1922 James made his application. At the interview with the awarding committee in November, he expounded a proposal to study the rapid growth of the shipping and ship-building industries in the United States. No doubt coached by his teachers, he named the American professor Emory Johnson as the reason for choosing the University of Pennsylvania.

This application for a scholarship to take him to Philadelphia was a major turning point in Frank James' career. It is ironic that the topic chosen and the choice of university have all the marks of A.J. Sargent, a teacher with whom he was not particularly impressed. However, by his own account, he was sent as a junior bank clerk on an errand to the Great Eastern Railway head office. Perhaps a receipt required the signature of the chairman of the company, Sir Henry Thornton; at any rate, for whatever reason, James was introduced into the chairman's office. In conversation, it came out that Sir Henry, who was an American, had been captain of a famous football team at the University of Pennsylvania in 1894, and he warmly approved of James' choice. In telling this story, James added, "Many years later, I was to know him even better as the President of the Canadian National Railway." In commenting on the form of his proposal to the Cassel's Awarding Committee, he wrote, "How much this prospect was inspired by Sir Henry Thornton, how much by Sargent and [Emory] Johnson, I do not now remember." The likelihood is that Sir Henry had very little to do with the matter; as for James knowing him even better in his later career, Thornton had fallen into political disgrace and had died in March 1933, six years before James arrived in Canada.

When the all-important letter arrived at 92 Nevill Road on 2 December 1922, informing Frank James that he had been successful and would receive a bursary of £230.00, almost three times his bank salary, he was overjoyed. He applied to Barclay's Bank for a year's leave without pay, to the University of Pennsylvania for admission, and to Irene Leeper for her hand in marriage. His intention was to spend his third university year in the United States, and then return to England and a banking career. He and Irene were engaged in June 1923, and in September he sailed for Philadelphia.

CHAPTER TWO

The Young Philadelphian

The story of Frank James' first year in America reads very much like one of the G.A. Henty adventure stories popular in the 1920s among British schoolboys. The young hero goes off to a strange country, faces all kinds of new and exciting experiences, is threatened many times because of his inexperience by potential disaster, but each time escapes the danger in a way that greatly benefits him, so that every incident unexpectedly furthers his career.

The theme began to develop while he was still in London. Five days before he was due to sail on the Red Star liner SS *Zeeland*, the shipping company wrote that it could not accept him as a passenger because the new restrictive US Immigration Act made it unlikely he would be allowed to land in New York. James immediately went to the US Consulate where he was received by no less than the Consul General himself, who volunteered to give him a letter to the immigration authorities, proposing he be allowed to land in New York and wait a decision on his case by the Secretary of Labor. Shown a copy of this letter, the shipping company allowed him to travel, but he nevertheless faced the prospect of a stay of indeterminate length on the notorious Ellis Island. However, a fellow passenger and his wife were so taken with young James that the husband, a lawyer, offered to post an appropriate bail-bond so that he might spend the waiting period in their home on Long Island. In the event, the immigration authorities allowed him to land as a student visitor and he had no need of the assistance so generously offered.[1]

After a brief look at New York, he travelled up the coast by steamship to Boston, and from there by train to Concord, New Hampshire: "in 1923 New England was a green and pleasant land of small farms, orchards and woodlands, dotted along the route of the railway with pleasant little towns where all the buildings, including the church, were built of wood and painted white."[2] For a young man whose previous journeying in Old England had never exceeded a hundred miles from London, this seavoyaging and train travel in New England was an odyssey of enchantment. His hosts in Concord were only friends of a bank-clerk friend, but they lavished hospitality on him, and at the end of his stay, the son of the family extended a further invitation to pass a week with him in Hartford, Connecticut. James comments that his diary was filled with names of those who, although complete strangers, "helped, entertained or befriended me during a period of nearly three weeks, so that I took the train to Philadelphia on September 24, carrying a sheaf of happy memories."

But James was by no means idle during this leisure time, either at sea or in the new country. At LSE he had paid particular attention to the business of marine transportation, and during the voyage across the Atlantic he took advantage of the opportunity to gain practical experience of a ship. "I managed while we were at sea to explore every nook and cranny of the ship from the bridge to the engine room and coal bunkers." Similarly, finding that Hartford was at that time a major centre of the US marine insurance interests, he contrived to meet some of the underwriters, "So that I was pleasantly able to combine business and pleasure."

Knowing no one at the University of Pennsylvania, he picked from a lodging list a room in a boardinghouse simply because it was the cheapest offered. Had he received the best of advice, he could not have chosen better. The owners were a kindly couple and the other two roomers congenial young men who befriended him and gladly showed him the ropes of American university life. One, Sydney Hernandez, was a medical student and the other, Chester Comer, a dental student. The latter's home was on the New Jersey coast, and it was not long before all three roomers were taking occasional Sunday day-trips to enjoy the warm hospitality of Chester's parents.

An organization called International Students' House also provided James with social activities, including the activities of the Women's Hospitality Committee (held on Friday evenings).

The whole thing was voluntary and independent of the University, but it worked splendidly. During the academic season I seldom missed a Friday evening, and was entertained – usually on Sundays or holidays – at several Philadelphia homes ... I also met several foreign students studying in other faculties, with whom I should otherwise have had no contact and ... more than a score of us got together to create l'Académie Cosmopolite. I was elected President ... we wanted to return some of the hospitality that we were receiving, by taking over responsibility for some of the Friday evening sessions and offering to our American friends an entertainment that was specifically Chinese, Japanese, Philippine or typical of some country. When it came to my turn I could think of nothing more typically British than a program of readings of modern English poetry, but my effort was well received...

James had found his way back into the student world from which he had been earlier excluded, and in a gracious setting far removed from the plebian grime of Clare Market, he was settling into its pleasant patterns very happily.

Pennsylvania was quietly proud of its history and I was proud to be a member of it. In 1765, it had established the first Medical School in the United States and more than a century later, in 1881, the Wharton School was created as the first university school of business administration in the world. There were many other firsts, and many great names in its history, so that almost from the day of my arrival, my affection for and loyalty to the institution grew steadily.

But James' new life almost ended before it had begun. Naively he seems not to have realized that he would have to pay tuition fees; certainly he was not prepared for the American scale of fees. He had registered in the fourth year BSc (Econ) class, and was asked to pay $325 for the year. With the costs of lodging and subsistence as additional items, this sum was quite beyond his resources. He took his problem to his professor, Emory Johnson, who was also dean of the Wharton School of Business in the university. The dean produced a remarkable solution: after studying James' academic record from LSE, he declared James eligible to register in the graduate school. In the curious ways of academia, graduate fees happened to be much less than undergraduate – in fact, only $110. Disappointed that he could not be a candidate for the BSc (Econ) but relieved that his student career had been salvaged, James registered in graduate courses the next day. He quickly found that what he had lost by way of academic diploma he had more than gained in quality of academic experience. Graduate seminars were conducted in small groups offering opportunity for close relationships with senior professors.

But the decline of his bank balance force him to seek some additional income. Naturally he turned again to banking, but since his seminars took place in the daytime the only job he could accept was as a member of "the night clearing staff" at the Corn Exchange National Bank. Although this meant he had to work from midnight to seven A.M., he found the work not only enjoyable but also an excellent source of practical banking information. Nevertheless, after only four weeks, his academic work had suffered noticeably and he had more than once fallen asleep in class; reluctantly he resigned his position.

The same day he resigned, one of James' professors, E.M. Patterson, called him into his office. Although he knew nothing of this banking episode, Patterson had noticed the deteriorating quality of James' work and wanted to spur him on to renewed effort. He pointed out to James that if he did well in his seminars and presented an acceptable thesis topic, he could qualify for an MA degree. In a moment, all regrets for the missed BSc (Econ) degree vanished, and James immediately began to look for a thesis subject. The $130 he had earned during the four weeks at the bank would be enough to carry him through. The dean readily accepted the subject "A review of the international shipping situation, with special reference to the policy of the United States and that of the United Kingdom."

James found his university courses challenging but enjoyable. He was required to participate in six seminars weekly, each gathering fifteen to twenty-five students to read papers in rotation for group criticism and discussion. Taking part in seminars, presenting papers, and joining in discussions came easily to the young Englishman. His basic preparation by Charles Davenport and the LSE lecturers had been of a high quality, and the years of participation in church societies and mission-hall preaching had honed his ability to organize his thoughts quickly and express himself clearly.

So the academic year passed pleasantly on its way. Friday evenings were spent at the International House, Thanksgiving in the home of Chester's parents, and Christmas Day and New Year's Eve in the warm hospitality of a Philadelphia family. When the Pennsylvania baseball team went to West Point to play the US Military Academy on 14 May, James and his friends made the excursion up the Hudson River, not so much to watch the game as to see that lovely part of the country and wander around the splendid buildings of the campus. On 28 May 1924, having passed examinations in all his courses, James submitted his thesis and presented himself for oral examination by a committee of graduate faculty chaired by Dean Johnson, who subsequently informed James that he had fulfilled all the requirements for the MA degree.[3]

With his first university year in the United States completed with success far beyond his initial expectation, Frank James was now more than ready to postpone returning to England in order to have further experience of this land of golden serendipity. The only problem was money. For the summer, his problem resolved itself in a manner once again unexpectedly advantageous. Chester Comer's family had political connections, and Chester had received a minor patronage vacation appointment at Valley Forge, by favour of the local congressman. There was a position available for another person on the team, which Comer sought and received for James.

This summer employment was another stroke of good fortune for Frank James, but the introduction it gave him to American history was perhaps even more important. It takes more than a book or two or a visit to Williamsburg to enable an Englishman to comprehend the depth of feeling engendered in American patriotism. During that summer at Valley Forge, James had an unusual opportunity to loosen the bonds of prejudice and find the freedom to appreciate and admire the achievement of American independence.

Suburbia had not reached Valley Forge in 1924. It was a small country village, twenty miles from Philadelphia, that nestled between the Schuykill River and the wooded hills behind it. Near at hand was the 'Battlefield' – more accurately an encampment – where George Washington and his army had spent the winter of 1777–1778, which was the turning point in the American War of Independence. One could wander for hours in pleasant scenery accompanied by a sense of history ... Dr. Burk,[4] whom I came to know well, might almost be called the creator of Valley Forge ... the hours that I spent wandering around the encampment with him as my guide, or sitting of an evening in his book-lined study at Defenders' Gate, were my introduction to American history. The preservation of the Memorial Chapel, and the tribulations of Washington's army during that terrible winter of 1777–1778 were his only subjects of conversation, but on each of these he was well-informed and eloquent, so that I was an eager listener.

The boy who had spent a summer poring over the medieval parish registers of Stoke Newington was now responding to voices from the eighteenth century, and was not at all dismayed by their American accents. It was the accent of a country that had warmly welcomed an unknown young visitor and offered him advantages beyond anything he had expected. James was probably unaware, in the excitement of it all, that he was being weaned from the

England of his upbringing; a slow, deep change was occurring, which was to make him, like so many others before and since, a loyal and eager participant in the life of the United States.

The emotional inclinations of the summer were reinforced by practical considerations of a most persuasive character. In a formal report to LSE on his year's performance, Dean Johnson had written: "Mr. James is a student of exceptional ability whose record with us is a most enviable one." Johnson and two other professors, E.M. Patterson and Wendell Philipps, had also pointed out to James the advantages of returning to the university in the fall and registering for the PhD degree. When James raised the inevitable questions of resources, he was introduced to another time-honoured feature of North American university life: the employment of graduate students in junior teaching posts. The intention is both to provide doctoral candidates with the means of subsistence and an opportunity of apprenticeship and also to relieve professors of some of their less-pleasant chores, such as marking examination papers. The system accomplishes these ends with such considerable efficiency that no one has found a way to replace it; it also means that many undergraduates receive less than first-class instruction at a critical period in their intellectual development. In his own teaching career, James tried consistently to develop the advantages and to minimize the disadvantages of the teaching-assistant system, but in 1924 he was naturally only too happy to avail himself of its benefits.

Dean Johnson recommended him to Professor Frank Parker as a suitable candidate for employment as an "Instructor in Finance." James had the honesty to point out to Parker that he knew practically nothing about the American financial system but this admission was brushed aside. He had the whole summer to learn enough about American financial institutions to keep well ahead of the first-year class he would be facing. Parker was more concerned with the suitability of his mind and character. But after talking with James in his office one morning at some length and then entertaining him as a dinner guest that evening, Parker told James he would be pleased to have him working in his area and would recommend his appointment. The salary was to be $1800. Later, James was asked to teach an additional evening course, for a further $400. For a young man who had survived his first year on something around a thousand dollars, this was the prospect of riches indeed.

But he was not yet ready to burn his boats. He took the precaution of writing to Barclay's Bank in London to ask for a further year's unpaid leave, which the bank readily granted him. James does not mention the fact, but he must also have written to Irene Leeper to explain why her fiancé, absent for a whole year, was now proposing to prolong that absence for at least a further twelve months. Presumably he wrote persuasively; the engagement continued.

One other matter deserves comment. In England he had been unusually active in religious organizations and was presumably personally committed to their faith and practices. In the United States, however, he appears to have made no relationships with any religious persons or groups. That aspect of his life slipped away from him, apparently with no sense of loss. It was a choice he never reversed, though in his later years there were occasions when he dearly wished he could. As it was, a friendly benevolence toward the Christian religion and an interest in its welfare remained with him all his life, and at the end, one suspects he was left regretting that the River Jordan is, like all the others, one in which you cannot bathe twice.

Officially registered as a candidate for the PhD degree, James returned to the University of Pennsylvania in the fall of 1924 to continue the exhilarating life of a graduate student. He was still very young – he celebrated his twenty-first birthday shortly after the beginning of term – but he was already included in the academic roster as "Instructor in Finance." The next two years would see the completion both of his doctoral thesis and of his student status. Equally important, they would see James launched upon his future career. It was to develop not in the world of banking but in academia.

Unfortunately James' autobiography was terminated at this point by his sudden death, and his narrative diaries do not begin until 1936. There are pocket appointment books, scrap-books with numerous newspaper cuttings, his thesis and considerable publications and his lecture notes, which record, or allow to be reconstructed, his public activities, but they reveal little of the private man. They do, however, allow us to see that in the years 1924–31, he developed an enjoyable, productive, and professionally successful career. At age twenty-four, he was appointed assistant professor of finance.

Fairly early in his career, the young professor had ceased to be Frank James or even, in a style at that time more American than British, Frank C. James. He had become, as he was ever after to remain, F. Cyril James. There are many possible and even probable explanations for this change, not the least of which might include the streak of showmanship he by no means lacked – a readiness to let his name and his faintly British accent add a touch of class to his public performance. If his American colleagues and students assumed he had a modestly aristocratic background, he saw no reason to disillusion them. Another consideration must have also been a factor. In his activities outside the university, James followed his earlier bent and cultivated acquaintances with bankers. But his name was not one that would readily commend itself to that particular profession. The nineteenth century's most celebrated bank-robber, already something of a cult-figure, was Jesse James, and his brother Frank, who had daringly liberated Jesse from jail, shared his notoriety to the full. In the late twenties and early thirties, a young man named Frank James, seeking to gain acceptance in banking circles would first have to overcome a serious public-relations problem and suffer the brunt of many jokes in the process. But the young Professor F. Cyril James was free to create his own image. When many years later he arrived in Montreal, the university news-release gave his name in full; a reporter at the *Montreal Star* assigned to an interview, asking his editor how he should refer to the newcomer in his story, was told, "Call him Dr Frank C. James – anyone with a name like Cyril would surely want to keep it quiet." The editor obviously did not know the style of the man Montrealers had received among them. James (although he always remained Frank to his family) was flamboyantly F. Cyril from the time he first began to achieve prominence in North America. We can date the change fairly closely. In November 1924 he was admitted to the American Academy of Political Science as Frank C. James; in December 1925 he was initiated a member of the Kappa Alpha Phi Fraternity as F. Cyril, and Frank C. disappeared from public view.

As a lecturer, James quickly revealed his gifts of clarity, cogency, and restrained eloquence. His students soon found that what their young tutor lacked in expertise was compensated by his commitment and his remarkable ability to communicate. The *Faculty Sketch Book* of the Wharton School for January 1928 includes the comment: "Dr. F. Cyril James, recently appointed Assistant Professor of Finance ... is brilliant, colorful, and clever, and teaches in a thorough and convincing manner, making his subject clear and showing an authoritative and colorful background. His flow of English is impressive; his accent is delightful; and his appearance is immaculate." The accompanying photograph shows a clean-shaven James, wearing rimless pince-nez spectacles, his hair parted high and plastered down, so that his appearance, though undoubtedly neat, is as typically American as any Philadelphian could achieve. A little later, when he recognized the subtle advantage of looking as he sounded – unobtrusively but distinctively British – he brushed up his hair, discarded the glasses except for reading, sported a small Guards-officer moustache, and smoked a pipe. But in either guise his image impressed itself on his students. Many years later, they remembered his distinctive appearance.

F. Cyril James was probably the best dressed and groomed man on campus. He fancied British-style striped shirts, with the fashion of that time – tab collars ... He brought, therefore, an urbanity of impressive proportions into his classrooms and was, in fact, a rather splendid role-model for the budding captains of industry and finance that the Wharton School aspired to turn out.[5]

His professorial standards were high, and so was his regard for students. Fifty years after graduation, two of them wrote:

Dr. James was the most articulate professor on the Wharton campus. He could always explain a complex, difficult banking problem lucidly, clearly and easily.[6]

I was not a brilliant student so Dr. James had to work awfully hard with me. He was such a patient and understanding man ... He was the only man in my four years at Penn whom I really got to know well enough to develop an admiration and affection for. In those days, in your senior year, the thesis was the most important work one did. He took the time to teach me how to organize such a thesis and even to write a more understanding report.[7]

James was probably remembering the debt he owed his own generous teachers, and especially the great kindness of Charles Davenport. Students at the Wharton School and later at McGill benefited, as all students do, from the commitment of bygone teachers of whom they had never heard.

James' career as a teacher at the Wharton School was not wholly uneventful. At least two incidents occurred that taught him academic judgments and debates are not always determined on academic grounds alone. In 1932, after five years as an assistant professor, James was in line for promotion. Dean Emory Johnson, from whom he had received considerable help in the early days, now raised objections to his advancement on the grounds that James was not an American citizen. Earlier he had raised the question whether James had a legal right to reside permanently in the United States. These are the kind of objections often raised when the real reason is something that cannot be stated openly. It may be that James was a little too bright, a rather too polished performer, for all his older colleagues to view him with equanimity. Presumably the objections were not withdrawn because he had to wait another two years for the promotion. However, further promotion came quickly: he was made associate professor in 1934 and full professor in 1935.

The other incident, which taught the future university administrator that campus politics and academic relationships can sometimes heat up to truly explosive pressures, also occurred early in his teaching career. It would appear that the Wharton School in the late 1920s was showing signs of age. In particular, the younger instructors were frustrated by the lack of communication between themselves and the senior members of the staff. Years later, James commented: "As a matter of fact I never met Professor Thomas Conway, who was Chairman of the Department of Finance, until after I had been serving for five years as one of his juniors."[8] Although it was Professor Frank Parker to whom James was immediately responsible, his statement regarding Conway does suggest a very odd situation, and one likely to engender jealousies and poor relationships among all members of the department.

Matters came to a head in the 1928–9 session, a year after James had been promoted to assistant professor. He summarized the incident.

One of the assistant professors wrote a book on *Branch Banking in England,* which the University of Pennsylvania Press accepted for publication. When it was already in page-proof form, it came to the attention of the Liberal thinker among the senior members of the hierarchy, who discovered to his own satisfaction that a substantial portion of [the] book had been plagiarized from United Kingdom publications. He sent letters of protest to the University of Pennsylvania Press and enlisted the support of several junior members of the Department, including myself. The whole controversy blew up to considerable proportions and completely disrupted not only the Finance Department but several other departments of the Wharton School. In the long run, before the flames had died down, two of my colleagues had committed suicide, one had gone to the University of Pennsylvania and another to the Department of Commerce in Washington. The only reason that I survived the holocaust was that my contract of appointment did not expire at the end of the 1928–29 session ... So much conflagration can arise in a tense atmosphere from so small a spark.[9]

It was an experience from which Cyril James learned an important lesson: It pays to establish good relationships with junior colleagues. One of his characteristics at McGill in his teaching years was to give particular attention to his graduate assistants.

Two other events early in his Philadelphia years must also have been significant experiences. In June 1925, when he returned to England to sit the final examinations for his London B Com degree, he took the opportunity to travel to France. Unfortunately, he left no record of his reaction to what is always a memorable experience, the first encounter with a truly foreign culture. His travels must have brought home to him how basically akin, despite all their differences, the British and American lifestyles are. The other event followed a year later when he returned to England a second time to marry, on 18 August 1926, his sweetheart of six years, Irene Leeper; photographs suggest that the petite Irene was lively and attractive.

As for James' thinking when he was not preoccupied with his own discipline, a lecture on the subject of "Progress" in 1928 gives some insight into his development. The audience was "the Rydal Forum," which seems to have been one of the numerous literary or discussion groups found in American society. The lecture begins with a familiar time analogy, although it may not have been so familiar sixty years ago. If, said James, the whole history of human existence were compressed into fifty years, forty-nine years would be required to bring the nomadic hunters and food gatherers to the beginnings of agriculture and settlement; six months through the fiftieth year some groups would have invented writing; the printing press would be only two weeks old. He continued:

Only yesterday would they have discovered the magical possibilities of electricity. Within the last few hours they would have learned to sail in the air and beneath the waters ... If we remember those hundreds of thousands of years of human history before the dawn of civilisation, the development of the last three thousand years will assume so wonderful a procession that the simple word 'progress' is hardly great enough to describe them.[10]

Because his subject was so vast James took three themes as illustrative of the whole: international relations, creative thought, and religion. Each one he treated descriptively, hastening over great periods of time, painting his pictures with a broad brush. He then concluded:

If I had to analyse the chief elements that have aided the progress [of mankind] I would say 1. creative and critical thinking; 2. tolerance of new opinions; 3. the ideals of Christianity ...

At the end of his manuscript, there is a list of books that obviously supplied James with his ideas and their illustrations: James Bryce, *International Relations;* J.H. Robinson, *The Mind in the Making:* G. Unwin, *Studies in Economic History;* H.G. Wells, *Outline of History;* H. Van Loon, *The Story of Mankind* and *The Liberation of Mankind;* Frederick Soddy, *Wealth, Virtual Wealth and Debt.* Judging from these examples, James can be described as standing squarely in the general Christian-humanist tradition. But for all his emphasis on "critical thinking," his own thought had not been very critical. He did not, for example, stop to define "progress," appearing to equate it with technological advancement and what he broadly calls "civilisation." However, we have to remember that in 1928 the future looked a good deal brighter than it did after the stock market crash of 1929, the beginning of the Great Depression, the emergence of Naziism and Fascism, and the threats of World War II. Our own somewhat jaundiced assessment of "progress" has the dubious benefit of hindsight. What the lecture does reveal is that James was continuing to read broadly, beyond the confines of his own specialty. In his early years at McGill, professors were often disconcerted to discover that James could discuss their own disciplines with considerable knowledge and understanding. Attempts to lecture to his ignorance were countered with two or three pertinent questions; some of the older professors were inclined to resent this until they learned to take him seriously and accord him a considerable measure of intellectual respect.

So the early years in Philadelphia passed very pleasantly and with a considerable measure of success. But the young Englishman's career in the United States did not really take off until the final years of the decade – more particularly until after the stock market crash of October 1929.

CHAPTER THREE

The Rising Star

Cyril James could not have arrived in the United States at a more exciting period for a political economist than the mid 1920s and early 1930s. He entered the country at a time when a rising tide of prosperity for business and commerce was beginning to encourage the spread of financial speculation to an extent that in a few short years could only be described as reckless gambling. A particularly serious feature of the activity in the year 1929 was the unchecked extension of credit, for buying farms, machinery, commodities, even services such as education, and above all equities on the country's stock exchanges. It was possible to buy large quantities of stock on as little as 10 percent security – and even that was probably borrowed; in a constantly rising market such practices seemed wise investments.

Another dangerous element in the situation was the chaotic state of the American banking industry. Most banks were chartered by individual states. Distrustful of large banking interests and multi-branched corporations, many rural states in particular insisted on single-branch institutions, run by a well-known local resident, whom (the theory ran) friendly neighbours could know personally and trust. Senator Huey Long of Louisiana, for example, stoutly defended "the State banks at the forks of the creeks of this country." Senator Carter Glass of Virginia on the other hand was already calling for drastic measures against "the little corner grocery men who run banks," claiming they were not qualified for the responsibilities they had undertaken.[1] The operation of the Federal Reserve Banks, established by Congress in 1913 and located in twelve major centres, each with one or more branches in neighbouring cities, was intended to supplement and to assist the local banks by evening out the flow of currency and by regulating to some extent the availability of credit. But the banking system as a whole lacked coherence and agreed-upon professional procedures.

When the stock market crash came on 24 October 1929, it was soon discovered that this catastrophic loss was but the beginning of a whole series of unparalleled commercial and economic disasters, plaguing not only the United States but world trade in general. In an attempt to isolate the country from "the European sickness," prohibitively high tariffs were adopted by the US in 1931, with the result that England and most other countries devalued their currencies and departed from the gold standard, while world trade shrank and the American share of it was cut to one-third of what it had been in 1929. Borrowers were called upon to repay their loans, and when they could not do so, local banks, unable to meet their liabilities, were forced to close their doors. State authorities found themselves impelled to intervene. In 1933, Louisiana was the first to close its banks, declaring a "bank holiday," followed by Detroit. After a short interval, Chicago, Philadelphia, and finally New York were also forced to close their banks, ostensibly as a temporary measure. "On March 4 [1933], the banks in all states but one were completely or in great part closed. The central nervous system of the greatest capitalist country in the world had ceased to function."[2]

The people of the United States had elected Franklin Delano Roosevelt as their new president in November 1932 almost as an act of panic. At that time (and for the last time), the inauguration of a new administration took place the following March – for Roosevelt the date was the ominous fourth of March. It is significant that in his first speech "FDR" included the words, "The only thing we have to fear is fear itself." He knew that his priority task must be to restore national self-confidence. The one piece of legislation everyone recognized as most urgent was a new banking law. The Glass–Steagall Act of 1 June 1933 forced a separation of deposit from investment banking, empowered the Federal Reserve Board to further curb speculative credit expansion by member banks, and, as its most novel feature, authorized the creation of a federal corporation to insure small bank deposits.[3] In due course, there followed the innumerable agencies of "the New Deal." But recovery was heart-breakingly slow. For a decade, unemployment, poverty, and homelessness were prevalent in rural areas and city centres alike. Even nature joined in the debacle, producing in the western plains the worst drought in recorded history. Foreclosures on debts were everywhere forcing farmers off their land; "hobos riding the rails," seeking illusive employment became commonplace; nomadic groups of boys and girls, rootless and demoralized, dismayed both social workers and volunteer organizations.

Cyril James, who had come from a working-class home, and had been a barely funded student, had no great wealth to lose. His only income was what he could earn but that, though relatively modest, was fairly secure. In 1926, he married Irene Leeper and brought her back with him to Philadelphia, and as she had (as was then usual) no gainful occupation, he had a household of two to maintain. But there were no children, and he could supplement his regular salary with night-school earnings, with lecture honoraria, and, before long, with book royalties. So there are no signs that the "Great Depression" severely affected James personally, although he must have seen its evidences everywhere around him. H.G. Wells has been contrasted with Charles Dickens as a writer, in that he escaped working-class origins with thankfulness, while Dickens revelled in them with nostalgia. James was undoubtedly more akin to Wells. He was not indifferent or callous about unemployment and poverty – they were the facts of life he had grown up with; as a political scientist he recognized them as major elements in the economy; but he was, in all probability, thoroughly glad that he personally could leave them behind him and go on to better things.

The lecture on progress had been given in January 1928. His PhD thesis, *Cyclical Fluctuations in the Shipping and Shipbuilding Industries*, published in 1927, had drawn favourable comments in both trade and professional journals. But, ironically, it was the stock-market crash in October 1929 that brought James into local prominence. The subject was one he could talk about fluently and with confidence; it was in his field, and there were many who wanted to hear some rational explanation of the troubles that had befallen them. He came forward at that time with bold assurances of future stability. Anyone who could offer prospects of improvement in those bleak months in the fall of 1929 could be sure of an attentive audience, and James began to receive invitations to address business and banking organizations, radio audiences, and women's clubs. In October of that year, for example, he told the Philadelphia Credit Men's Association: "I feel the complete stabilisation of the [stock] market will occur in two or three months, and prices will remain at that lower figure (30% below the pre-crash level) for about a year or two before rising." He added, "There is one cheering thing to remember in this collapse of the market, and this is that credit will be liberalized for the use of industry. Bank rates will be eased, and although business may suffer temporarily from the Wall Street disturbance, it will be greatly helped in the end by the money available for productive instead of speculative purposes."[4]

In the days before radio and television, when newspapers were the main medium of communication, the report of a meeting or banquet was expected to convey the major substance of an address or lecture. Universities were a good source of copy, and some papers assigned a particular reporter to tour a major institution regularly, looking for stories; professors who had acquired a favourable reputation could expect two or three reporters from the various journals to attend their public occasions. Newspapers were also more numerous than they are now; in the 1930s Philadelphians could choose between three or four morning papers and two evening publications, apart from the weekly, trade, and professional journals. As a result, James began to find his name in the newspaper headlines more often. Not only the Philadelphia papers but also those of Rochester and New York began to feature his name at the top of long columns reporting his speeches.

The publication of his second book, *The Economics of Money, Banking and Credit*, in May 1930 was also very timely. This textbook, intended to make his name and to enhance his fortunes, succeeded in both these endeavours, partly because of the immense interest at that time in the subject. The *American Economic Review* gave it careful but favourable consideration, concluding, "The book will find many friends among teachers and students as well as among bankers who do not confine their interest to the immediate details of their own institution."[5] By January 1931, the publishers were advertising the book as having been adopted as a recommended text in thirty-two schools, spanning the states literally from coast to coast and including such prestigious names as Wellesley, Duke, and Brown. At this point, Cyril James had been in the United States a mere eight years and was still two years short of thirty. It was becoming a dazzling performance.

No one, of course, believes in astrology, but when the horoscope for the day printed in the newspaper suits our purpose, there are few who can resist taking note. When Cyril James read the horoscope for 8 October 1931, his twenty-eighth birthday, he thought it worth preserving.

Born on October 8th you are far-seeing and practical. The signs indicate that a business career is the one in which you will shine and succeed. In order to bring out the best that lies in October 8th subjects, they must be in continual touch with the whirl of affairs, and will show great aptitude in out-thinking others ... You are destined to travel a lot. You are attracted by and attractive to the opposite sex, and there is a magnetism about you which invites confidence, esteem and admiration. You should not marry until your position is assured, as you could not tolerate the atmosphere generally engendered by any degree of privation.[6]

James evidently knew himself well enough to recognize that in many respects, the astrologer had drawn a bow at a venture and had scored something very near a bull's-eye.

It is possible, too, that he had already begun to recognize the wisdom of the last remark, but in this instance the warning came too late. One cannot help wondering though, if his brief flirtation, also in 1931, with the idea of returning to Britain, was not prompted by the desire of his wife to be nearer her family. In any case, he applied for and was offered a post at a college in Dundee. But Scotland had little to offer him in competition with the heady life in the United States, and in the end he declined. It would have been an uncharacteristic retreat from beckoning opportunity.

James now launched into a busy period of teaching, lecturing, and writing. Most of his addresses, delivered at meetings of bankers and their associates, dealt with the procedures of credit and the practice of banking. He was particularly concerned with the Gold Standard. Britain had cut itself loose from this sheet-anchor of international stability, and James was at pains to explain to his audiences that this action could offer only short-term advantages. But, he told the Bond Club in Philadelphia the current situation did point to the need for an international revaluation of gold, so that a general rise in prices world wide might result and stimulate production. This, he believed, was the best cure for the depressed economy.

But let me emphasize that the cure must be carried out by skilled doctors. The control of the gold standard, and the formulation of monetary policy must be in the hands of skilled bankers, not in the hands of political parties or Governments. The evils of inflation in the past have been largely due to the fact that it was used for political rather than economic aims.[7]

Many economists would agree that history has shown the general soundness of his views. Government should maintain an arm's-length distance from the day-to-day control of central banking policy. But the notion that economic aims could be separated from political intentions and that the control of the former should be left solely in the hands of bankers sounds rather naïve. The idea, however, naturally appealed strongly to members of "the Bond

Club" or "the Credit Men" or similar audiences. James was soon invited to address an even more prestigious organization, the Investment Bankers Association of America, by contributing an article along the lines of his Bond Club speech to their journal *Investment Banking*.

Also in the fall of 1931, James was encouraged by the appearance of the four-volume encyclopedia *American Business Practice*. The second of forty major sections was devoted to "Money, Credit and Banking" and was contributed by that indefatigable young economist, F. Cyril James. This was a major publication, and participation in its production was a further feather in a cap that was beginning to look like an Indian headpiece.

Early in 1932, his third book appeared – an analysis of Britain's economic woes that, despite a formal disavowal of the intention, offered a prescription of remedies to cure them. Entitled *England Today* and published in Britain, the volume was widely and, on the whole, favourably reviewed in British periodicals. The *Times Literary Supplement* gave a short but typical notice.

Mr. James has given a simple and comprehensible account of the modern industrial, commercial and monetary systems, without introducing any misconceptions of his own under the guise of original discoveries, or appearing to have any particular social or theoretical axe to grind. The purpose of the book, according to the Preface, is "not to lament or advise but to describe". Mr. James is not deterred by this self-denying ordinance from discussing such troublesome topics as protection, government interference in business and the influence of banking policy on the price level; but he succeeds, at the expense perhaps of a certain inconclusiveness, in maintaining a remarkably balanced and moderate point of view.[8]

James was already at work on his next book, *The Road to Revival*; it was published only six months after its predecessor. In this 235-page volume, James set out to do for the United States what he had already done in *England Today*: point the way to a planned economy as an intelligent attack upon what was already beginning to be called the "Great Depression." A comment in the October 1932 *Journal of Business* reflects the favourable reception accorded his ideas in many commercial circles. "At present politicians largely control the economic destiny of the United States; but not a single influential politician appears to have any plan comparable to the plan set forth by Professor James. Not every economist to be sure is ready to follow Professor James all the way; but agreement is so general that if economists were to gain control of the federal government ... the country would soon be on Professor James' *Road to Revival*."[9]

Annals of the American Academy reviewer Alvin Hansen, of the University of Minnesota, was not so unreservedly commendatory.

The medley of reforms suggested by Mr. James is, at present, seriously open to question with respect to its self-consistency ... Social engineering is in the stage that medical science was in a hundred years ago, and economists had much better admit it.[10]

If that was true, James and his contemporaries could hardly be blamed for not knowing all the answers. But James had set out the problem in a clear and comprehensible fashion, and the mixed economy style of society he advocated, a middle road between free enterprise and socialism, appealed to many as an intelligent and practical solution. As one critic put it, James pointed to a middleway between Adam Smith and Karl Marx. A similar comment came from the executive director of the Adult Education Council of Chicago, F.A. Moore, who wrote to James in January 1933: "I have just finished my first reading of your *Road to Revival*, and heartily thank you for such a masterly, clear, reasonable analysis and program. It is most helpful to have a possible course of procedure without tearing our present economic system to pieces."

Moore went on to say: "I wish to know whether you do any or much public lecturing. If you can talk as well as you can write, you can help a lot in the vitally needed endeavour to widen the popular understanding of our economic problems and their possible solutions."[11] The author in question could indeed talk as well as he could write, and consequently received a flood of invitations. A significant engagement was to debate the subject "A Road to Revival under Capitalism" in the Chicago Forum on a Sunday afternoon in February 1933 with Maynard C. Krueger, professor of economics at the University of Chicago. Krueger was billed as "one of the ablest leaders of the Socialist Party, and intimate associate of Norman Thomas," the party's perennial candidate for the US presidency, while James was described as "author of a most important contribution to economic thought."[12]

As 1933 drew to a close, the major concern of the American public in general was whether the "New Deal" promised by President Roosevelt was going to cure the economic crisis, or whether the measures proposed would make matters worse. At the 1933 annual meeting of the American Academy of Political and Social Science, some three thousand economists, bankers, and politicians listened to another major debate. The main speakers were Professor Irving S. Fisher of Yale, who may be fairly described as the then doyen of the American economists, Senator Elmer Thomas of Oklahoma, a prominent Democrat, and F. Cyril James of Pennsylvania. The significance of the occasion for James' development is that it reveals him taking his place, even if modestly, on the American national stage. He was finding his way not only into newspaper headlines but also into the cartoons that commented daily on public life. The Philadelphia *Public Ledger*, for example, regarding the occasion as a triumph for its local champion, printed an apt "steal" from the London magazine *Tit-Bits*, in which a girl is saying proudly to her boyfriend, after he had won prizes at a fair-ground game: "I *knew* you could do it, Cyril, if you tried!"[13]

A significant aspect of this debate was that James supported the point of view of the professional bankers. This was to prove increasingly characteristic of his pronouncements over the next few years and was to make his acceptance by bankers and their associations all the more easy and understandable. Yet the overall economic politics he advocated were not simplistically conservative. He advocated the international control of banking through an institution very like the International Monetary Fund, that was to be established in 1946, and he believed that the use of gold as the international standard for all currencies offered the best support of stability in world markets. He recognized that a degree of inflation was necessary within the United States, but urged that if the federal government was going to create three billion dollars of credit, it should be used not for the payment of debt or the settlement of obligations, but for social programs such as public works, unemployment, and poverty assistance. Raising prices and increasing wages and social welfare payments, he argued, would effectively reduce the value of capital instruments such as bonds and mortgages, and this would put more money in the market place. This in turn would encourage production, because once again things could be made more cheaply than they could be sold.

Cyril James was very ready to admit in these years that neither he nor any other economist could fully comprehend the operations of international finance. But others were not so modest. At the end of 1933, the man with whom he had debated at the AAPSS meeting, Professor Irving Fisher, published a list of nineteen men in the world "who understand the real meaning of money."[14] (He did not include his own name but nineteen is one short of "only a score of men," and he undoubtedly expected readers to make the correct addition.) Among the nineteen names was that of Frank

All the doctors are practicing on Uncle Sam.

Chicago *Tribune,* 7 November 1933

London *Tit-Bits*

"I *knew* you could do it, Cyril, if you tried!"

Philadelphia *Public Ledger,* 23 November 1933

Cyril James – an accolade that, deserved or not, must have made the celebration of that New Year's Eve a particularly happy occasion. If the next decade were to prove as successful as the preceding, the young assistant professor of finance had much to look forward to.

In January 1934, President Roosevelt decided to devalue the dollar. Whereas since 1834 the dollar had been the certificate for 25.8 grains of fine gold, it would now be the guarantee of 15.23 grains. Whereas previously an ounce of gold had cost $20.67, it would now cost $35.00. The currency, while not freely convertible, had at least a fixed gold value; in that modified form, the views endorsed by James had prevailed. The House of Representatives Coinage Committee in Washington had intended hearings on ways to "stabilize the dollar on a metallic basis," at which Irving Fisher, James P. Warburg, a prominent international banker, and F. Cyril James were to be called as expert witnesses. On 17 January, however, the chairman, overtaken by events, announced the cancellation of those hearings, in order to allow the committee to consider the president's devaluation bill.

The proposal to change the value of the dollar and the accompanying plan to transfer into the US treasury all gold holdings in the United States aroused considerable alarm both in banking and commercial circles and among ordinary citizens. Anyone who could explain what was going on was in great demand, so it is not surprising that one of those most sought after was the young economics professor of Pennsylvania. He had decided and clear-cut ideas on the subject and was very ready to expound them. For the next four years, that is, for as long as he remained in the United States, James was busy teaching, writing, addressing societies and organizations, and making authoritative pronouncements on the economic questions of the day. In May 1935, for example, he told the Philadelphia Association of Security Salesmen:

My greatest qualms over the New Deal (and by that I mean the developments not only in the United States, but in England, Germany, Italy and other countries) are over the rapid growth of economic nationalism, the shutting out of international trade. Human progress on this earth, whether you measure it in terms of books, culture and music or in terms of economic improvement, has resulted from the increased supply of goods which came from international intercourse.[15]

To those who read his words fifty years later, the discussion sounds very familiar and the argument just as cogent.

In the summer of that year, a revised and enlarged edition appeared of his book *Money, Credit and Banking*, with a new list of academic adoptions. The text, now in use in some seventy colleges and schools across the United States, was enhancing not only his reputation but also his bank balance. That same year, his appointment as full professor was announced. There could be no question he had earned this promotion.

In March of 1936 and again in May, in interviews and speeches, James could be heard, somewhat surprisingly, still criticizing the financial policies of the Roosevelt administration, which was pre-paring for the November elections.[16] One might have though a political scientist with roots in the London School of Economics tradition would have welcomed Roosevelt's general democratic policies to the point of muting if not silencing criticisms of par-ticular measures, but for James and many of his colleagues the financial policy was the heart of the matter. They formed a group of some eighty economists, who called themselves the Economists' National Committee on Monetary Policy and chose as their pres-ident Professor Edwin Kemmerer of Princeton University, and as their vice-president, Professor Cyril James. Together with Kemmerer and three others, James attended the Republican Convention held in Cleveland in June to urge adoption of a resolution constituting a gold-standard "plank" in the Republican Party's election platform. In accordance with their non-partisan standing, they told reporters, a similar deputation from the Economists' National Committee would attend the Democratic Convention to urge the same policy upon that party; but it was evident to all that their chances of being successful were far greater in Cleveland than they would be in Philadelphia. In the event, the Republican Party adopted a watered-down version of the Kemmerer–James resolution, but added that the return to gold-standard currency would not be adopted until "the conditions were such that the change back would not impair agriculture and industry."[17] In an interview published in a Philadelphia newspaper, James expressed his dis-satisfaction with this weakened version. Later in the month he and two colleagues from the Economists' National Committee duly appeared in Philadelphia before the Resolutions Committee of the Democratic Party Convention, but later that day his only comment was, "I think that it had even less effect than we did at Cleve-land."[18]

The more thoughtful among the bankers noted that James had made various references from time to time to the need for self-reform within the American banking system. These remarks were to have important consequences. In the spring of that same year, 1936, the Association of Reserve City Bankers invited Cyril James to advise them in the matter of banking research, a proposal welcomed by the American Bankers' Association and the National Association for Economic Research, both of which associated themselves with the initiative. As the idea took root that a reform of the banking system from within was overdue, a movement spread throughout the country to study in each state the present condition of the banks and to plan for their future needs. The events of March 1933 were too recent and too sore a memory for anyone to resist the idea. The proposal that emerged in New York was that during the summer vacation, James would tour the interested states, meet with the bankers to receive and share information of their operations and prospects, and report his findings with recommendations to the Reserve City Bankers. For this work, he would receive $1,000 and expenses – this at a time when his annual salary was $3,500. As one state after another climbed on the band wagon, the tour soon began to assume major proportions. In August, the *Southern Banker* reported:

From its start in the State of New York, the study of the banking structure has within a short half year not only assumed national proportions but the nature of the study has been virtually transformed ... As a missionary worker in the cause, Dr. F. Cyril James of the Wharton School of Finance, University of Pennsylvania, is lending a directing force to the task, the beneficial effects of which cannot be overestimated. He is visiting every state in which the movement is taking cohesive form ... The nature of the problems Dr. James has encountered present an almost unlimited variety, and the separate study of these problems, before and after consolidation into a nation-wide survey, will bring to the bankers of the country an implement of immediate utility and value, which can be translated into increased profits, as well as increased efficiency in defeating or forestalling injurious legislation.[19]

This comment on James' visits having a missionary flavour was perceptive. Understandably, the bankers saw his tour as an attempt to improve their efficiency and consequently their profits, but James, with his background of social responsibility and academic training, undoubtedly saw it as the reform of an extremely important element in modern society. Believing in banking as he did, he was sincerely convinced that anything he could do to improve its self-understanding and its administration of the financial aspect of the commonwealth would constitute a positive and constructive contribution. But just as the bankers accepted reform as good for society because it was also good for profits, so, too, although he was preaching a message in which he truly believed, James could not have been unaware that this nation-wide tour was also very good for his career.

Nevertheless, he had to pay a heavy price in undertaking the program. On the road for fifty-one days, he visited twenty-four states. At the time of his visits, the Mid-West was suffering temperatures of 110 degrees Fahrenheit – reportedly 130 degrees in one town his train passed through. On the other hand, outside Denver he saw snow and experienced temperatures in the thirties Fahrenheit. Some of his trains were crowded and not "air-cooled," as he terms it; some plane rides were extremely bumpy (routes did not in those days seek altitudes above 12–15,000 feet); and one plane flew through a severe electrical storm that gave him considerable anxiety. When his hired car broke down in the desert outside Las Vegas, many cars passed before he could get one to stop. On one occasion, at least, his fortitude was sorely tested: "A hellish day! I started out at midnight by plane [from Salt Lake City] and did not reach [Topeka] until 11:10 this morning and, since the trip was bumpy and I had no sleep, I felt sort of weary. When I reached here it was as hot as the inferno (and still is) so that I was not improved in spirits! To crown all, the hotels I wanted to go to were full, so that I had finally to come to this little commercial dump!"[20]

So it was not all first-class travel and luxury hotels, and even if it had been, the effort of so much travelling, constantly meeting new people and adjusting to new surroundings and to different time-zones, would have dampened the ardour of most missionaries, however highly motivated. But James seems to have survived physically without too many negative effects and, apart from an occasional remark about a hot, crowded train or a tiring flight, maintained his equanimity remarkably well. Moreover, he appears to have lost none of his mental energy – at least not until toward the end of his trip, when he confesses to having to whip himself up to face the last one or two hurdles in Baltimore and Greensboro.

In trying to assess what he gained from his immense effort, we must begin by saying that it gave him a breadth of knowledge of the United States that few Americans could rival. We have to add that a side-benefit of great importance to our understanding of Cyril James is that about this time he began to keep diary notes of his activities and thoughts, which give not only glimpses

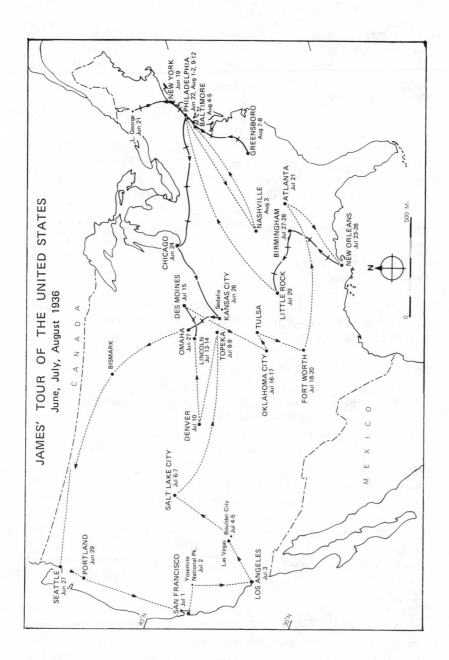

James' Tour of the United States, 1936

of the cities and states he passed through and of the people he met but also insight into the man himself. He was particularly impressed with the north-west states of Washington and Oregon.

This afternoon, between the meetings I had a chance to drive around Seattle a little – and it has captured me. The glorious trees all over the town, and the unusually brilliant colouring of the flowers are unique; so are the beautiful lakes – and so is the stark majesty of Mount Rainier seen across Lake Washington! The whole town is delectable, with its gardens and lawns and its stately trees that are really green – and strangely reminiscent of England ... This N.W. (of Washington and Oregon) has a real character of its own. The people are more independent of politics than most of the rest of the country – and more philosophical! They love gardens and lawns so that their cities are a glory to behold – and they are frank! Moreover, I am told that living is very cheap. I must investigate further ...[21]

His visits to Yosemite, the Grand Canyon, and the Boulder Dam drew more considered impressions, for example his diary entry for 11 July, written at Grand Lake, Colorado.

After we left Este's Park (where I had lunch) the weather cleared – but we found that the higher mountains had experienced snow instead of rain this morning, so that it was bitterly cold after we had passed 10,000 ft. The road actually goes as high as 12,500 ft. in its efforts to get across the great continental divide, and the peaks that flank it are much higher. But all the landscape was a fairyland of snowy mountains, rising up to dizzy peaks above the green pine forests, while occasionally through a pass one would catch a distant glimpse of wheat fields gleaming in the sun, 10,000 feet below and fifty miles away. Iceberg Lake was frozen solid; so was Crater Lake, and there was not much water showing around the edges of the Gorge Lakes – but Poudre Lake, the last body of water on the Eastern side of the continental divide was full of deep blue water that reflected a richer blue sky than I have ever seen before. I go to bed contented and happy: if only Irene were here it would be perfect.[22]

Irene, however, had left for England six weeks earlier, at the beginning of June, and her absence left him somewhat vulnerable. Just as he was responsive to the natural beauty of the places he visited, so too he was not unresponsive to feminine charms. The remark above is the only time in his travel diary that he mentions his wife, but several times he makes comments that reveal his sensitivity to female companionship. As early as the first of July he writes: "But how I am missing feminine society on the trip!" and three days later: "I spent a couple of hours in Las Vegas, one of the really wild and woolly western towns, where the saloons are open all day and all night, gambling flourishes openly and women are licit and unashamed! It was a strange sensation to encounter in real life a place where one could not drink a whiskey and soda without the accompaniment of a blandishing demi-mondaine (and a tantalizingly pretty one at that!)." Two days later he records: "Tonight George Eccles gave a dinner for me on the Starlight Roof of the hotel, with his wife, Mr. and Mrs. Vise and Mr. and Mrs. Fred Smith. It was a grand party – and a real luxury to have feminine company again!" One of his travel comments conjures up a less conventional picture.

After dinner at the Des Moines Hotel R.F. Kauffman took me out to visit Jimmy Darling – a perfectly fascinating man, with a delightful home, where we had a grand time despite the heat. We talked about politics en famille with Mrs. Darling (clad only in a nightdress because of the heat and looking very seductive) and a son and daughter – but later we adjourned to the bar in the basement where we drank highballs and talked about archeology and the lost continent of Mu. I was sorry I had to leave to catch my train.[23]

But on this extended trip, crisscrossing the United States, he could only note the one or two mixed social occasions that came his way, before hastening on to the next all-male luncheon or bankers' conference. That, too, was part of the price that had to be paid.

As for the men he met, he faithfully records their names and makes the briefest of comments about them. One would think he must have become very tired of the heartily warm welcome, the professional bonhomie, and the flattering presentation when he was introduced, but he seems to have taken it all in his stride. Perhaps, although his early days in Stoke Newington and his struggles at the LSE were now over ten years behind him, the fragrance of affluence had no more lost its seductive charms than had that of elegant women.

One notable incident briefly chronicled in his travel notes occurred in Seattle, when he took time off from lunching and dining with bankers to visit with "Florrie." Introducing her without explanation, he says merely, "Florrie arrived from Vancouver today to spend the day with me. She is much more smartly dressed than she used to, and even more loquacious."[24] This is the elder sister or half-sister James omitted from the autobiographical sketch of his early childhood. A letter to James from his mother, dated a decade earlier, mentions that Florrie in Canada "cannot come home until her debts are settled"; the young woman had obviously not found her first years in Canada easy. But by the time she met with her brother in Seattle, she was better off financially and had been happily married for four years, living in North Vancouver. It would not seem the two found much in common to talk about; after they had dinner together they elected to spend the rest of their evening at the cinema. James commented in his diary: "It was very pleasant to see her again – but I fear I should not want to be with her long." However, it could only have been he who set up the arrangement that they should meet, finding time, in the midst of all his travels to think of his sister.[25] They had probably not met since before he had left for Philadelphia fifteen years earlier; it was to be another twenty years before they met again.

Included with the diary of his travels is the original copy of James' report to the sponsor of his travels, the Reserve City Bankers' Association. Fifty years later, we can still sympathize with the typist who had to struggle with his handwriting. But the thought is clear. The area covered is huge – in effect the whole United States – and the interests involved were naturally diffuse, but James succeeds in bringing all his records into focus and makes of them one presentation, from which two or three simple and straightforward proposals for further activity can be drawn.

He begins by emphasizing the novelty of the idea of banking research and the consequent lack of defined goals or well-designed plans of attack. Each state has tended to concentrate on its own concerns, and each state research committee is at its own stage of development. His role has been to encourage the formation of committees where there were none, to enable each of these committees to define its most pressing problem, and to consider how the problem may be overcome. This perceived problem varies greatly from state to state. "Government competition worries a California banker, but not one from Oregon, while branch-banking is an ever-present spectre in Kansas, but concerns Alabama very little." James' solution is to encourage this diversity rather than to attempt imposing a centrally designed and well-coordinated plan, with regard either to goals or to methodology. At this early stage, he recommends, commissions should use the data already available to them, rather than embark on costly new enquiries, and should be encouraged to publish their conclusions as they reach them. James then documents his view of the situation with a state-by-state description of local research structures, including in some cases the people involved, a description of the perceived problem, and (where the commission had got so far) the proposed line of approach. James' draft report, included in his diary, deals with twenty-two states in this way, but the final version probably lists the full twenty-four he visited. If his recommendations were accepted, the role of the Association of Reserve City Bankers would be to encourage this activity, to send an observer each year to the local committee meetings, and to circulate the regional reports nationally. At a later stage, the association could expect to fulfill a coordinating and directing function, bringing all the disparate parts into one unified plan. In the meantime, James' blitz-tour had in his opinion made two things abundantly clear: the need to encourage fresh thinking on banking, and the need to circulate the new ideas widely.

To anyone who has studied banking conditions throughout the United States and is familiar with banking theory and economic history, there can be no question but that this effort to solve banking problems constructively is among the most important things that are going on today. Upon such research activities as this we must depend for any improvement not only in our financial system but in our whole economic environment.[26]

This conviction was James' central concern at this time: economic prosperity cannot be attained without an intelligent, self-aware, well-organized banking system. Whether the bankers would respond to the opportunity he had created for them must be their own decision.

As for James, he was due to join Irene in England. He boarded the newly launched SS *Queen Mary*, marvelling at her size and luxurious appointments. He renewed his energies by lazing on her decks for four days while the ship attempted at thirty-plus knots to win "the Blue Ribbon of the Atlantic." This she failed to do on that trip because of fog in the English Channel. Even so James was in another world, at home in Barnet, Hertfordshire, with his wife and her parents, five days after leaving New York.

After eight weeks of ceaseless travel across the United States by car, train, and plane, being dined and wined on starlit rooftops or "en famille" in affluent homes, James found it hard to cope with the shock of returning to the domesticity of his England-loving wife and her family and to the suburban delights of the Finsbury Park Empire music-hall. Four days after arriving in Hertfordshire, he returned to London to spend all day with

some American acquaintances, showing them the city and the
Whipsnade Zoo and entertaining them to dinner at the Red Lion,
St Albans – but, says the diary, "Bay did not like the whole thing
one bit and was decidedly angry when I reached home around
11:15 p.m."[27] It is clear that Cyril's lifestyle in the United States
was already being seen by Irene as a threat to their relationship.

When Cyril and Irene went off by car to tour Devon and
Cornwall for a week, he recorded his pleasure in the splendid
scenery; otherwise the only times he mentions his wife are when
he is listing the members of a family group engaging in some
social activity.

Last night Bay, Mum, the two Dads and I went to the Finsbury Park
Empire to see a revue, with some very good tunes – and tonight we are
going to see an even more glorified one at the [London] Hippodrome
with George Robey in the cast ... Somehow it seems to have been a very
short holiday this year – all bits and pieces with no sensible pattern. A
few hours at Barnet or Southgate, a few meals at the club with various
people, a very few theatres, a glimpse of Devon in the rain ...[28]

James senior was living at this time in the house in New Southgate
that Cyril had provided for his parents. The absence of reference
to his mother can only mean that she had died, although this
event evoked no record or written expression of bereavement. This
may be due not to a lack of feeling, but simply to the general
lack of written records for that period. At some date in those
"silent" years, the ones between the end of his autobiographical
chapters and the beginning of the hand-written diary notes in the
summer of 1936, an even more important event had taken place
that also evoked no written expression. This was the birth of a
baby girl, who sadly died shortly after birth. James did, on at
least one occasion in later years, muse in his diary with regret
that neither he nor his brother Douglas had left a son to carry
on the family name; but even then he did not refer to the daughter
that might have been. One must think either that in the middle
1930s he was too busy with his career to feel these personal
matters deeply and that they left little mark, or that they were
too traumatic for him to express them. For all his frankness in
his private papers, there are some shadowed recesses that he did
not choose to illuminate, or probably to explore.

Returning to Philadelphia, with Irene, after this holiday in Britain,
Cyril resumed his life of teaching, lecturing, and writing. He also
assumed the chairmanship of the graduate faculty in the social

sciences for the 1936–7 year. But this first introduction to the business of academic administration does not seem to have been particularly important to him; he was quite ready to leave it to accept another invitation from the banking fraternity, this time to take a year's leave of absence from the university to write a history of the banking industry in Chicago. As his diary for February 1937 reveals, Cyril had expected a half-year's leave with pay in 1937–8 and Irene had looked forward to a six-month residence in England.[29] It was only the fact that Cyril was to receive $15,000 for his year in Chicago, almost three times his regular salary, that reconciled Irene to the proposal. She had to spend the year in England on her own.

The outcome of the year's work, commissioned by that city's First National Bank, was two massive volumes, *The Growth of the Chicago Banks*, bound in handsome maroon cloth, embellished with gilded page-tops.[30] In the inscription in the copy he gave to his wife (it should be noted, he was still "Frank" to her and she still "Bay" to him), he wrote:

To Bay,
I offer with my love these ponderous volumes which could never have been written if she had been with me in Chicago but which would have had even less chance of creation if the thought and spirit of her had not been with me.

Frank

It is a loving sentiment, carefully expressed, but it smacks a little too much of the traditional absenting husband's self-exculpation: "I could not love thee, dear, so much, loved I not honour [or fame or riches or whatever] more."

Yet we should not be too quick to judge him harshly. He undoubtedly allowed his work and his career a primary place in determining his choices, but he also maintained an appreciation of things beautiful. As a young man, he had found a ready pleasure in poetry, and in these Philadelphia years, especially, he sometimes tried his own hand at little verses, not always unsuccessfully. They were often an appreciation of femininity, not in any erotic way but certainly with warmth and affection – and the name invoked and embellished was not always Irene. One, written in Chicago in 1938 is short and evocative enough to bear quotation:

Stephanie's poetry
Brings to my memory

Pleasing, but daunting, me
  Stephanie's self.

Friendship invitingly
  Offered, not slightingly
Ere shall refused be,
  Dear little elf.

The friendship of other young women was, then, not always to
be "slightingly refused." But other lines, also written in Chicago,
were obviously intended for Irene. A small poem on day-dreaming
ends:

Those dream-worlds find their centre, love, in you
And, with you near, life is an ecstacy.
I feel your soft hair pressed against my cheek,
And see your deep, brown eyes that tell so much.
Such dreams are joy, dear heart, but, being weak,
I wish for more, and long to feel your touch.

Cyril clearly had a strong sense of deprivation when he was away
from Irene, although he could often seem oblivious of her when
she was present.

The pile of clippings, James collected relating to *The Growth of
Chicago Banks* are almost all book-trade announcements – short
notices in banking and commercial bulletins or in the Chicago
newspapers – and do not include serious reviews from learned
journals. The Chicago *Journal of Commerce*, for example, gave two
full columns to a notice that summarized the content in some
detail but offered no critical comment. The *Chicago American*, an
evening paper, was a little more forthcoming.

The book is really a history of Chicago, at times almost an economic
history of the United States, but always through the eyes of the Chicago
banks. Despite the great detail which makes the book invaluable as a
work of reference, the author has succeeded in dramatizing events sufficiently to make interesting reading.[31]

The one notice James kept that was written by an academic
rather than a journalist or banker also appeared in a newspaper,
the New York *Daily News*. It was contributed by Professor Melchior
Palyi of the University of Chicago, who produced an amusing
example of how to damn with disingenuous praise.

The book is very readable and expensively illustrated ... the author should be congratulated on the completion of so great an undertaking within the short space of one year despite the fact that he is an Englishman who teaches in Philadelphia and has not hitherto been either a student or even a resident of the Chicago area.[32]

Obviously, his disgruntlement at the choice of James over himself or his Chicago colleagues had influenced his review. The reference to James as an Englishman was particularly uncalled for, since Palyi himself had emigrated from Germany only three years before! James, who had met Palyi at a lunch in December 1936, had noted in his diary that he was "a pleasant fellow with ... none of the hauteur which Ralph's prior description had led me to expect."[33] James perhaps revised his assessment when Palyi's review of his book appeared under the headline: "Big Opportunity in James History Missed, Palyi Says."

Notices from other academics were more ready to stress the positive aspects of James' achievement. The reason James did not preserve them is no doubt that, appearing in journals (in the days before photocopiers), they were not so easily excerpted. The two-page notice in the *American Economic Review* by Howard Preston of the University of Washington judged the work to be "virtually a history of national monetary and banking developments with special reference to Chicago's part therein," and adding that there were "so few shortcomings that it would be ungracious to mention them."[34] The reviewer in the *Journal of Political Economy*, Benjamin Becker of Columbia University, gave the work a full three-page, decidedly favourable review.

In an interesting and forcefully written two-volume study, Professor James has provided us with a scholarly account of the development of credit institutions in Chicago ... Whether one agrees with Professor James's forecasts of Chicago as a serious competitor of New York City or not, there can be no disagreement that he has made a distinct contribution to banking literature.[35]

James could in fact derive considerable satisfaction from what he had achieved. To master an immense amount of detail and produce two volumes totalling almost 1,500 pages, with full bibliographies and careful indexing, in only one year's leave of absence from other duties, constituted an outstanding accomplishment. The final judgment on the abiding worth of his work was provided in 1969 by the Allan Nevin's Reprints in American Economic

History series, which reproduced the two volumes thirty years after their first appearance. The introduction to this second edition begins:

The literature on American banking history published in the late nineteenth century and in the first four decades of the twentieth is, on the whole, not impressive ... There are, however, a few exceptions, such as some books on the beginnings and early history of the Federal Reserve System. Among these one is especially outstanding – F. Cyril James' brilliantly written two-volume work, *The Growth of Chicago Banks*, published in 1938.[36]

In his retirement, James must have read that introduction with particular satisfaction.

After this effort, James returned to Philadelphia for the academic year 1938–9, expecting to resume his usual program of teaching, public lectures, and writing, and so to continue for many years to come. But hardly had he settled back into his former patterns when a new distraction intervened – an invitation from a university and a country of which he had practically no knowledge. The invitation was to visit Montreal, Canada, to consider, and be considered for, appointment as director of the McGill School of Commerce. Initially the idea had little to commend it, and it was with some reluctance that he agreed to travel north across the border to give the proposal at least a first, cursory examination. To accept would interrupt, if not break off, a very promising career.

Other important considerations had to be taken into account as well. During the years they had lived in Philadelphia, Cyril and Irene had made a number of friends, particularly among university colleagues. James belonged to a group called the Sunday Breakfast Club (though whenever we hear of its activities they occur on a week night), which seems to have been at least partly social in nature. A fair number of dinner invitations went to and fro, and there were theatre visits, either in Philadelphia or up to New York. James was particularly friendly with Joe Willits, a fellow professor some fourteen years his senior, who had become dean of the school at the same time James was promoted to full professor. The two men remained friends until after they had both retired. Another long and affectionate friendship was established with a surgeon and his wife, Sumner and Nan Cross; again they were of an older generation than Cyril and Irene, but the friendship continued until age and death intervened. Irene had also developed a social life of her own and, with frequent summer trips back home to England, she appears to have found life in Pennsylvania by no means uncongenial. Of course, we do not have her diaries or letters to tell her side of the story. But when the idea of moving away from the Wharton School arose, they both realized it would mean leaving behind a way of life that had become very much a part of themselves.

The three James boys, Cyril, Mervyn, and Douglas, ca 1911

The Boy Scout, 1914

The first suit, 1917

The LSE student, 1921

The young Philadelphian, 1924

Mary James (Mrs Frank Senior)

Frank James Senior, 1934

Irene Leeper, 1924

Douglas James, 1937

Irene James, 1939

Cyril James, 1939

CHAPTER FOUR

North to Canada

James had visited Montreal at least once before, to board a ship bound for England, but the city evidently made no great impression at that time, and when he returned in March 1939 to examine the McGill offer more closely, the judgment he formed was not very favourable. The city, he wrote in a diary note, was encased in a layer of dirty ice and embellished with piles of frozen snow along the edge of every sidewalk. It was cold, too, with the thermometer at 10 degrees Fahrenheit. Nor were his first impressions of McGill any more positive.

The purpose of my visit was to consider the post of Director of the School of Commerce at Magill [James was to go on misspelling the name in this way for the next two months] and to be considered by the Selection Committee for this appointment. The student-body is smaller than that of Toronto and the faculty appears weak, so that it would be an uphill job, particularly in view of the fact that the School has no autonomy at present and the Director little power. The whole thing is simply a sub-division of the Faculty of Arts and Science, and under the general control of the Dean of the Faculty (C.S. Hendel) ... On the whole I do not think that Hendel is enthusiastic about the School of Commerce ... Hemmeon [Chairman of the Economics Department] I am not sure of: at breakfast he seemed anxious to encourage me, but by dinnertime he insisted that I should probably be disappointed if I went to Magill, and told me that he was sorry he ever left Harvard ...

Most of the day, however, was spent with Principal Lewis Douglas, who was evidently convinced of the need for considerable development in the school and left James in no doubt that Douglas would be a tower of strength to the new director. But James remained unpersuaded. "As a result of these conferences and reactions I am far from decided in my own mind as to the relative wisdom of accepting the post (should it be offered) or of staying at Pennsylvania a while longer."[1]

These first references in the James diaries to "Magill" point up the main elements in the situation. Dean Hendel of Arts and Science (who was planning to leave McGill for Yale) was prudently keeping his distance from a matter in which he saw no reason to get deeply involved; Professor Hemmeon representing Economics and Political Science was suspicious that favouring the School of Commerce might detract from the influence of his department; and Principal Lewis Douglas was strongly in favour of a thorough-going reformation.

There were, however, deeper currents flowing across the McGill campus during the inter-war years than a one-day visitor could readily discern. The influence of the old-style imperialism of Principal William Peterson (1893–1919), Dean Charles Moyse, (1879–1921), and Professor Stephen Leacock (1901–36) had had its last grand manifestation in the principalship of General Sir Arthur Currie (1920–33). Currie, however, had died in office, and Leacock, the last of his breed, had been retired, volubly protesting, in 1936. Meanwhile, born of the ferment of the 1920s, the stock-market crash of 1929, and the mounting misery of the Great Depression, a small breath of socialism had begun to stir among some students and younger members of the academic staff. Although the numbers were few, the voices were persistent and – for the governors of the university, who were heads of great corporations or establishment professionals – decidedly disturbing.

The earliest manifestations were found in some student publications, notably the *McGill Fortnightly Review,* which ran from 1925–7.[2] In 1930, financed by a Rockefeller Foundation grant of $100,000, the McGill Social Science Research Project was established and Leonard Marsh, a young economist from the London School of Economics, brought in as director.[3] For the next decade the project produced studies dealing with the current dislocations in the economic structure of Western society. They were written mostly by Leonard Marsh, by the pioneering sociologist Carl Dawson, and by a lively flow of social science students, who were also producing among them several graduate theses each year. Other teachers who were actively propagating what were considered to be socialist views were Eugene Forsey in the Economics Department and J. King Gordon of the United Theological College; the latter was active in the Student Christian Movement, which had become strongly imbued with Christian Socialist ideals. No one irritated the Board of Governors more than Professor Frank Scott, at that time an associate professor in the Faculty of Law. Scott frequently addressed political meetings and conferences and wrote provocatively in Trade Union publications.

After Currie's death, the Board of Governors had somewhat incautiously appointed an Englishman, Arthur Eustace Morgan, to be principal of McGill, without a sufficiently close inquiry as to his political leanings. When the chancellor and others appealed to the new incumbent to take steps to counteract the worrisome socialistic influences, it appeared Morgan himself had considerable sympathy with them. Fortunately, from the governors' point of view, Morgan fell out with them on financial matters, and succeeded on yet other grounds in making himself very unpopular on campus. He was therefore persuaded to resign less than two years after being appointed. The strong man on the board at this time, who had dominated the administration of McGill since Currie had first fallen ill in the late 1920s, was the chancellor, Sir Edward Beatty, president of the Canadian Pacific Railway. After Morgan's departure, Beatty undertook to find a principal who would share the governors' viewpoint and who would be able to correct the undesirable influences at work on campus. His candidate, Lewis Williams Douglas, named to the vacant position on 1 January 1938, was very much the style of person a businessman would choose as president or principal of a university. In addition to having a good military record in World War I, he had enjoyed considerable political and business success. True his only academic experience was teaching a little history at his own alma mater, Amherst College, but he had also studied as a special student at the Massachusetts Institute of Technology. In 1924, he had been elected a member of the Arizona State Legislature for three years and then served as a Democratic member of the House of Representatives for seven, before accepting appointment in President Franklin Roosevelt's administration in March 1933 as director of the budget. In August 1934, however, in protest against Roosevelt's New Deal fiscal policies he had resigned and left politics for a business career, becoming vice-president of the American Cyanamid Company. He was also elected a trustee of the Rockefeller Foundation. When he came to McGill, he had, therefore, a sound political record and a good business experience and could be expected to deal judiciously and effectively with the socialistic influences causing concern to the governors.

Deciding that the place to begin was with the reform of the

McGill School of Commerce, Douglas' attention was soon attracted
to Cyril James. Here was an academic with an excellent scholarly
reputation, a proponent of enlightened capitalism who had scored
in debate with socialists, an associate and confidant of bankers,
and, as a bonus, one who like himself had been critical of the
New Deal. Having once got this prize on his hook, Douglas was
prepared to go to considerable lengths to make sure it did not
get away.

Through the rest of March 1939, James wrestled with the problem
of reaching a decision. Although he did not know the whole story
of the influences and counter-influences at work on the McGill
campus, he sensed they were there, and this increased his reluctance
to accept the university's offer. By the first of April he had decided
(despite, he observed, the inauspicious date) to stay in Philadelphia.
A few days later, however, Douglas was phoning to arrange a
further meeting in New York. James was persuaded to reconsider.
In favour of going to Montreal there was the prospect of increased
income, the opportunity to create "the first outstanding school of
business in Canada," and the possibility of starting in the Dominion
a National Bureau of Economic Research. In favour of staying in
Philadelphia were the friendships he enjoyed in the Wharton School
(he mentions in his record of deliberations "the gang" and the
Sunday Breakfast Club) and the greater professional prospects.

The matter of citizenship was yet another consideration. Still a
British Dominion, Canada did not confer a separate nationality;
Canadians were British nationals living in Canada. An emigrant
from Britain was, until 1948, able to exercise full citizenship from
the moment of landing, so in Canada James would be as British
as if he had stayed in England. Despite his success in American
society, he had never acquired US citizenship, but now he saw
clearly that if he was going to opt for remaining in the United
States he could delay no longer. One result of the struggle to
come to a decision was that he took the initial step of applying
for naturalization. It would be five years before the process was
completed, but the move indicated that he was leaning toward
staying in Philadelphia.

But Lewis Douglas was persistent. Another telephone call led
to yet another meeting in New York. Douglas was proposing a
compromise, and at the same time enriching the bait. By 18 April,
James was writing to Dean Alfred Williams, the new dean of the
Wharton School, that he would agree to go to "Magill" for two
years provided that the university gave the necessary leave of
absence, that James' departure would not interfere with the dean's

plans for the Wharton School, and that the US Department of Labor would allow James to keep a residence in the US so that his application for citizenship would not be affected by his Canadian appointment.

Meanwhile, Douglas had raised the annual salary he was offering to $10,000. (Cyril commented in his diary: "As Bay insists, I have never had anything handed me on so large a silver platter."[4]) When he had James' reply, Douglas used his influence to persuade the president of the University of Pennsylvania to grant the unpaid leave and secured the agreement of the US Department of Labor regarding James' residence. Under such favourable conditions, James saw no reason to hesitate any longer. After spending the summer in England, he and Irene returned not to Philadelphia but to Montreal – just at the time of the outbreak of war in Europe.

Although the response of the country and the university in 1939 was more sober and realistic than it had been in 1914, it was, nevertheless, whole-hearted and intent. McGill's chief officer and natural leader, however, could not share this determination. Lewis Douglas was an American and therefore neutral; his country was not at war. Douglas had, in fact, already concluded some months earlier that he had made a mistake in accepting Sir Edward Beatty's invitation to serve as principal of McGill. At the same governors' meeting in May at which he had reported to the board on the final details of the deal he had worked out with Professor Cyril James of Philadelphia, he intimated that he wished to resign and return to the United States as soon as his successor could be appointed. But events had moved faster than he had anticipated. War had broken out in Europe and here he was still firmly in place in Montreal. At this point, his attention was again drawn to Cyril James.

Soon after his arrival, James began considering the possibility of upgrading the School of Commerce to the level at which it could offer a master's degree and eventually a PhD. This led him to larger ideas. He worked with Dean C.S. Le Mesurier of the Law School to prepare a memorandum that became a proposal to reorganize all graduate studies at McGill in the field of the social sciences. Attached to it was a comment that a Canadian Bureau of Economic Research, "comparable to the National Bureau at present operating in New York and to the National Institute of Economic Research in London," was the most effective way of achieving the necessary improvements in staff and funds. He also drew up plans to train lawyers and economists to assist most effectively in carrying out the national war effort.

But after producing, in the office, page after page of memoranda on these and other aspects of the war situation, he would return to his apartment and Irene to face problems of a different kind.

Saturday, September 15, 1939

Yet I cannot escape from the feeling that the urgent and immediate needs of the struggle will soon become so great that long-range viewpoints will be impractical. In such circumstances I should not be able to carry on even if I wanted to, and should have to take up some service of a more immediate kind. Probably that means fighting – for which I have no enthusiasm whatever – since I do not think that there is any governmental service for which I am so well qualified that my brains would be worth more than the cannon-fodder utility of a reasonably healthy body. It's a sad reflection after all these years of academic eminence, but when I look at myself realistically I know that it is true.

And the prospect of fighting worries me. If I could be sure that I should be killed reasonably soon, there would be no problem since my insurance is adequate to take care of Bay and the old folks. But if I were not killed how am I going to meet the financial obligations of the two houses and take care of Bay and the Leepers? It cannot possibly be done on army pay – and even though my problem is not so very different from that of thousands of other men I cannot worry over it the less on that account.[5]

His problems were to be solved in quite an unexpected way. He found that he and Irene were being invited to lunch or dinner with a surprising number of members of the Board of Governors, including Chancellor Beatty.

Thursday, October 12, 1939

After dinner tonight I went round to Sir Edward Beatty's, at his request, and stayed for three hours discussing the School of Commerce and my ideas of the immediate future of the University. At first I must admit that I was ridiculously nervous – but after a while I began to enjoy myself and found Sir Edward charming. I think he means what he says, and if that assumption is right he is enthusiastic about the reorganization of the School of Commerce. I want to crystallise my ideas on paper a little further and then go to see him again.

The next entry is for a week later, Wednesday 18 October.

I am seeing so many Governors, and spending so much time with Douglas these days, that I am convinced either that the Board is much more enthusiastically interested in the School of Commerce than I had ever dreamed, or else they are putting me down in the long list of people to be looked over as potential candidates for the Principal's job. Either assumption is gratifying ...

At this stage James was not taking seriously the wild thought the he might be a candidate for the principalship, but he was certainly beginning to conjure up visions of himself not only as director of the rejuvenated School of Commerce but also as associate dean of the Social Sciences School. In such a position, he would be able to suggest ways the university could play its wartime role more effectively. As he had been ready to cope with Britain's postwar problems in *England Today,* and with the United States' economic depression in *The Road to Revival,* and with the American banking industry's need for self-reformation in his twenty-four state missionary journey, so now he was ready with ideas to reform McGill and supply the Empire with the trained personnel it would sorely need when victory had been achieved. When he appeared before the Executive Committee of the Board of Governors to explain his ideas, he was in his natural element. He had been lecturing to bankers and business leaders for years, and one can believe the members of the board received an impressive exposition.

But even is his wildest imaginings, James was not prepared for the rapidity of the outcome.

Thursday, October 26th

A day of unexpected happenings! At lunch Hendel and I met with the Executive Committee of the Governors to discuss the plans for reforming the [Faculty] – a meeting that was not exactly unexpected since Sir Edward invited me two days ago, but it did surprise me to find the Governors so unanimous in their approval of the plan.

The real surprise came this afternoon when Douglas called me in to ask if I "would consent to allow my name to be put before the Governors as a candidate for the Principalship" – a line of diplomacy much higher than Sir Edward's suggestion this evening that if I would accept the post, the formal arrangements could be completed next week!

Even though I had suspected something, the offer still surprises me. The salary of $17,500 is grand; the opportunity for service is tremendous – but can I do the job? And am I justified in breaking my ties with Pennsylvania? I am still in a whirl!

As he had every right to be. Even from the financial point of view alone, the prospects were intoxicating. In August his annual salary at Pennsylvania had been $7,296; in September, as a result of his coming to McGill, that had risen handsomely to $8,500; and now, a mere month later, he was being offered more than twice that amount.[6] But quite apart from the money, the professional opportunities were such stuff as dreams are made on. As executive head of a greatly respected university, he would have responsibility not merely for the School of Commerce or even the Faculty of Arts and Science, but also for Medicine, Dentistry, Law, Engineering, Agriculture, Education, Music, Graduate Studies, and Research. Moreover, McGill, together with Toronto, was a member of the select American Association of Universities, which meant James would attend its exclusive meetings and rub shoulders with the foremost members of the academic world; he could expect to be consulted by governments; he would be part of the imperial estab-lishment. James made a decent show of consulting friends and advisers; on Wednesday, 1 November, he was writing in his diary: "Tonight I am Principal-designate of McGill."

The events of those tumultuous days at the end of October later became somewhat telescoped in his mind. Writing a contribution to Edgar Andrew Collard's book *The McGill You Knew*, James told the story of how he was called to the principal's office, where Lewis Douglas and Sir Edward Beatty awaited him. According to James, Beatty said, "You already know that Lewis Douglas wants to go back to Washington. In normal circumstances McGill would search for a really distinguished successor in Canada and the United Kingdom, but at the present time all such people are being absorbed into the war effort. The Board of Governors would there-fore like you to take on the job."[7] The actual events, it is clear from the diary, were played out at a somewhat slower pace, but the bland assumption of the formidable chancellor that, once he had offered and James had accepted, the board would duly confirm the appointment is more than a little breath-taking.

That evening, James' mind was, as he said, in a whirl, and the events of the next few days did little to allay the excitement.

Wednesday, November 1, 1939
The evening radio programmes announced [my appointment] at the begin-ning of the news and the early editions of tomorrow's papers blazon it forth in one-inch headlines across the front page!

Even though I realise that there is lots of work ahead, I am thrilled to my back teeth, thrilled more than I have ever been before. At lunch today

I met the Deans: at the dinner given by Dr. Chipman tonight we celebrated more gaily. But my excitement is too great for me to think or write much.

The following Saturday, General Andrew McNaughton, a McGill graduate, former president of the National Research Council, and now GOC First Canadian Overseas Division, came to review the Canadian Officers' Training Corps (COTC), and university dignitaries who were veterans of World War I took their place wearing their medals alongside the general on the reviewing stand.[8] McNaughton also spoke at the ceremonial stone-laying of the new gymnasium by Lady Currie, and then the honoured guests were entertained at a large luncheon hosted by the chancellor, after which everyone proceeded to a McGill-Queen's football match. Cyril James attended all these functions modestly and retiringly in his new role as principal-designate but naturally was showered with introductions and congratulations. And more was still to come.

To complete the day's functions we went on to George McDonald's where there was a gala tea for Bay and myself – so that we arrived home at 7.15 delighted but very weary. It has been doubly pleasant to sit at home quietly and listen to Toscanini on the radio tonight.

Quickly finding the pace and the social demands made upon her too much to cope with, Irene left for a holiday in New York. Her reaction is understandable, given the number of dinner and speaking engagements James records, as well as the lunches Douglas was arranging for him to meet various heads of departments. His next entry is not until Saturday, 25 November.

Life has been very busy during the three weeks that have passed since the last entry, and I have not been in the mood to reminisce or even record the swift march of events. Even now I can do little more than record the impressionistic picture of all that has happened because the kaleidoscope has changed so quickly that I have lost much of the detail.

As to the appointment itself, congratulations still pour in, although the stream begins to abate somewhat. Everybody appears to be very pleased, and I have had warm receptions from the graduates at Ottawa and Toronto, where I journeyed to make speeches, as well as from the council of the Parent Society, which I met at dinner the other evening. Moreover, the time is rapidly approaching when I shall have to descend out of the pleasant clouds where congratulations are the chief result of the news, since Douglas leaves for the west at the end of this month ...

James was indeed going to have to descend out of the clouds; Lewis Douglas made his trip to the west at the end of November his final departure from the university, leaving James to assume full responsibility as acting principal. Even more disastrously, Chancellor Edward Beatty, the Board of Governors' strong man, was suddenly removed from the scene on 17 December by serious and, as it turned out, prolonged illness. As a result, Cyril James was left on his own to learn a new university, a new country, and a new job, without the guidance or period of tutelage he might reasonably have expected.

If this were not enough to occupy all his waking moments, he had other concerns, on a quite different front. In an emotional rebound, Irene was finding consolation from the unpleasant realities of Montreal elsewhere. James continued the 25 November diary entry:

What I most need at present is an opportunity to get away from everything so that I can have a chance to think clearly, and formulate proper policies. Ten days ago I went down to Philadelphia for a long weekend, with the hope that it might give me such an opportunity, but the result was not what I had expected. In the first place there were too many business details that had to be attended to ... The second trouble was much more serious. Irene, who came down to the Cross's to spend the weekend with me, is not at all pleased by the prospect of all that the new job entails and has also fallen for Nina's brother in New York, so that she was none too sure that she wanted to come back to Montreal at all. In the end, I persuaded her to come back with me, but I do not think that she is particularly happy here and there is no question at all that she is very much worried and highly nervous ... I suppose (perhaps with a wish that is father to the thought) that we shall find some way to straighten things out – but it is going to be an awfully hard job to arouse any enthusiasm in Irene, and harder still to get her to enjoy life. I am in the position of needing to think out the problems of home almost as much as those that arise out of the office, and have more than a suspicion that between the two I shall make a very bad botch of the whole thing.

James no longer had to worry about being called to serve in a fighting unit of the armed forces, but would he be able to retain his new appointment if his wife left him for another man? Marital discord, a hint of scandal, certainly divorce, were not taken lightly in pre-war Montreal society. While he was publicly meeting deans, learning the niceties of university–hospital relationships, and discovering the rural charm of Macdonald College and the cloistered reserve of the women's Royal Victoria College, James knew privately that his appointment tottered on the brink of disaster. He could only show a brave front in public and carry on, hoping all would turn out well.

There was no shortage of administrative matters to engage his attention. No sooner had Douglas left Montreal than James found himself in a delicate situation involving Sir Herbert Holt and the board of the Royal Victoria Hospital on the one hand and Dr Lyman Duff and the McGill Pathological Institute on the other. The hospital was seeking to safeguard its rights in the matter of pathological testing and autopsies, which the institute, administered by Duff as the university's professor of pathology, had hitherto undertaken in return for service fees. It required considerable diplomatic skills on the part of the new (still only "acting") principal, but he managed to bring all parties to agree to what he calls "a *modus vivendi*." On 11 December, he was cordially welcomed for the day at Macdonald College, but there was so much to see and learn that it proved a long and tiring experience. "At teatime I met the student council, and the staff later gave me a very pleasant dinner, before I took the train back to a lonely apartment (since Irene left for New York [again] this morning)."

The 1939 diary ends on 15 December, and James does not resume his notes until 14 January, after he had been formally installed as principal and had plunged wholeheartedly into McGill life with a dedication that left little room for anything or anybody else. He had persuaded Irene once again to return from New York and done his best to patch up the relationship. Irene had been enthusiastic for the move to Montreal when they had contemplated the director's increased salary, but now that she experienced the demands the principalship made upon her, and especially the loneliness it entailed, she bitterly regretted having left Philadelphia. That first winter established the pattern of Irene's dislike of Montreal and of her long absences in the United States or England.

The formal installation of Frank Cyril James as the eleventh principal of McGill University took place on 12 January 1940, in a crowded Moyse Hall, in the presence of the Visitor to the Royal Institution for the Advancement of Learning,[9] His Excellency the Governor-General of Canada, Lord Tweedsmuir – better known as the novelist John Buchan. James was greatly impressed by Tweedsmuir, who he thought measured up in real life to the image he had formed of him by reading the novels. When Tweedsmuir died unexpectedly, only one month later, James was personally affected.

Lord Tweedsmuir is dead ... Perhaps it sounds silly to say that I miss him. I have only seen him twice, once at the Installation and once at the luncheon of the Canadian Forestry Association eight days ago. But I do feel a sense of personal loss ... He had a charm and wisdom – and a determination that made him do well any job to which he put his hand. He might have lived longer if he had worked less hard, but he would not have made that compromise with fate.[10]

In making this assessment of Tweedsmuir, James was revealing his own attitude to the morality of responsibility. When a man finds himself in a position of trust and leadership, he has to respond, James believed, with a total self-commitment – a commitment of time, talents, and energies. This was the ideal he took with him to the installation in Moyse Hall that January afternoon and expressed with considerable force in his inaugural address.

This Installation Ceremony, in a sense, may be regarded as the descendant of those solemn occasions when men swore fealty, and, in like manner, I wish now, publicly, to dedicate myself to the service of McGill. The Office of Principal and Vice-Chancellor carries responsibilities that are commensurate with its distinction, and although I recognize my own unworthiness for the honour that you have conferred upon me, I am resolved that such talents as I have shall be devoted to the University, in the hope that its progress during the years that lie ahead of us may be a worthy continuation of the great story of its past.

Amid the rustle of academic gowns, the soothing cadences of "Hail Alma Mater," and the pompous ceremony of a governor-general's visit, those words may have sounded a fitting response to institutional formalities, but Cyril James meant them sincerely and expected them to be taken literally. In the quiet of his office the following Sunday morning, he wrote:

January 14, 1940
I worked harder in the preparation of [the installation address] than on anything else that I have ever said or written, and it represents as nearly as words can express it the work that lies ahead of me. To dignify it by the title of a personal philosophy would be grandiose, yet it offers the framework of a philosophy more accurately than anything else I have ever written. And if travail of soul and mind can be said to sanctify a document, this one is well worthy of presentation: never in all my life have I been as near to collapse as I was during last Friday's ceremonies.

Somehow, despite all my hopes that I may return to Pennsylvania, or some other university, to become again a simple teacher with leisure to spend on the writing of books I feel in my bones I shall have to retain this position until I die. There is so much to do that is worth doing that I shall never accomplish it all, and unless McGill finds another Principal who is better-fitted than I am to undertake the task, it will demand all the best I can give it for the rest of my life.

These are strong words from a young man of thirty-six, but James meant them and he lived them – through two decades of war, postwar reconstruction, expansion, and social revolution.

The installation address gives the clue to why James saw McGill in such an exalted light that he was ready to offer himself in this kind of dedication. He characterized the new decade as one offering "more question marks than sign posts." The external struggle of war, he believed, reflected a deeper division within each of the great democracies on the issue of whether private initiative or government regulation offered the best hope of "adapting human society to the new environment that has been created by two centuries of scientific progress and mechanical invention." Many voices, he acknowledged, were ready to proclaim private universities as certain casualties of the coming changes. In his view, however,

the circumstances of today do not necessarily imply the elimination of private universities. But they do constitute a challenge. If our great universities are content to offer traditional instruction of a kind that evades all troublesome issues … they will soon cease to be a vital force … Perhaps it is not too much to say that our great universities hold the future of civilisation in their hands.[11]

At one time James might have said this about the Christian Church. But he had lost touch with the church that had been so influential in his own development; after Tweedsmuir's funeral he commented, "Somehow the service seemed strange to me, who have not been inside a church for many years." In place of the church he now put the university – the ideal, liberal, self-directing, self-scrutinizing university, of which McGill was the particular embodiment he had been called upon to serve. He never changed that view of himself and his vocation.

Whether he always went about his assigned task in the wisest ways may, however, be open to question. Certainly the price he paid privately and domestically was enormous. How far he and Irene had drifted apart before he became involved with McGill

can only be guessed, but sometimes the bright lights dimmed even
for him.

Friday, April 21st

These latter days have brought a feeling of weariness and disillusionment
that I find hard to fight off ... For many years I have been an individualist,
making few close friends and not leaning on Irene at all. I was proud
of my independence, proud of the fact that I could run my own life.
False pride discovers its nemesis and since I have not the courage of Sir
Edward – I find life desperately lonely now that Irene is far away,
spiritually as well as physically, and there is nobody else at hand.

Beatty had recently returned to Montreal after an enforced
absence of four months, and James had formed the habit of dropping in after dinner to talk over university affairs. He was greatly
impressed with the courage and cheerfulness of Beatty in facing
alone the trauma of a severe illness and long convalescence. But
Beatty had long been a bachelor by choice. James was a married
man, missing the support and encouragement of his wife. This
diary entry is particularly significant in that it shows that James
had a pretty clear idea of himself and knew that his present lack
of close friendships was no new thing. On the other hand, the
McGill situation, which place the principal on a pinnacle above
his colleagues, undoubtedly exacerbated what was already an
unfortunate characteristic.

However, James was to receive some help, particularly for the
next few years, from the somewhat unexpected direction of the
Royal Victoria College, an institution that served as the women's
dormitory of the university. The choice of a new warden for RVC
is mentioned casually enough in James' diary, but it brought to
the university a colleague who throughout James' career at McGill
was to complement his activities most fully and, in a working
relationship, give him more support and probably more friendship
than any other one person. Muriel Roscoe, a botanist from Nova
Scotia, came to fill a position corresponding to what many universities call dean of women; all women students at McGill, resident
in the college or not, were regarded as members and as part of
the warden's responsibility. Appointed early in James' first year
and remaining in office almost to the end of his principalship,
Muriel Roscoe matched James in presence and, in her own sphere
of responsibility, in competence. James felt he could leave the care
of women students safely in her hands, and it is probable, he did
not always realize how much he depended on her.

The end of term and the month of May brought little respite. James created new problems for himself when on the first of the month be bought a house at 3575 Peel Street, only to find that despite his greatly increased income he was short of funds to furnish and run it. Engaging a cook and two maids in the absence of Irene, he ran headlong into "servant trouble," and had to send the cook off with two weeks' wages in lieu of notice. At the university, he found himself confronted with the overwhelming tasks of presenting to the board a university budget that would keep the deficit to an absolute minimum yet also not cut expenditures back in a way that would alienate his academic colleagues. With William Bentley the bursar, he went over the budget sheets, item by item; with the deans he went through their faculty accounts name by name; and with his office staff he investigated the tax claims from the City of Montreal and the grant promises and defaults of the provincial government. He managed to cut $17,284 from the 1939–40 budget, presenting proposals for 1940–1 that, he noted, were $26,200 below the 1938–9 budget, but still leaving a "best case" deficit of $18,759 or a "worst case" deficit of $121,709. The amounts may sound small in the 1990s, but in the war years they loomed extremely large.

Also in May, the news from Europe was particularly bad. When James flew to Boston to address the Annual Convention of Savings Banks, he heard at the conclusion of his speech that Germany had invaded Belgium and Holland. A week later, when he went to London, Ontario, to address the Royal Society of Canada on "Science and Society," he heard that the French were on the point of collapse. Two days later it was headlined that Belgium had surrendered, leaving the French and British flanks undefended. To James' problems in the university and his private anxieties were now added premonitions of disaster for Britain and for his relatives at home. The newly appointed young principal, for whom everything had seemed so bright in October, was by May on the brink of emotional collapse.

Sunday, May 5th

Chipman gave a very pleasant lunch for the Hendels[12] today, and I spent most of the afternoon with Sir Edward who sets out tonight for his holiday. Both of them, in different contexts, said very nice things about me and the work that I have done – but I must confess that I feel unworthy of the compliments. For several days now I have done nothing but potter, without being able to put my mind to anything. Perhaps the psychologists would say that I had a bad case of nymphomania and, if any of them could read and publish my thoughts, I should certainly be kicked out of Montreal. Everything that wanders through my mind centers around women, and they are not soft sentimental thoughts, but somehow in the scramble of the years that have brought me here I seem to have lost the art of making love either to Bay or to anybody else – so I just go on thinking fiendish thoughts that harm nobody but myself.

But whatever he was feeling inwardly he still had to appear confident in public. In particular he had to face the festivities of convocation week and to ensure that everything went off without a hitch. If the weather held, the ceremonies would be celebrated in accordance with custom in the open air on the lower campus.

Thursday, May 30th

This has been my first Convocation and, by reason of Tweedsmuir's death and Sir Edward's absence, I officiated all by myself.

The weather was ideal, sunny yet not too warm, while the lawns and trees of the campus were a perfect setting for the ceremonies. (Even the crab apples were in blossom). Everything moved along beautifully, although I felt self-consciously regal as I sat there and capped the students, but since nobody else knew my thoughts they seemed to enjoy the proceeding. Doré[13] spoke a little too long, and not quite enough to the point – but I could not have done as well in French.

Since dinner I have been sitting in the garden for a rest, so that I feel better now and shall be quite awake again when we go down to the Convocation Ball at 11.0[0] p.m.

The picture of the thronging crowds of graduating students, the professors in their colourful gowns and hoods, and the parents and friends glowing with pride and satisfaction, all joining happily in the academic rituals orchestrated with calm dignity by the handsome figure in his vice-chancellor's robe, contrasts strongly with the black moods of the diary and the tragic news from Europe. None of those present knew on what thin ice their young principal was skating, but some of them, alerted by the carefully chosen words of his opening address, may have paused to think, even in the midst of their celebration, that their whole style of civilization was dangerously near to collapse.

But with convocation behind him and the war news settling, for a while at least, into a watchful lull, other matters also began to resolve themselves. The budget he presented to the Board of Governors was accepted with out cavil and the chancellor agreed to sanction a loan of $5,000 to enable him to furnish his new house. James arranged for Irene's niece, Doreen, to come over from England to live in his home and continue her education at Trafalgar School, and later in the year he was able to bring his father and Irene's parents away from the dangers of the air raids on London. He settled them in a house in Notre Dame de Grâce in the western suburbs of Montreal. James realized that this was not an ideal situation for the young girl Doreen, seeing that she had no youthful companions other than those at school. But the arrangements at least solved some of Cyril's problems about Irene, who now had her parents at hand to visit and care for.

The long summer vacation from May through September brought much-welcomed relief from university engagements. True, Cyril did not help matters by being under pressure to finish a complete revision of *The Economics of Money, Credit and Banking*, which he had been working at, off and on, since the preceding September. The actual writing occupied him well into July, he was still wrestling with galleyproofs deep into August, and then he had to compile the index, so that it was a triumph of publishing skills that the book was ready in September, in time for the all-important "fall-adoptions."

By the beginning of term at the end of September, James was feeling more "acclimatized," as he put it, and could face the new academic year with more confidence. He also felt confident in receiving, at the fall convocation, the university's new Visitor, the recently appointed governor-general, the Earl of Athlone, and his wife, HRH the Princess Alice, so the boy from Stoke Newington was playing host to royalty for the first time. This is probably the place to introduce James' secretary, Dorothy McMurray. She had come to McGill in 1929 to temporarily replace Sir Arthur Currie's regular staff for a few days, and she stayed as secretary in the principal's office for thirty-two years. The four typewritten sheets she placed in the principal's hands on the morning of this convocation were typical of her work both in their meticulous detail and in their slightly managerial tone.

Principal's Programme

Monday, October 7, 1940

10.00 a.m. Your car should be approaching the Champ de Mars back of City Hall.

Newspaper instructions were: DRESS: Morning Coat (without spats, without gloves, I presume you carry the latter).

Attached yellow ticket must be presented at Champ de Mars parking place, and presented again at entrance to city hall, either by main, Notre-Dame St. entrance, or by elevators in basement, to Hall of Honour.

You also take with you your Principal and Vice-Chancellor's visiting cards, and Mrs. James' cards, if she accompanies you, and give them to the person appointed to take them at City Hall (two of each, I think).

Princess Alice is Her Royal Highness, The Earl is His Excellency.

10.15 a.m. Civic Reception, in Hall of Honour, by Acting Mayor, E. Hamelin.

There will be a great crush. I presume no one can leave until His Excellency does.

This is the first of four pages, and the instructions continue step by step through the business of getting the governor-general and the Princess Alice from City Hall to the Arts Building, reviewing the guard of honour at James McGill's tomb, away to the Gymnasium, and through the Convocation Program. Item No. 6 on the last page reads:

Your own address
Glad to have the Chancellor back
Any other remarks
Formal introduction of His Excellency

James quickly learned to rely upon Mrs McMurray's capacity for work, her dedication, her shrewd perceptions – in these qualities she matched him, step for step. In one matter, however, she was a good deal wiser than her superior: when she went home at the end of the day (and they were often long days) she devoted herself to the care of her husband, and Alexander McMurray responded with affection. In retrospect, speaking of their life together, she said they "got married and loved happy ever after." She also jealously guarded her month's holiday every August. But in the office, she typed furiously on her manual typewriter, arranged the principal's appointments, turned away undeserving callers, drew up intricate itineraries, searched back files in order to write informative papers on all kinds of subjects, and offered him, often unsought, much sound advice. Her memoranda ranged from the shortcomings of the provincial government in matters of finance to the history of teacher-training in Quebec or the tangled story of the Graduates' Society support for the Sir Arthur Currie Memorial Gymnasium. Whether Cyril James could have achieved what he did without her help is highly doubtful. She was a Scot from Nova Scotia, with strongly inbred traditions of loyalty and industry; he was an Englishman with private demons that he harnessed to the service of McGill; together they made a formidable pair. Yet Mrs McMurray never presumed upon her position. Certainly she would never have thought of herself as on a par with the principal. It was simply her job to look after him, and look after him she did. Mrs Mac, as she was widely known, managed at one and the same time to boss Cyril James, to mother him, to guard him jealously, and to defer to his exalted position; she made sure other people also deferred. In her own sphere, she was as remarkable a person as he in his.

The fall convocation marked the end of one academic year and the beginning of another. For Cyril James, it had certainly been a year to remember. At its beginning he had experienced a most unexpected, indeed thrilling, promotion; in the spring and early summer he had come perilously near to collapse; by the fall he had, somewhat precariously, recovered his emotional balance. But the sense of loneliness remained and was intensified by the prolonged absences of the chancellor, Sir Edward Beatty. After Beatty returned to the city more permanently in June 1940, James increasingly made it a practice to call upon him in the evenings to discuss university business. But the following March, Beatty suffered a severe stroke, and this time James was permanently deprived of his advice and support. Beatty struggled on for two further years, battling illness and repeated surgery until his death on 23 March 1943. Walter Chipman, a distinguished physician, who was a governor both of the Royal Victoria Hospital and of McGill, succeeded Beatty as president of the hospital. In these early years, he, more than any of the governors of McGill, worked readily with the young principal and in small measure played part of Beatty's role. But by the middle of 1941, Cyril James was getting more and more confirmed in the habit of thinking that he would have to accomplish his major goals alone.

University administration is rather like steering a small boat in a heavy swell. Each wave is critical; as it approaches it engages all one's attention and skills; when it is past one wonders why it seemed so threatening; but then the next wave approaches, and one has little time to look back at the waves that have gone by. As the events of each day crowded one after another, James took time to observe in his diary that only a small haphazard selection of them received notice in his nightly jottings – anyone seeking the consistent record, he wrote, should turn to the office files, where everything was carefully documented. But on 28 April 1941, he does spell out a typical day.

A busy but not exciting day. Budget all this morning; military executives committee at 12; lunch to discuss the Lachine Rowing Club at 1:00; History Selection Committee at 2:30; George McDonald at 3:30; Professor Holecki[14] at 4:30; Ross Clarkson at 5:00; a little gardening before dinner and most of the evening spent working on the French text of the address that I have to give at Laval on Wednesday. Certainly not exciting, scarcely inspiring and certainly a crazy exercise in mental gymnastics – but a fairly typical day.

The conversation with Ross Clarkson, vice-president and general manager of the Royal Trust Company, concerned the organization of the McGill Associates. The notion of gathering a group of business executives, mostly men who like Clarkson himself had no formal connection with McGill (or probably any other university), giving them a yearly dinner, supplying them regularly with information about the university's activities, and generally making them feel part of the McGill community, had been around for two or three years, but little action had been taken. James, wanting to revitalize the idea, enlisted the help of Clarkson, who had recently become a governor of the university, to make the necessary business contacts. He also secured the organizing skills of the young Lorne Gales of the McGill Graduates' Society to plan a dinner at the Ritz-Carlton Hotel. James himself provided the emotion of the evening by making a fine speech on his favourite theme: that educated men and women would be the next generation's leaders of Dominion and Empire – hence the need for businessmen to support universities (especially McGill!) and so save both Canada and Western civilization. It was what James would describe as "a grand evening," its success due not only to good food, good wine, and good feelings, but also to the fact that the McGill principal really believed in what he was saying. Certainly since that evening the associates have continued strongly and given excellent support to the university for half a century.

Other items on James' daily agenda reveal him in more delicate relationships. At RVC, Muriel Roscoe wanted to replace two middle-aged residential assistants, one a lecturer in English and the other a senior worker in the registrar's office, with two or three graduate students, one of whom preferably might be a postdoctoral fellow; her hope was to upgrade the academic atmosphere and function of the college. Some of the women students rallied to the cause of the residential assistants, sending a round-robin letter of protest to each of the governors. Although in favour of academic upgrading in general and of supporting his new warden, of whom he was coming to think more and more highly, James was well aware that the McGill community might close ranks against a new principal seen as a ruthless innovator. It behoved him to move warily.

He took the problem to the Executive Committee of the Board, explaining that neither of the displaced residents was losing her employment and that the new warden's plans should be supported. He had met with the students and they now saw the matter in a different light and apologized for writing and distributing the letter. The executive accepted the principal's explanations and agreed to the new appointments. Presumably, they also graciously accepted the apology. The accepted view at that time clearly was that students should not attempt to interfere in administrative matters, even when their own interests were involved![15]

On the other hand, when the male students of the Zeta Psi Fraternity indulged in a "drunken party on Saturday night," James took "summary action," suspending the worst offenders from classes for a week and placing them on conduct probation for a year. Privately he doubted whether he had the statutory powers to take such action and expected his judgments might be challenged. He was right – Dean Le Mesurier of the law faculty came in next day to argue that he had no such power; "a fairly litigious and friendly argument since he agrees with the sentence." James stuck to his guns and that was the end of the matter.

It is when we turn to James' copy of the agenda of the 28 March 1941 meeting of the Executive and Finance Committee of the Board that we see how multitudinous the minor, and the not so minor, crises truly were. In its closely typed pages we get a glimpse of Cyril James in action and realize that he was a meticulous administrator, despite the self-deprecation of the diary. The extended agenda setting out his personal notes for that March meeting is a long document – twelve pages of typed material – that deals first with the Principal's Report, covering such matters as the university's tax exemption and the Macdonald College Bill, currently before the Provincial Assembly. The agenda then goes on to deal with negotiations with the Morgan family relating to McGill's possible acquisition of the Morgan Woods and farm; necessary changes in the management of both the Royal Victoria College and Douglas Hall, the men's residence; the possibility of McGill taking over the Lachine Rowing Club; the vaguer possibility that McGill might set up a School of Marine Engineering and Naval Architecture; a list of persons to receive honorary degrees; a list of academic appointments and reappointments; increases in the board and lodging fees at Macdonald College, with provision for much-needed bursaries for the poorer students; the sale of Westmount Mountain Summit to the City of Westmount; the report of the Real Estate Investment Committee, concerning the purchase of houses on University Street; a scheme to cooperate with the Ayerst, McKenna and Harrison Company in the manufacture of bacteriological products in great demand by the government; revised financial estimates for the university's operation in 1940–1; a forecast of the financial situation for 1941–2; and a list of Gifts, Grants, and Bequests.

Under item 15, "Other Business," – largely matters of information – one matter is particularly significant: someone had had the temerity to nominate a woman for election by the graduates to the board. James recognized the difficulty, but had a solution. Not only by proposing to encourage "private pressure by the Graduates' Society on the branches" for the election of Mr Hugh Crombie, but also by suggesting to the society amendments to ensure that such proposals could be eliminated at an earlier stage. So much for "women's rights."

In the absence of the chancellor, James as vice-chancellor took the chair, guiding the committee with masterly competence through the whole complicated maze of business, knowing what he wanted and making sure that the members of the committee were left satisfied that what they had concluded was also what they wanted. Those who saw James in action in such a setting were always impressed; as one governor once remarked: "It was difficult ever to disagree with James; he always knew all the facts."

Normal university business affairs were not the only matters that required the principal's attention. The fact that Canada was at war made increasing demands upon him, with regard not merely to his own time and effort, but also to making good the deficiencies caused by the departure of other men and women into the armed or civil services. An early problem involved the introduction of military training into the McGill program for all male "British nationals" (i.e., Canadians) aged eighteen and over – there were the inevitable conscientious objectors who needed special provisions. One young man had to be sent home for a term until a sufficiently flexible accommodation with his conscience could be reached. A more difficult matter involved the question

of military conscription: which students should be granted deferment from national service until their degree work was complete?
This subject required consultation with colleagues in other universities and then the presentation of a common point of view to
the appropriate governmental authorities. J.S. Thomson, president
of the University of Saskatchewan during the war years, has
stressed in his memoirs how quickly agreement was reached and
how readily the minister of defence accepted the universities'
proposals. "Hitherto, the Conference [of Canadian Universities]
had been what the title suggested: a series of annual meetings to
discuss topics of common interest in higher education; now, it
became the recognized means for agreement on accepted policies."[16]

But Cyril James, who was considerably younger than most of
the other executive heads, did not view the slow pace of the
discussions with the same equanimity.

Last Monday [24 February 1941] I went to Ottawa for another meeting
of the Canadian Universities Conference on the subject of military training
– and came away with the feeling that we had wasted a great deal of
time without arriving at any real conclusions. Ralston and Gardiner both
made pretty little speeches that did not mean anything – but they could
scarcely have conducted a confidential discussion in what was practically
a public meeting.[17] I have today written to all the University heads
suggesting that we should set up a small committee of them to keep in
close touch with the government – and if that idea is approved we may
really get something. Half the trouble lies in the fact that Cody[18] is not
the right man for President [of the Conference] – even though he is a
thoroughly pleasant person when there is nothing more urgent than marking time and going through the tardy democratic motions of a meeting
that is in no hurry to get anywhere.

After further discussion, the universities agreed on military training
for all "British" males over eighteen; engineering, science, medical,
and dental students were to be exempt from call-up until the end
of their degree programs; law, humanities, social science, and commerce students would be accepted and continued only if they
were fully qualified and if they maintained their standing in the
upper half of the class – an ambiguous but generally accepted
phrase. James' idea of a small negotiating committee was accepted,
and of course he was named a member. When the committee met
to discuss its tactics in laying the universities' ideas before the
minister of national defence, Cody paid James the compliment of
asking him to be their spokesman.

It was the first attempt of the Universities' small committee to negotiate with the government, and frankly I do not think that we attained much.

Cody I met at Lunch, in order to talk over the problem – and he promptly suggested that I present the matter to Ralston this afternoon. Wallace [of Queen's] and Maurault [of l'Université de Montréal] agreed later. As a result we all sat in Ralston's office, he being flanked by [civil servants] – while I held forth. Ralston first suggested that we take the matter up with others – and then suggested a written memo and a later conference. Results of the meeting: nil!

But as Thomson's summary of the situation recorded, in the end, the universities' proposals were accepted and the relationships established with the federal government were cordial. It is evident, however, that despite his junior age and inexperience, James was already drawing attention to himself among Canadian university presidents by his initiatives and leadership.

But in his private life there was no improvement. The diary entries for the years 1940–1 show that all through this period, affairs in the James household continued in what can only be described as a precarious condition. In April Cyril feared Irene was on the verge of a nervous breakdown; he grumbled that she could not manage the household accounts, complained that they were without servants in the house and that their financial affairs were in a mess – they were overdrawn at the bank. In August he was once again questioning to himself his fitness for the position of principal.

A major problem undoubtedly was that in order to provide for a style of living thought to be appropriate for a university principal, James had severely strained his resources and that, as a result, Irene was being asked to cope with situations beyond her abilities. But his pride – or perhaps genuinely the social etiquette of the day – would not allow James drastically to reduce his level of expenditure. Fortunately, James was distracted from the cares of his household and the nagging questions of self-doubt by another major call upon his energies, professional skills, and above all his imagination. It presented itself in the form of an exciting invitation from the federal government – an invitation that, especially in wartime, it was unthinkable to decline.

CHAPTER FIVE

The Committee on Reconstruction

The opportunity that presented itself in the spring of 1941 must have seemed to James one for which the whole of his previous career had prepared him. The federal government of Canada, led by Mackenzie King, was devoting its energies to the prosecution of the war, but it also had time, when it was prompted, to think of the conflict's aftermath. It was essential that the chaos and recriminations that had followed World War I not be repeated. Under the aegis of the Cabinet Committee of Demobilization and Re-establishment, a committee was appointed to advise the government on postwar reconstruction policies. Its members were to be Principal R.C. Wallace of Queen's University, Kingston; Edouard Montpetit, directeur de l'École des sciences sociales, économiques et politiques de l'Université de Montréal; D.G. McKenzie, chairman of the Board of Grain Commissioners; J.S. McLean, president of Canadian Packers Inc.; and Tom Moore, president of the Trades and Labour Congress. But the important decision was to name the chairman, upon whose leadership the committee's effectiveness and achievements would largely depend.

From many points of view, it would have been difficult to suggest a person better fitted to chair the Committee on Postwar Reconstruction than Cyril James. A graduate of that home of social planning, the London School of Economics, PhD of the Wharton School of Business, writer of perceptive memoranda on the training of the leaders of society, friend and mentor of bankers and businessmen, author of volumes on the economic reconstruction of the United Kingdom and of the United States, well known in influential circles in Ottawa and Washington, James must have seemed to many the ideal man for the appointment. Equally, from his own point of view, the job was most desirable; after so much preparation and paper-planning, he was going to be given the opportunity to test out his ideas in the real world of people and politics.[1]

It was not to be an easy task. On 22 March James wrote in his diary:

All day has been spent at Ottawa or on the train – so that I am tired tonight and my mind oppressed with a sense of new responsibilities. I have been appointed Chairman of a new Committee to advise the Cabinet on all aspects of postwar reconstruction policy ...

It is, I think, a good committee, but the task assigned to it is a stupendous one, since the Cabinet (even if it does not take our advice) is much too busy to develop long-range policies on its own account. Even though we are a purely advisory group, there is a very real challenge which demands careful thinking and hard work. In my heart I suppose that I wanted the Chairmanship, but now that I have it I realise how great a job there is for the chairman to do since other members of the committee, although enthusiastic, will require wise leadership and much prodding.

Professor R.A. Young of the University of Western Ontario has studied the operations of the Committee of Reconstruction closely and has given a perceptive account of the committee's growth and activities.[2] As early as 8 December 1940, the Cabinet had established by Privy Council Order 4068–1/2 a committee to consider the problems arising from demobilization in the postwar period, and in February 1941 the committee reported "that the problem of the rehabilitation of ex-servicemen is a part of the general question of postwar reconstruction" and asked that "the scope of its duties should be enlarged to include an examination and discussion of the general question of postwar reconstruction, and to make recommendation as to what government facilities should be established to deal with this question."[3] PC 4068–1/2 was amended by PC 1218 to include this wording, and Ian Mackenzie set up the Committee of Reconstruction to tackle that agenda. Later the terms of reference were more modestly described as "to collect, receive and arrange information with regard to reconstruction policies and activities in Canada and abroad,"[4] but by that time James had already written the first draft of a Basic Memorandum, which set out his overall view of the subject. It is clear from the beginning that if the politicians and bureaucracy expected a tidy essay with a few statistics thrown in for appearance' sake, they were in for a considerable surprise. James, taking advantage of the broad terms of PC 1218, was already re-drawing the patterns of Canadian life, so that the Dominion might be ready to play its full role in the hoped-for "efficient global economic system that will permit relatively free movement of commodities, immigrants and capital funds across existing national boundaries."[5] The successive drafts of the memorandum reveal the impressive scope and detail of his concerns. Employment and unemployment, redeployment of industry, agriculture, forestry, public works, housing, education, taxation, and fiscal policies are among the many factors taken into account – and in case the "efficient global economic system" should not be attained and postwar depression should result, reference is included to the corrective and restorative measures that might be taken. James obviously thought that if postwar planning was to be effective it had to be done on a grand scale, and he took full advantage of the wording of PC 1218 – in his own excerpted copy the words "what Government facilities should be set up" are typed twice in capital letters.

When working with and for the American bankers, or when criticizing the Roosevelt New Deal policies, or indeed when talking to the McGill Board of Governors, James had kept well in check any socialistic tendencies he might have inherited from his early training at LSE. When, however, he drafted this memorandum on the economic reconstruction of postwar Canada, he seems to have allowed these tendencies to emerge; possibly his new vantage-point enabled him to see things in different perspective. In the fourth draft of the document, for example, he discussed the possible need to control the civilian demand for consumer goods immediately after the war had ended.

Admittedly this aspect of reconstruction will demand very careful consideration, because it becomes increasingly apparent that absolute decontrol will not be possible at the immediate conclusion of hostilities and may in fact never become possible again during our lifetimes. Even though we may as individuals regret the passing of the older order of free trade, competition and capitalism, the available evidence concerning the impact of industrialism on a democratic-capitalistic order of society suggests that the attainment of reasonable economic security for the average individual will demand a large measure of coordination and governmental control.[6]

To be effective, this "coordination and control" would have to penetrate every aspect of the economy. The committee, prompted by this conviction and guided by its energetic chairman, quickly established sub-committees on such foremost matters as employment, natural resources, public construction, and agriculture. Professor Young wrote: "These flexible groups, along with more informal panels in other sectors, heard the views of interested organisations and authorities, and stimulated and informed them. In this way the James Committee penetrated all functional sectors of society, motivating them and drawing their leaders into a consultative framework of the kind which is now commonplace in many fields."[7]

The committee also commissioned a number of more detailed studies of various aspects of Canadian life, deemed important at a time when a predominantly agricultural economy was becoming more industrialized. Many of these studies were written for the committee by Leonard Marsh. James had come to know Marsh at McGill, where the latter had worked for ten years as director of the McGill Social Science Project.[8] When the Rockefeller funding had not been renewed at the beginning of World War II, the Board of Governors, never in favour of the project, had made no effort to continue it. One of Lewis Douglas' last actions before he handed responsibilities over to James had been to write Marsh a letter informing him that his appointment would terminate in 1941. It is ironic that while the governors were breathing a quiet sigh of relief at Marsh's departure from McGill, their own whiteheaded boy, Cyril James, was engaging him for a role in which he would disseminate his ideas throughout Canada.

The diary for 1941 shows in abundant detail that each day James was busy with very few intermissions on the complicated business of the university, which he dealt with in extraordinary detail. His concerns ranged from such things as the acquiring of Stoneycroft Farm at Ste Anne de Bellevue (including the problem of a labourer's widow occupying a cottage with her nine children) to the PhD candidate who ascribed the rejection of his thesis to his being transferred without consultation from his own research to war work conducted by Professor Otto Maass. James' attention to postwar reconstruction could therefore have been only intermittent. There are indications as early as June of that year that he saw the problems as requiring the close cooperation of the provinces with the federal government, and that he envisaged the need to establish a network of committees across Canada that might effect in each province what his committee was attempting at the federal level. He must have known that such activity would involve trespassing on very sensitive grounds, but he probably judged that if the task assigned was to be undertaken seriously, the risks were inherent in the commission. If he was convinced that a scheme was right, James tended to minimize difficulties and to be optimistic about the outcome.

At the same time, his thoughts and relationships were extending far beyond the Canadian borders. In the United States, there were social scientists whose views on the re-ordering of society were worthy of careful consideration, while in Britain there were many governmental and non-governmental agencies, such as the Royal Institute of International Affairs, whose ideas and goals should be taken into account in Canada. In the first draft of the Basic Memorandum James wrote: "In view of our hope that a world economy may be restored at the end of the present war, it seems desirable that this committee should familiarize itself with studies of postwar reconstruction that are now being made in Great Britain and the United States." It was relatively easy to consult with American social scientists; getting over to Britain was another matter. James' friend from the Wharton School, Joe Willits, now with the Rockefeller Foundation, suggested when they met in Washington in June that if the Canadian government would not finance a trip to Britain, perhaps the Carnegie Trust would. That same month, however, when James met the prime minister in Kingston, his hopes received a severe check.

Tuesday, June 24th – Kingston
I am down here in order that I may orate on British-Canadian-American relations tomorrow morning – but the most significant event for me is the fact that I failed to convince the P.M. that I should go to England. Ian Mackenzie telephoned tonight to say that he is flying over to do various jobs, including the presentation of the "Victory Torch" to Churchill, and that he is going to look after reconstruction in his spare time. Of course I am annoyed: I want to go to London very much indeed. But even apart form my own annoyance, I do not think that Mackenzie is knowledgeable enough to really accomplish anything in the way of coordinating British-Canadian thinking in the matter of planning for reconstruction. I realize that I should have found it a tough assignment, [but I would have been] beginning with greater knowledge of the field and spending all my time working at it. I cannot, however, convince the P.M. of that!

In July he heard that a Joint Economic Committee had been established in Washington and Ottawa to deal with postwar problems. Thinking this must either conflict with or at best duplicate the work of his committee, which seemed not to be very effective anyway, he proposed to resign. But by the first week in August he had convinced himself that the Committee on Reconstruction still had a worthwhile task to do, if it was separately constituted by Order in Council. This was accomplished by PC 6974 on 2 September 1941. So, in the midst of all his other preoccupations, James continued to give considerable thought to the committee's concerns.

His interest was strongly encouraged in October by two visitors from Britain, both involved in postwar reconstruction planning, Sir Geoffrey Shakespeare and Sir Ivison MacAdam.[9] Calling upon him at different times, they both agreed, no doubt at his prompting, that a visit by James to Britain would accomplish a great deal. Another visitor of the same kind was Lord Barnby,[10] whom James had had no time to receive in Montreal, but arranged to meet in Washington, where they both planned to be shortly. The account of their conversation reveals James' thinking at this time very clearly.

By arrangement, I met Lord Barnby on the four o'clock train and we went to Philadelphia together. He confirms my earlier impression that Greenwood is completely hopeless, and Reith operating upon a very narrow single track in his approach to Reconstruction.[11] Barnby himself is very much interested in the question of postwar emigration from England. During the course of a talk that lasted nearly three hours, I emphasized to him my own feeling that coordinated discussion of reconstruction problems among the Dominions is absolutely essential at this time. I reiterated the fact that Canada, England and Australia must understand one another's minds before they approach the United States, and insisted that it was woolly thinking to imagine that the United States was going to finance British reconstruction after the war without a quid pro quo ...

Greenwood and Reith were outstanding political figures with long experience of social administration, but their accomplishments had evidently not earned James' esteem. He was reaching out far beyond their narrower visions to an imperial concept, with Britain, Canada, Australia, and no doubt other dominions, working in close concert with the United States for the postwar resuscitation of international trade. Organized emigration from overpopulated Britain to underpopulated dominions, willing and prepared to receive skilled members of the work-force, was one element of the grand concept, so Lord Barnby, who was a member of the British Overseas Settlement Board, was an appropriate person with whom to discuss such not wholly fantastic notions.

Certainly these ideas were not new to James. Since his earlier Philadelphia days, he had looked forward to a peaceful world in which commerce and trade flowed freely, unhindered by nation-alisms or tariffs. He knew that others did not share his optimism, but even in the darkest days of the war he had an inner conviction that because such a world was reasonable and right, sooner or later it would come to pass. In March 1941, for example, he heard in the morning visiting British economist Gilbert Jackson prophesy that since postwar Europe and Britain would not be able to afford imports, Canada must face a serious depression. In the afternoon, he himself spoke to the Canadian Women's Club on "Canadian Universities in Wartime," later commenting: "I tried to hit an optimistic note and suggest that Canada had an important role to play in the postwar world." But then he asked himself:

Am I degenerating into a superficial thinker and a professional optimist? Or is it true that my ideas spring directly from the assumption of a world society, politically and economically integrated, while Jackson begins from an assumption of continuing national sovereignty? Even if the latter assumption is true, which of us is right?

James could not answer that question: he had to make a choice and go on in faith. This he did, holding to the same hopes, right through to the end.

Whether James had given serious thought to the mountains that would have to be moved to persuade governments to work in such international harmony is, of course, open to question. But faith does at least conceive that mountains are movable. Given the initial premise of a postwar world re-born into an era of peaceful international economic cooperation, the ideas James poured out to Barnby on the Philadelphia train were not too wildly unrealistic. Roosevelt and Churchill had already proclaimed their countries' determination to establish such a world in the Atlantic Charter, signed at sea in August 1941. Moreover, the United States did eventually propose and implement a wide-ranging scheme, the European Recovery Plan, commonly known as the Marshall Plan, not dissimilar in scope to James' own. But it was one thing for a powerful government to propose international economic policies and quite another for such a scheme to be proposed by a bright young academic. However, at least one consequence of having circulated such ideas was growing support for the idea that James should be sent to London to explore the situation (and, as he interpreted the commission, to propound his ideas) in the heart of the Empire. He was to receive further help from other and less desirable directions.

Great events were taking place on that larger stage of world affairs, and these inevitably influenced the smaller scene in which James was playing his minor part. Japan suddenly attacked the United States on 7 December 1941, and America was thus brought into the war as a fully declared ally of Britain and Canada. This great increase of Allied strength was welcomed as fervently in Canada as in Britain, despite regret at the wider proliferation of war into the Pacific. But the Canadian prime minister, Mackenzie King, soon had further concerns of his own. All through the earlier months of the neutral but increasing support of the United States for the British war effort, King had been suspicious that the United States and Britain were entering into secret agreements from which Canada was being excluded. This suspicion became a full-fledged worry after the United States officially became an ally. King welcomed any opportunity to gain further knowledge of the policy formation of the two countries. This business of planning for postwar international economic reconstruction, for example, touched Canada's interests closely, and while it was not yet a major subject of debate, internally or internationally, King thought (or could be persuaded by advisers such as Ian Mackenzie to think) that a Canadian inquiry into the ideas on reconstruction circulating in and around Whitehall would not be a bad move, and might possibly prove a good one.

When Churchill announced his plan to pay his new ally a visit in December 1941, King characteristically expressed concern over the possibility of a meeting between Churchill and Roosevelt without himself being present – not, he wrote in his diary on 22 December, that he was anxious to participate, but his opponents would "seek to have it appear that all that had been said about my being a link between the two amounted in reality to nothing ... I said that Churchill must pay us a visit here."[12] Churchill duly came to North America and addressed the United States legislature; but to appease King he also visited Ottawa and addressed a joint session of the houses of Parliament. James followed all these events with great interest.

Thursday, 1 January 1942
Another year has begun, heralded by Churchill's speeches and the cooperative determination of the British Empire and the United States to fight this war to a finish. Even Hitler seems less cocksure than he was: his New Year proclamation does not promise victory during 1942 but prophesies bitter fighting.

This will undoubtedly be a bleak year. Nobody expects that it will see the attainment of peace, and it is generally admitted that we may suffer serious reverses during the coming months because our maximum output of armaments will not be attained until 1943. There can be no doubt therefore that this will be a year of greater sacrifice and suffering – and yet I think that everybody feels happier than they did twelve months ago. The atmosphere is clearer, the issues more definite and the spirit of the people stronger.

In addition, his personal planning prospered. On 7 January 1942, James received a letter from the prime minister, authorizing him to make the visit to Britain.

I have now had an opportunity of discussing this matter with my colleagues, and we have agreed that such a visit might serve a useful purpose in connection with the work of the Committee.

I hope that, if you go to the United Kingdom, you will be able to make a detailed investigation of British plans for internal, social, and economic reconstruction. You might also, perhaps, find it useful, prior to your departure, to discuss with Dr. W.A. Mackintosh, Chairman of the Canadian Committee of the Joint Economic Committees, the possibility of your being able to obtain information in regard to the way British thought is running in the wider field of international reconstruction.

On 12 January, James had a long conversation with Mackintosh, who was serving as special assistant to W.C. Clark, the deputy minister of finance.[13] Mackintosh reported that King was very perturbed that "Canada is completely in the dark at the present time about English ideas on current and future economic policy and does not even know the gist of the present conversations that are going on between Great Britain and the U.S. in Washington." He added: "In brief, we would like to find out what is the policy of London in regard to the economic organization of the whole world at the end of the war." This conversation, of course, encouraged James greatly and increased his eagerness to get to England.

There was, however, still a great deal of delay before he could begin the journey. Accommodation on flights to Britain was very difficult to come by, but at last, after much wire-pulling by influential people in Montreal and Ottawa, he was told to prepare himself for the great adventure of flying the Atlantic in a bomber. Noise would be a major problem, so it was advisable to bring earplugs; oxygen would be required continually and therefore passengers must not fall asleep; but the greatest danger was cold. To avoid frostbite, loose warm clothing must be worn under the oversized flying suit and boots provided. Above all, there must be no careless talk, especially on the telephone, about airport locations, times of departure and arrival, destinations, and particularly the weather. On Friday, 6 February James was packed and ready to go, but the weather was unsuitable. The flight was postponed one day, then, two, then three – a week passed and still James was waiting (eating lightly, and avoiding, in accordance with his instruction, "gas-producing foods such as beans, cabbage, etc."). On Friday, 13 February, although the weather was fine, the pilot would not fly because if *was* Friday the thirteenth. St Valentine's Day, however, proved no obstacle, and that morning James finally took off.

An RAFFC [Royal Air Force Ferry Command] car picked me up at home at eight prompt, and took me out to Dorval, which we left at 10.15 in a four-engine Liberator bomber. There were nine of us, including Alexander Korda [the film-director] … The plane is quite roomy and comfortable, outside of the bomb racks (where we stayed only for take-off and landing). Incidentally, just before the plane left I was given three diplomatic pouches from the Embassy for delivery to the F.O. – becoming for the nonce a courier.

We reached Gander at 3.30 – flying all the way at about 7500 feet over the snowcovered land and the Gulf filled with pack-ice. Gander itself is huge, efficient and desolate: we had nothing to do but sit (on hard chairs), eat and talk – but the latter was interesting. I had a long chat with Korda, about [James Elroy Flecker's play] *Hassan* – which he likes personally but has not filmed because he thinks the people prefer things like the *Thief of Bagdad* or what he calls "tear-jerkers". He is an amazingly simple person, and interestingly enough he made that same comment about Charlie Chaplin.

The eight-hour flight across the Atlantic at 24,000 feet was noteworthy only because of the oxygen masks, which were "unpleasant but not uncomfortable." The plane landed at Prestwick, twenty-four hours after departure from Dorval, and then, after a bath and dinner, the party drove to Kilmarnock to catch the night train south. "The RAFFC took First Class sleepers for us – and I must say I enjoyed the luxury, sleeping like a top right through to 9 a.m., when I was wakened" by a steward with a cup of tea. James was back in his native London, arriving in a style that contrasted greatly with the manner in which he had originally departed twenty years earlier.

After taking a room at the Savoy Hotel in the Strand, he went immediately to Canada House

... where I had a long chat with Massey.[14] In regard to my request that he get me bomber passage for the return trip, he was frankly doubtful, but he promised to try. In regard to Reconstruction he is very much interested, but thinks that Canada is already ahead of England in the matter. When I have picked up a few of the threads, we are going to have another chat – and he has raised the interesting suggestion that he might appoint a special secretary at Canada House to collate all of these things and serve as a permanent specialised channel of communication between London and Ottawa.

It is becoming clear that many of these helpful proposals by persons in high places coinciding so neatly with James' own ideas arose from the fact that he was adept at suggesting actions and arrangements that would favour his planning. He then recorded in his diary, and possibly in his own memory, apparently spontaneous reactions that were in fact the reflection of his own enthusiasm for the scheme in hand.

As for Massey's comment, when James talked later with an American resident in London, Daniel O'Brien of the Rockefeller Foundation, he received the frank assessment that in Britain few people, if any, had clear thoughts on the nature of the postwar problems or were likely to commit themselves to definite statements.

One person who did have ideas on postwar reconstruction was Sir John Reith, as James discovered in a visit with him the next morning. Reith was ready, even eager, to discuss these ideas. However, James also discovered that Reith was, as he had suspected "operating on a very narrow single track" and thinking almost wholly in terms of physical reconstruction. When James tried to introduce his idea of an international dimension, Reith replied that building materials were not something Britain needed to import, but he would have somebody look into the matter. Although obviously not receiving the Reith support for his vision of empire-wide planning, James found much else in common with the former Director of the British Broadcasting Corporation.

Reith is tall and sturdy, but very energetic. He walked up and down the room all the two hours that I spent with him, never sitting down and seldom ceasing his continuous conversation. Since he was in Swarthmore [College, Pennsylvania] for two years in the last war, we have many

Philadelphia friends and American experiences in common – We were still talking when he had to leave for Buckingham Palace, so I went along in his car. He is going to draft a couple of memoranda for me regarding present problems, and will arrange a meeting of his senior staff so that we may have a general discussion.

How very nice to be dropped off at Buckingham Palace!

Amid all the talk of planning, Reith told James the story later included in Miller-Barstow's biography of Sir Edward Beatty.[15] After the death of Sir Arthur Currie in 1933, the university had taken its time looking around for a replacement. Two governors, William Birks and Walter Chipman, sent to scout possible candidates in Britain, consulted Lord Beaverbrook the Canadian-born newspaper proprietor. He recommended John Reith, and telephoned Reith asking him to consider the position and at least to receive the two governors to discuss it, to which Reith agreed. This was on a Sunday afternoon, and an appointment was fixed for the following Tuesday morning. Reith consulted his mother (an invariable practice) and with her encouragement decided to accept the position. But his expected visitors neither kept nor cancelled the appointment. Reith decided that between Sunday afternoon and Tuesday morning the two governors had communicated with the Chancellor, Sir Edward Beatty, who had vetoed the proposal. Certainly, two strong-minded characters such as Beatty and Reith operating on the same campus were likely to have clashed vigorously.

As James continued on to his next appointment – tea with Lord Kemsley, editor-in-chief of the *Sunday Times* and proprietor of the *Daily Sketch* and many regional newspapers – he probably reflected that had Beatty not intervened, it might well have been Reith visiting London as principal of McGill, with he himself still a professor in Philadelphia. Over "a sumptuous tea (fruit cake, petit fours and marzipan!)" Kemsley introduced James to four of his editors. In response to James' question, the editors agreed that "the man in the street" was more interested in postwar reconstruction when the war was going well than when the news was bad – a comment that does not seem to require profound insight. All present "agreed on the desirability of an international order after the war" – but recognized the difficulties and spent a good deal of time discussing them. Kemsley then sent for a more lowly member of staff and James was photographed before being sent on his way with promises of any further assistance he might need.

Returning from the "sumptuous tea," James telephoned Lord Barnby and was promptly invited to dinner. "After drinks at the flat we went out to a Club where we had (my record of food again!) soup, whitebait, roast turkey with potatoes and artichokes, jam tart and coffee. A sumptuous meal." It certainly does not sound as though wartime austerity lay heavily on the ruling classes of Britain.

So began a quite remarkable month. Although it was wartime, and all the energies of the empire were being unremittingly committed to the desperate struggle, yet Dr Cyril James from McGill University, Montreal, enquiring into plans for postwar reconstruction found that Cabinet ministers holding some of the most important portfolios still had time to give him personal interviews and to talk to him freely and at length about governmental and international affairs. Similarly, senior civil servants, front-ranking editors of newspapers (including *The Times*), powerful Trade Union officials, the foremost academic persons (including those of London, Oxford, Cambridge), the highest banking authorities (including the Bank of England), all welcomed him for personal interviews, lunches, dinners, teas, and even weekend visits.

But James also had warning of how swiftly some of these potentates might find themselves shifted from their seats of power. On a Friday morning, only two days after an interview with Lord Cranborne, under-secretary for the Dominions, and Greenwood, minister without portfolio, James was surprised to read in the morning newspaper that both these long-time political leaders had been dropped overnight from their posts; on the following Monday he learned that Reith, in the midst of all his confident planning, had also been fired. Undaunted, James wrote in his diary: "I shall have to do some of my work again."

If some of his connections were becoming suddenly disconnected, the others performed excellently. Among political leaders he was given interviews by Reith's successor, Lord Portal, by Herbert Morrison, the Home Secretary (they discussed air raid precautions mostly), Clement Attlee, secretary for the Dominions, L.S. Amery, secretary for India, R.A. Butler, president of the board of Education, Sir John Anderson, lord president of the Council, and Sir Archibald Sinclair, secretary for air. He spent a great deal of time with senior civil servants from numerous departments and with semi-official government consultants and advisers, men such as John Maynard Keynes, G.H.D. Cole, Arnold Toynbee, Alfred Zimmern, and William Beveridge. He stayed a weekend with Beveridge at University College, Oxford, in the Master's Lodgings. "These," he wrote in his diary "like King's at Cambridge, are palatial – but not very warm!"

Strangely enough, while James records with care numerous inter-views with other men whose names at that time appeared in the newspapers daily but who are now mostly forgotten, he records no details of his conversation with this Oxford host whose repu-tation grows rather than diminishes. Beveridge, however, appar-ently spoke freely of his work during that weekend; in his report to Prime Minister Mackenzie King, James was able to describe Beveridge's intentions in considerable detail.

In the specific field of social security, the matter is now being studied by a Committee of Officials under the Chairmanship of Sir William Beveridge who has, for the past quarter of a century, been one of the outstanding experts in this field. The Committee is working out a programme that coordinates the present schemes covering old age pensions, unemployment insurance, workmen's compensation, national health insurance, maternity benefits, care of child health and preventive medicine, while some attention is also being given to such recent proposals as family allowances. Since the task is not yet finished, no detailed scales of the benefits proposed under each head can be offered at this time, but Sir William insists that the unanimous aim of the Committee is to provide a comprehensive programme that will enable Britain to attain for its people a greater measure of "freedom from want"[16] than has yet been realized in any other country; while a secondary (and closely related) result is expected in regard to the improvement of the national health.

This was the pattern the Committee on Reconstruction would follow when their research director came to set out their plan for social security and "freedom from want" for the people of Canada. No doubt James discussed with Leonard Marsh what he had learned at Oxford in even greater detail than he did in this report to the prime minister.

Two of James' interviews stand out in their revelation of how misguided could be the international expectations of well-informed, experienced bureaucrats and political leaders of the war years. The first was with a senior official of the Treasury.

I met Sir Richard Hopkins at the [Athenaeum] Club and walked back to the Treasury for a further discussion. His view is that immediately after the war there will of course be temporary unemployment in various areas as a result of the shift from war to peace industries, but that this can be met constructively and will not cause any end to the postwar boom ... As to international matters, Hopkins feels that the British policy will be to make trade "as free as possible" after the war – but he does not expect free trade in the old sense, or a gold standard. An international monetary standard will have to be developed by Anglo-American corporations, but other nations should be admitted to participation at exchange positions offered by England and U.S. This will create some potential problems – and Russia in particular is apt to be obstructionist!

This vision of an Anglo-American alliance graciously arranging affairs for the rest of the world was to prove far removed from reality – but at least the misgivings about the attitude of the Soviet Union were amply confirmed.

The other notable interview was with Sir Walter Citrine, the president of the Trades Union Congress, a man of a very different political background from that of Hopkins.

His plan was clear cut. In the first phase he insisted on "international homogeneity". After the war ends, there must be an armistice of five years (or even ten) during which Russia, Britain and the U.S. will police the world and enforce order by armed force if that be necessary. During that period the immediate measures for the relief of famine and sickness in Europe will be carried out by an international body composed of those three countries – since it would be dangerous to use national governments at a time when revolutions are possible in many nations. At the end of five years, the three nations would call a peace conference at which all the nations would meet to draft a really constructive peace – but it might be desirable for the three nations to police the world for another five years in order to provide an opportunity to try out the peace treaty and ensure its revision if it were unsatisfactory.

Such international homogeneity would not be possible without "national homogeneity", so that, in the second place, it would be necessary in each country to attain this end. Any attempt on the part of a political party (he mentioned specifically the Labour Party) to precipitate a general election for its own ends would be contrary to the general plan. An election exacerbates national disputes. A coalition government must therefore continue in existence in all important countries.

There was even time, in this unreal, wartime London of "scrumptious teas" and "homogenized" political blueprints, to indulge in social calls. James was able to make a number of brief calls upon relatives at Barnet and to invite one or two old friends to join him for dinner at the Savoy and, on one occasion, even to visit the theatre. The play was a musical called *Lady Behave*. Although James makes no comment on the play, he does remark on the early timing: because of the black-out, the show began at 6.00 P.M.

and ended at 9.00 P.M. On a rather different level was an invitation for Sunday, 22 February.

Took the 10.5 from Paddington to Taplow in order to spend the day with the Astors[17] at Cliveden, which is the most beautiful place I have ever seen, even on a cold and frosty morning. It must be Elysium in summer ... Astor himself is a simple soul, wholeheartedly interested in the work of Chatham House and the public service generally – Lady Astor is utterly different. She is full of life, talks incessantly and has clear cut opinions about everything. She is delighted by the recent Cabinet changes since she did not like "Churchill as Czar" and particularly hates Beaverbrook.[18] I judge that her contacts with Stafford Cripps[19] are good since she says that she will now be able to work with Churchill through Cripps.

We cannot refrain from commenting that Churchill must have been greatly relieved.

It turned out that the underlying reason for this invitation was that Lord Astor wanted "to give Cliveden to the nation," but the presence of No. 5 Canadian General Hospital, which occupied Astor's grounds, created complications. These, he had decided, could best be eased if Canada would agree to give the hospital as a going concern to Britain, so that after the war it might continue as a public general hospital – and Astor thought that James might have influence in the matter. James promised to look into the matter and took the opportunity in the afternoon to visit the hospital, mostly staffed by doctors and nurses from Winnipeg. Lady Astor, on the other hand, took the opportunity to warn James against Lady Zimmern, whom she knew he was to meet later. When he did visit Sir Alfred Zimmern,[20] and dined with the lady in question, she reciprocated with a warning against Lady Astor.

Dinner with Sir Alfred and Lady Zimmern – the lady is overpoweringly verbose and enthusiastic so I can understand why Lady Astor does not like her. (Incidentally I despair of making this diary a reasonable record of my trip. I did not mention Lady Astor's long conversation about Lady Zimmern having impaired her husband's career, nor Zimmern's threat, to sue for libel and the Astors' appeal to Lionel Curtis[21] who finally pacified him. I did not even record the long conversation about Churchill who is certainly none too popular with the "Cliveden set" – nor the Astors' self-consciousness about the epithet!).

Since both ladies were charming and vivacious, James felt able to cope with their contradictory admonishments, and they certainly each added to the number of his memorable experiences.

After this excursion into Restoration comedy, none of his social occasions was as significant for James as a lunch in the city given in his honour by the chairman and directors of Barclay's Bank. Twenty years earlier he had been a junior clerk in the bank; now he was being graciously entertained by the chairman of the board as an important visitor from Canada. The reminiscences of his early days in the bank must have gratifyingly emphasised the contrast between his former lowly appointment and his present eminence.

Halfway through his visit in London, James became aware of international developments that had the effect of robbing his mission of its intended purpose. On 25 February, just ten days after he reached London, he read in the newspapers the announcement of the Anglo-American Lend-Lease Agreement. There was no longer any secret to be delicately explored: the United Kingdom and the United States had openly entered into a most far-reaching agreement. The further terms of the announcement, however, fully justified Cyril James with regard to the importance he had placed on the need for postwar regulation and management of the international economy; they were directed toward "the elimination of all forms of discriminatory treatment in international commerce and to the reduction of tariffs and other trade barriers; and in general to the attainment of all the economic objectives set forth in the Atlantic Charter."[22]

The announcement also revealed that Mackenzie King's wary suspicions had been fully justified. One clause directed that "articles and information so supplied might not be transferred to others by the British Government without the President's consent." Where did that leave Canada? The matter was raised in the British House of Commons. "Replying to supplementary questions, Mr. Attlee [the deputy prime minister and Dominion secretary] said that the representations of the Dominions had been taken into consideration ..."[23] – a vague phrase that indicated that Canada, despite her intermediary role, had not been invited to participate in the shaping of the agreement.

Although this announcement deprived James' mission of its underlying purpose, its ostensible reason of exploring ideas for postwar rehabilitation remained intact, and he continued with his planned program of interviews.

Interspersed with the continual flow of interviews and conferences were one or two university occasions. When James met

Colin Russel from the Montreal Neurological Hospital on a visit to No. 1 Canadian General Hospital, he was able to deal with some small matters regarding engagements and promotions for several McGill members of the medical staff, who no doubt appreciated this direct contact with the university. This was followed by a tea-time meeting of the McGill Graduates' Society of Great Britain at the Mayfair Hotel, arranged by James and the secretary of the society, at which Sir Harry Brittain[24] presided and James himself spoke briefly on the current state of affairs in Canada and the university. He was pleasantly surprised to find the meeting attended by sixty members, despite the short notice and the difficult transport conditions.

It was, however, becoming urgent that he should return to Montreal. He raised the matter during his visit to the secretary of state for air, Sir Archibald Sinclair, who was more than willing to help. It turned out Sir Archibald had personal ties with McGill and with Montreal that stemmed back to World War I: he had served with Sir Arthur Currie and been friends with the Canadian senior chaplain, now archdeacon of Montreal, F.G. Scott[25] – to whom he wanted to convey greetings. But stronger influences than these old wartime connections were also apparently at work; someone behind the scenes had obviously indicated that Dr James should receive VIP treatment. Group Captain Sir Louis Gregg was called in to arrange transportation back to Canada by ship. James was also to be given a special tour of the bombed areas of London, and, if time permitted, he should also be taken to visit RAF headquarters in the south of England.

That afternoon he was picked up at his hotel and driven through London on a carefully planned route that included a great part of the City area around St Paul's Cathedral, the Bermondsey and Southwark Boroughs close to the Surrey Docks, through to Kennington and Lambeth, and back to Westminster and Whitehall. The route stretched some fifteen miles, and as a result James had an extremely good idea of the destruction the German bombing had caused. The ocean transport became available for Friday 13 March (ships' captains were evidently not as superstitious as ferry pilots), and this gave James an additional day in which to accept Sir Archibald's invitation to visit Royal Air Force installations.

Air Commodore Curtis, RCAF, called for me at 9.30 and we drove into the country to visit Bomber Command where we were received by Air-Marshall Harris and Air Commodore Harrison. After showing us the photos of the recent raids on the Renault works in Paris, and the German tank factories in the Ruhr, both of which demonstrated complete devastation (200 British bombers dropped thirty tons *more* bombs on the Renault works than 500 German planes had dropped in London during the heaviest raid last year – and only one British bomber was lost), we went down to the big operations room underground. We inspected the big map which records hourly the weather at each of the flying fields in U.K., the "mozaic" standard air maps of German towns, and the vast chart on which the strength and position of the various squadrons is shown as of the exact moment.

From Bomber Command we drove straight to Coastal Command, which has no dugout as yet. After lunch with Air Chief Marshall Sir Philip Joubert, who is a very charming person, we went down to the operations room for an inspection. On a great wall-chart are plotted the position of all convoys, coastal and trans-Atlantic, as well as individual ships – while a companion table gives the details of each. The position of all aircraft of the Coastal Command is also plotted, as is that of the submarines spotted. Joubert showed me the historical charts of several recent convoys, illustrating the way in which and the extent to which air escort had been provided as well as the way in which air escort at a given point might break the contact between submarine and convoy, thus preventing further sinkings. He also showed me a chart showing all sinkings during the past three months – which with the present information of reported U. Boat positions is not encouraging for one who is about to put to sea.

In the middle of the afternoon we drove over to Fighter Command, where we were entertained to tea by the Chief of Air Staff, in the absence of Sir Sholto Douglas. The magnificent operations room, sixty feet underground, is more or less familiar from the published descriptions of it and the movies – but it is fascinating to watch the actual work of keeping an up-to-the minute record on the great table map. I watched one German aeroplane intercepted and sunk in the Irish Sea, and saw two others chased back to France.

Clearly, James was not being treated as a run-of-the-mill visitor. Received by Air Marshal Harris of Bomber Command, lunched by Air Chief Marshal Sir Philip Joubert, shown the secrets of Fighter Command by the Chief of Air staff, he was being given very special treatment indeed. Nor did the courtesies end there. That night on the crowded troop-train to Liverpool, he was speedily ensconced in a single first-class sleeper, and on the even more crowded troop-transport, the USS *Neville*, he was given "the luxury of a cabin to myself." Evidently Sir Archibald Sinclair had sent down signals that James was to be sent back to Canada as comfortably as possible, and as replete with understanding of Britain's aerial warfare as could be achieved. Mackenzie King and the Canadian government may have supplied James with impressive credentials, but it is unlikely their emissary would have rated this degree of care and concern. This treatment seems rather to have come from a more personal network of obligations and requitals, of which one in particular becomes apparent.

In the early months of the war, when the United States was neutral but benevolent, the American aircraft industry could provide the great four-engined bombers that Britain needed to reach into the heart of Germany. But how were they to be transported across the Atlantic? The man who came up with the answer was Sir Edward Beatty, president of the CPR and also of the company's airline.[26] The British Ministry of Aircraft Production gladly accepted his offer to organize the Canadian end of the run. Aircraft were flown by American pilots into St Hubert Airfield outside Montreal, and there Canadian and British pilots took over. The CP Air organization set up the Trans-Atlantic Ferry Service, and a contract between CP and the British Air Ministry was signed 6 August 1940 with the blessing of the Dominion Government. The flood of supplies destined for Britain grew constantly, so that by 27 May 1941, the Canadian and British governments cooperated to take over the operation with the establishment of the Royal Air Force Ferry Command. But Beatty's name and the Canadian connection were still remembered by the British Air Ministry authorities, and it was most probably a letter of introduction from Beatty, still chancellor of McGill despite his illness, that unlocked the secret doors of the Royal Air Force to James. Sinclair, Joubert, Harris, and the rest wanted a full, first-hand report of RAF activities and of the immense RCAF contribution to get back to Beatty and his colleagues, partly out of gratitude and partly because his name still represented a linchpin in the American–British air organization. Cyril James, in the luxury of his private cabin on the crowded USS *Neville*, once again had reason to be grateful to Sir Edward. He also had the grace to suffer pangs of conscience that he travelled in such comfort (he even had a private bath) when "those other poor devils, probably better men than I," had to endure such wretched discomfort as he saw on his rare visits to other quarters.

The voyage took twelve days, and was mercifully uneventful. The ship docked in Brooklyn, he was able to catch the night train to Montreal, and he arrived safely home on Thursday morning 26 March. Irene and Mrs McMurray were at the Windsor Station to meet him. It was the end of a visit to Britain that had been for him a vivid and nostalgic experience. It did not appear that the cause of postwar reconstruction had been greatly advanced, but he had had that significant weekend with Beveridge.

Upon his return, James immediately set about preparing a long, careful report on all he had heard and learned – a report that ran to thirty-three pages, with eight pages of appendices. He hastened to Ottawa to give a brief first-hand summary to Ian Mackenzie, the member of Cabinet to whom he was immediately responsible. He found to his dismay that Parliament was about to rise for a month's Easter recess and that Mackenzie himself was preoccupied with preparations for a trip to the west coast. In addition, those involved with Canada's postwar reconstruction plans were concerned with the fact that the House of Commons had recently appointed its own Special Committee on Reconstruction and Re-establishment and were busy discussing the implications and complications of this development. Nobody was particularly interested in what James had learned in Britain.

To return to Canada after many perils of air and sea, after having been welcomed so freely into the inner offices of the empire and after having conversed on familiar terms with the rich and famous, the wise, and the powerful, only to find that no one in Ottawa really cared, must have been disappointingly anti-climactic. But there were great gains to be recorded. He had established in Britain a valuable network of relationships that would stand him and his university in very good stead in the years to come. As for himself, his sense of kinship with England and his affection for his native land, which had been lying dormant during his American period, had been strongly renewed, and this was to prove important to him in later years.

Finally, we may comment that he left in his diary unpublished, probably not greatly considered, what (with all the advantage of hindsight) we may consider the most perceptive forecast he received of the postwar fortunes of Britain. It came from Ernest Bevin, the long-time socialist politician. "If a revolution *did* occur in England, the Amalgamated Engineers [Trade Union] would decide that it was not properly conducted according to paragraph 2 of Rule Seven, and want it done all over again."

A month after his return, James was given another opportunity to deliver his message in Ottawa. He appeared before the House of Commons committee on reconstruction and, to quote Professor Young, "he covered the field so thoroughly and so definitively that the parliamentarians must have felt even more redundant than was usual in those days ... Cyril James characteristically left the impression, not just that his vision of reconstruction was the official one, but also that rational men could hardly fail to agree with him."[27] In June, the Reconstruction Committee's agricultural sub-committee met with representatives from the provinces to propose the appointment of similar committees in the various regions. These could correlate their activities through the reconstruction committee's agencies, so that "any report which the [Agricultural] Sub-Committee will make to the Committee on Reconstruction for consideration and recommendation to the Government should represent the support of all the Provinces."[28] The sub-committee on the conservation of development of natural resources also held meetings with federal and provincial representatives and envisaged the preparation of programs to be approved by the federal government "and given to the Provinces for handling, committees being set up to carry them out."[29]

Late in August, Cyril James visited the western provinces, combining a holiday at Banff with university and reconstruction committee business. One purpose was to encourage the establishment of provincial reconstruction committees; their secretaries, he suggested, might also be attached to the federal reconstruction committee's staff, and regular conferences should be held with the appropriate provincial ministers. Even though debate on the Rowell-Sirois report on federal–provincial relations had been precluded by the concerns of war, James should have realized that he was trespassing on treacherous ground; since Confederation, the relations of the federal and provincial governments had been, as they still are, hedged about with susceptibilities and pride. But the obvious logic and inherent rightness of the proposals he was making lured him on.

One activity of the committee proved particularly important. It asked Leonard Marsh to prepare for Canada a blueprint for welfare planning of the scope and character of the Beveridge plan for Britain, which had been published as *Social Insurance and Allied Services* in Britain in 1942. Marsh's *Report on Social Security for Canada*, published by the King's Printer in Ottawa in March 1943, immediately attracted considerable attention, partly because of the obvious parallel with the Beveridge Plan but primarily because it dealt comprehensibly and constructively with Canada's own major social planning issues.

[This study] is an attempt to set out (a) the main features of existing statutory provisions for social security matters in Canada; (b) the methods by which these provisions can be improved and extended, particularly by transformation of the coverage and the technique to a social insurance basis; and (c) the principles which should be considered, if the construction of a comprehensive social security system, suited to Canadian conditions, is to be undertaken in a fruitful and effective manner.[30]

The study was well received by the public, and Marsh became the centre of much publicity, the journal *Saturday Night* inevitably dubbing him "the William Beveridge of Canada."[31] The book's historic character was established when in 1975, more than thirty years after first publication, it was reissued in the Social History of Canada series. In the preface to this edition, Professor Michael Bliss described it as "the most important single document in the history of the Welfare State in Canada." In a 1986 issue of *The Journal of Canadian Studies* devoted to the life and work of Leonard Marsh, Brigitte Kitchen noted that this judgment has been endorsed by other writers on the subject. She added her own support by way of a critical comment. "Today, the *Report on Social Security* still remains the most important single document attesting to the failure of Canadian governments to build a comprehensive social security system. The Marsh *Report* is a record of what could have been."[32]

In October the reconstruction committee submitted its own interim report, and although there was enough in that document to set alarm bells ringing in the offices of the senior bureaucracy, James forged steadily ahead. In December he organized a full meeting of the committee, its sub-committees, its research staff, and its many provincial representatives, including two provincial premiers. The meeting, held in the Railway Committee Room of the Senate, was a great success. James reviewed the committee's many activities, emphasizing again the urgent need for national planning that would reach on the one hand down into the provinces and on the other out into the world of Canada's allies. Provincial representatives responded to the persuasiveness of his advocacy, asking a great number of practical questions – many of them, predictably, related to the essential matter of funding. The federal government was in considerable danger of having a policy it had not proposed or even considered foisted upon it by general consent and enthusiasm.

An easy way to deal with the situation was to thank and discharge the committee and quietly to shelve its findings. Although the final report was ready only six months after the Marsh study, that is, in October 1943, it did not appear in print until March

1944. It then went through at least three printings, so it may be thought to have aroused a fair degree of serious attention. But the committee and its activities had offended many powerful susceptibilities, and there was no one to speak on its behalf.

Professor Young, assessing the activities of the Committee on Reconstruction from the point of view of a political scientist, describes it as a "spectacular example of the task force run wild."[33] James had, in dealing directly with provincial governments and in establishing relationships with official and unofficial bodies in Britain and the United States, far transgressed his terms of reference and aroused the territorial instincts of Ottawa's public service mandarins. Young points out that as early as October 1941 the Department of External Affairs had "delivered a stiff note of protest to Arnold Heeney, Clerk of the Privy Council: the Reconstruction Committee should restrict itself to domestic rehabilitation; otherwise the work of the [Canada–United States] Joint Economic Committees might be jeopardized." That concern found expression in the Economic Advisory Committee (EAC, a senior interdepartmental gathering composed of senior deputy-ministers, the governor of the Bank of Canada, and the chairman of the War Time Prices and Trade Board. Young quotes their memorandum of November 1942.

The [Economic Advisory] Committee believes that an outside or nondepartmental committee of the type of the Committee on Reconstruction can perform valuable functions in assisting with the development and promotion of postwar plans, but ... that postwar planning must be the responsibility of the Government itself ...[34]

Consequently the EAC recommended that the Committee on Reconstruction should have "Advisory" added to its title and that its future activities should be reported not directly to Cabinet by the minister of pensions and health, but through the prime minister, which in practice meant through Arnold Heeney, clerk to the Privy Council, and the regular bureaucracy. Further studies of the Advisory Committee on Postwar Reconstruction should only be undertaken in cooperation with EAC, and that body, somewhat enlarged, should be charged with "planning and organizing the activities of departments and agencies in the field of postwar planning."[35] James recognized that these manoeuvres effectively crippled the activities of his own committee, reducing it, as he put it in his diary in January 1943, to the role of a "fifth wheel." In this way the report of the Committee on Reconstruction was shelved before it could appear.

Yet the outcome of the Committee on Reconstruction should not be seen as one of failure. The opening section of the report itself places the matter in fair perspective.

When the Committee on Reconstruction began its work, very few public agencies in Canada concerned themselves actively with postwar problems. Victory appeared to be a distant dream and the energies of the nation were concentrated upon the immediate effort, so that the Committee found it necessary to instigate preliminary inquiries over a very wide field. In many cases it was also necessary to spend considerable energy and time in the task of stimulating others to give some practical consideration to postwar problems.

Today the climate of opinion has changed. In every province of this Dominion, reconstruction commissions appointed by the several governments are actively studying the problems that will confront them when hostilities have been brought to an end. In Ottawa itself, Committees of the Senate and the House of Commons have been listening to many witnesses, with a view to formulating specific recommendations to Parliament, and many of the cities in Canada have established special committees to study local problems. Canadians realize that the success which has attended the arms of the United Nations in recent campaigns brings the end of the war appreciably nearer, and they realize too that reconstruction is a gradual and continuous process, in which the immediate decisions made by government in some areas of public policy may have a profound postwar significance.[36]

This was a solid achievement, and the committee did well to emphasize it. With regard to social security, the report endorsed the major ideas of Leonard Marsh's study, but James and his colleagues had also concerned themselves with many other equally important matters, which appeared in the report under eight broad headings: the Impact of War on the Canadian Economy, the Problem of the Transition Period, the Role of Private Enterprise in Canada, the Role of Organized Labour, the Special Problem of Agriculture, the Area of Governmental Responsibility, Dominion–Provincial Relations, and Canada's Place in the World Economy. On the whole, the report can be characterized as a perceptive and comprehensive survey of Canada's anticipated postwar resources, obligations, and prospects.

In the event, the ideas of social and economic planning were taken up with considerable energy by Canadian governments at all levels, and history has proved to be on the side of the planners. Cyril James, R.C. Wallace, Edouard Montpetit, D.G. McKenzie, J.S.

McLean, and Tom Moore – as well as Leonard Marsh – had no reason to be ashamed of the ferment and stir they created in the minds of Canadians during the war years. Canada was infinitely better prepared for the postwar years because of their efforts.

James' own final comment on the reconstruction committee and its work, written in his personal diary Sunday, 30 January 1944, is appropriately modest.

One segment of my work ended this week when the P.M. tabled the full Report of the Committee on Reconstruction in the House of Commons on Friday. It will not, I think, make much stir because the Speech from the Throne on Thursday had already indicated the lines of policy which the government intends to follow – but it is pleasing to know that some of those lines were suggested when we handed in the report last October.

Although James did not personally contribute to the large international coordination of economies he had advocated in his Philadelphia years and again during his visit to Britain, he did significantly contribute, by means of this final report, to the dissemination of such ideas. Not surprisingly, he strongly approved of the Bretton Woods agreements reached in the fall of 1944 and was much encouraged by the creation of the United Nations in October 1945. The world we now live in – the world of the International Monetary Fund, the World Bank, the General Agreement on Trade and Tariffs, and the "global market" – is very much the kind of world James envisioned.

As for himself he was immersed in a constant deluge of university affairs, sometimes important, more often trivial, but always demanding and could emerge from these only occasionally to think about matters of national postwar reconstruction. In this situation, he had a choice: either he could be content to study the situation from afar, analysing and proposing large general ideas, as he had done in *England Today* and *The Road to Revival*; or, if he wanted to effect particular developments, he must plunge into the maelstrom of politics himself. He had recent memories to warn him of the uncertainties involved in a political career: the suave, competent Lord Cranborne, the confident, dynamic Sir John Reith, and the experienced, long-time party stalwart Arthur Greenwood, all dropped without warning from their offices only days after he had interviewed them. James took the lesson to heart. After this brush with the affairs of state, he chose not to become involved again in public affairs, other than as they related to universities. From now on he would stay with education.

CHAPTER SIX

Contributing to War

After his return from England in March 1942, James plunged once more into the work of running a university. Among the many trivial but nonetheless time-consuming matters, one issue of major importance engaged his attention and enthusiasm. This was an attempt to induce the different faculties of the university to provide "accelerated programs" so that students could finish their courses in a shorter time and be available to assist in the war effort. His determination in this matter was a direct outcome of his month in England, where the war and its grim consequences were a more immediate reality than they could be three thousand miles away in North America. His visits to the bomb-sites of southeast London and to the operations rooms of the RAF, where he had seen the war at firsthand, had left their mark. He earnestly desired to contribute to the war effort. Moreover, there was something he could do.

With Germany, Italy, and Japan aggressive on all fronts, and with the United States and the Soviet Union now fully involved, the call for armaments, navies, air forces, and armies increased, even in Canada, the demand for manpower – and womanpower – in every department of national life. Most of the combatants had resorted to some form of conscription, but MacKenzie King's government was constrained by the solemn pledge it had given in the National Resources Mobilization Act of 1940 not to introduce conscription. The Cabinet, resorting to an unparliamentary form of democracy, had therefore decided to hold a referendum on the question – the vote to be taken on 27 April 1942. The results, however, would not affect full-time students, since they were granted deferment of registration under the National Service Act. Looking at his university, an eminent source of men and women equipped with the qualifications most in demand, James saw that in many faculties the leisurely patterns of peacetime still prevailed. Classes ended in late April or early May and did not resume until mid-September. The whole summer was blank as far as these faculties were concerned, so that the universities were in effect a bottleneck in the supply of the men and women most likely to serve the country well.

It has to be said that there was another side to this story. McGill had lost some students by their own volition to the armed services, but it was the call-up of junior staff into the services, and of both junior and senior staff into work of national importance, that hit the university most severely. Class sizes had to be increased, lectures repeated to two sections of the same class, and in general heavier workloads undertaken. In the science and engineering departments particularly, higher registrations had to be served by a depleted staff; at the graduate level practically all research had been switched to war-related projects – especially in the chemistry department under the vigorous leadership of Professor Otto Maass – this research already being conducted on a twelve-month basis. Macdonald College had become the Eastern Training Centre for the Canadian Women's Army Corps – the School for Teachers being moved to the Montreal campus to provide the necessary accommodations. The medical and dental faculties, responding wholeheartedly to the call for volunteers, had provided almost all the professional services needed for the overseas Canadian General Hospitals Nos. 1 and 14 – McGill operations in everything but name. The university's contribution was thus a major one by any standards. Yet large areas of the campus remained almost wholly undisturbed by the national emergency: notably, the humanities and social sciences departments in the Faculty of Arts and Science, the Faculty of Law, and the School of Commerce. This situation, James believed, could and should be altered. A campus-wide, year-round range of accelerated programs should be available to the students.

On Monday, 30 March, five days after his return from London to Montreal, James raised the matter with the dean of arts, Cyrus Macmillan, himself briefly a member of one of King's earlier Cabinets and still a frequenter of the corridors of power.

Dean Macmillan came in at 3.30 ... We then discussed the question of acceleration of courses and Macmillan insisted that the government was completely unwilling to have anything to do with any acceleration. Even in the case of medicine it had been extraordinarily reluctant and had only responded to pressure from the universities. I told him that in that case I felt that McGill University had a major public responsibility for prodding the government and if necessary publicly disagreeing with it.[1]

Nothing further occurred until the deans' meeting on Wednesday, 8 April, when acceleration was the main subject of discussion. James gives a full account of the meeting, an indication of the importance he attached to it.

Dr. Roscoe came in for a brief chat about acceleration and I asked her to stay to the Deans Meeting since Dr. Shaw [Chairman of Physics] would also be present, in his capacity as Chairman of Arts Committee on Acceleration ... The Senate at its meeting in January had authorized acceleration and the Board at its last meeting had warmly approved the idea. The Medical Faculty, which is obviously one of the hardest to accelerate, has already developed a comprehensive programme and Dean Macmillan has written to me that the Arts and Science Faculty is eager to do so but nothing has yet eventuated. The women students in the Royal Victoria College have presented a petition requesting it and I have heard several opinions in the community that it ought to be carried out.

I pointed out that as a result of careful observation of English conditions I was convinced of an absolute need for trained professional men vastly greater than anything foreshadowed by official statements of the Canadian Government (a point on which Dean Macmillan confirmed my judgment by saying that the Government for reasons connected with the plebiscite did not desire at the present time to come out and say what it really knew). I further pointed out that the English universities were all accelerating their courses both in engineering and medicine as well as science ... and that no students at all were allowed to come to University excepting in fields where their training would be of use to the war. I followed this by referring briefly to the acceleration that has occurred in the U.S. and insisted that since Canada is also in this war we cannot allow matters to slide without reaching a formal decision.

A half-hour discussion followed, in which the dean of engineering stated flatly that acceleration was impossible for his faculty, and the dean of medicine observed "that he saw no reason why arts students should be considered exhausted after working halftime for twenty six weeks." Finally, it was agreed that each of the faculties should reconsider the matter, and that the next meeting of Senate should be delayed until Wednesday, 22 April, so that a comprehensive report regarding acceleration could be presented.

Besides working on his faculty deans, James had been writing letters to the ministers he felt should be active in this matter. This correspondence resulted in a telephone call the following Monday, 13 April, from L.E. Westerman of the Wartime Technical Bureau, who told James that a meeting of presidents, principals, and deans had been arranged for the first or second of May. James replied that it seemed desirable to him that the universities, and particularly McGill, should come to the meeting with definite plans for training additional people for the war effort, or accelerating the training of present students, plans that could be put into effect immediately if the meeting disclosed an urgent need for personnel.

James set about getting those "definite plans" approved by his colleagues. His effort is not only of interest in itself but also casts light on his relationships with the McGill staff; he was evidently a long way yet from winning their confidence. Deciding to face the opposition where it was strongest, he attended the engineering faculty meeting. After a tough session lasting nearly three hours, he won reluctant agreement that a special summer session provided by the Faculty of Arts and Science would take the place of the normal "pre-Engineering year," and that the engineering fourth year would begin in June, so that graduation could take place at Christmas. These arrangements would shorten the engineering course from five years to four and would make a class of graduates available in January 1943 rather than June, and so on in succeeding years.

This was the most difficult opposition he had to overcome. The next week James was in Toronto for a meeting of university presidents. Most of the discussion concerned the universities' relations with government and the military, and it was only over lunch that James was able to raise the matter that seemed to him the most important.

At this point the University Presidents ... adjourned for lunch at Hart House, and during the course of lunch I explained to them that I felt very strongly that Canadian universities were in a very invidious position at present. British universities had accelerated markedly for the picked students who were allowed to attend, and American universities were already carrying out large scale acceleration programmes. Once again, I was in a minority of one. Cody insisted that Toronto had quixotically accelerated medical training last year and was $23,000 in the hole as a result, a point on which I said that I found it hard to understand, since we had conducted a medical course on exactly the same principles for the last four years and suffered no financial loss as a result of it. His only explanation was that Toronto students were less wealthy than McGill students.

At the end of the paragraph there is a note inserted by Dorothy McMurray, who typed these journal entries each day and who occasionally added a corrective note when she thought the principal had his facts wrong. In this case, she had written: "(By DM: the loss of fees as a result of substitution of four year course here was about $30,000, was it not?)" However, basing a retort on an error of fact never hurt a lunch-table argument; the talk continued.

Wallace [of Queen's], although less definite, felt we ought to wait for the Government to tell us what to do and how much they would pay us for doing it, while Gilmour [of McMaster] and Fox [of Western Ontario] strongly followed Cody's lead.

It was clear from this conversation that James was going to be on his own in this endeavour, and the following week it was also apparent that he was not going to get strong backing from government sources either; he met with representatives of the Wartime Technical Bureau, who said that nothing could be done until decisions had been made at the planned meeting in May. That afternoon the arts faculty met to engage in "a great deal of desultory discussion about acceleration." James recorded the outcome in his journal.

Finally the rather vague resolution of Shaw's Committee [on Acceleration] was adopted with only three dissents, providing for the establishment of a summer session on a voluntary basis, [by] offering courses that would enable fourth year men and women to get their degrees toward the end of the summer whether the government asked for such a scheme or not.

Although these journal notes are in type, the record for Wednesday, 22 April is a private, hand-written, diary note. It refers to the crucial meeting of the University Senate, which had approved the reports from the faculties on the feasibility of acceleration and set the date for the commencement of a summer session in June. The diary note then continued as a fervent outpouring of relief. Obviously the tussle had cost James a good deal of nervous strain.

I feel strangely elated tonight – as a result of the fact that the first round of the acceleration battle has been won. Ever since I returned from England I have been trying to steer the various faculties (and the Dean's Committee) into the development of a proper programme for the acceleration of studies, and it has been uphill work. The reports have come from the various faculties reluctantly – and that from Arts and Science is so woolly that most of the detailed work still remains to be done – but Senate today accepted these several reports, and actually adopted plans that call for a summer session beginning on June 15th! I have already given the news to the press – and tomorrow morning McGill will either be the leader of a new crusade towards a greater war effort or else it will be a bitterly criticised object of scorn! I do not know which result will occur, but Muriel Roscoe (who came up for a chat tonight) tells me that the RVC students cheered the announcement at dinner time and I hope sincerely that this may be a happy augury.

The battle had indeed been won, but there was still much to do before victory could be claimed. On Monday, 27 April, James held a university-wide staff meeting to explain the details of the acceleration program, its financial implications, and the reasons for its implementation. There was "a good attendance of the higher ranks," though "Macmillan did not get back from P.E.I. for it" (he had gone to his home province to assist in the last moments of the plebiscite campaign). Only a few questions were asked – "quite simple ones of procedure." The next day, when Macmillan returned, he came in to see James, "very full of enthusiasm that the town where he had been in Prince Edward Island voted 96–0 in favour of the plebiscite," but James quickly brought him back to university priorities. "I pointed out to him that now that the plebiscite was over we had to do some hard work on the summer session, which was getting bogged down. Macmillan confessed to being extraordinarily surprised to hear this because it was his impression that all the faculty were strongly in favour of it. I suggested that he talk to some of them or to Bill Gentleman ..."[2] However, this simply moved the need for the principal's intervention a little further down the chain of command. Professor Shaw came in at 5 P.M. to complain that Macmillan was expecting him to write to all members of staff, asking what courses they would be prepared to teach in the summer session and to correlate the replies in time for a meeting of his committee on Monday morning. James explained that this would not do, that the committee must first decide what courses would be needed (otherwise they would be offering only a "hodge-podge") and then find the people to teach them. Shaw went off less than mollified, and Macmillan had to be coached in the preparation of the appropriate resolutions to be placed before the coming faculty meeting. The program then had to be steered through a lengthy debate in that meeting two days later, a matter that James conceded, Macmillan "handled very well indeed." Since the University Senate had already declared itself to be generally in favour of acceleration, the scheme, particularly the scale of bonuses to be paid to participating staff, was now ready to be presented to the Board of Governors for final authorization. The Board, which met on 20 May, duly approved. Summer sessions could be announced as commencing on 15 June, as the principal had planned. In view of the resistance and foot-dragging James had had to overcome, it was a considerable achievement. But the campaign had cost him dearly in personal terms. He had won his point but, as he himself recognized, he had strained his relations with his academic colleagues.

The "elation" of last Wednesday was probably compounded of weariness and too much whiskey: there was damned little to be elated about! The acceleration plan that looked so grand on paper is gradually fizzling out, simply because the faculty and the department chairmen are not eager to have it succeed. A little cold water can easily discourage an uncertain student, and Bill Gentleman says that there will not be six students from the whole Faculty.

If I were a Joe Willits [formerly dean at the Wharton School] full of wisdom and rich in personality, I should know my men, and gradually find a "band of brothers" who might help me in cases of this kind, but I have not spent enough time or energy with my men to find out those who are really good nor have I been patient enough to take them into counsel and earn their confidence. I get an idea and work like the devil for the short spasm necessary to force it through faculty and senate (thereby adding to the number of those who regard me as a fool, as well as to those who hate my guts) – but I have not the store of energy which is needed to build up that spirit among my colleagues that is needed to make a success of my innovation!

Certainly the innovation proved more of a gesture than a major contribution to the war effort. In his annual report of 1942, James commented on the 1941–2 student registration figures. There had been, he wrote, a welcome increase in registrations in science courses and a corresponding decrease in arts registrations. He did not comment on the further fact (although he must have noted it) that of the 155 students registered in the summer acceleration courses only 95 were men.[3]

Outside McGill, however, there were others who were also concerned by the anomalies inherent in the call-up deferment provisions.[4] In August 1942, the *Financial Post* asked its readers:

"Should we close all university courses except those training war specialists?" W.P. Thompson, dean of arts at the University of Saskatchewan, wrote in November to the secretary of the National Conference of Canadian Universities: "We can no longer defend encouraging students who are of military age and physically fit to take courses in the Humanities and Social Sciences subjects."[5] The Toronto *Globe and Mail* contributed to the discussion – in somewhat muted fashion, since the editorial appeared on Christmas Eve – with a piece headed "Arts Courses in Wartime." It argued that "those thousands of young men taking non-essential courses are not making any contribution to the winning of the war. In fact their very presence at the university makes for unfairness to those who have not the money to proceed with their education and who, on finishing high school, joined the armed forces."[6] The editorial drew attention to the fact that there had been acceleration of programs in medicine, dentistry, and engineering, but that programs in arts had continued unchanged. "It must be obvious that the even tenor of peacetime is very much out of place these days. The Government at Ottawa, together with the universities, will soon have to make up their minds about fitting the universities into the total war picture."

The reluctance to alter the existing patterns of university practice was characteristic not only of McGill academics but also academics at other universities. Teachers in both the humanities and the social sciences saw proposals to limit or deny deferment to arts students (along with those in law and commerce) as a veiled attack upon their own relevance in wartime. By the end of 1942, a memorandum signed by forty-one "anxious humanists" was circulating on Canadian campuses, with copies sent to Prime Minister Mackenzie King and Sidney Smith,[7] president that year of the National Conference of Canadian Universities. The memorandum, representing the views of both humanists and social scientists, made three points. "We recognize the primacy of the war effort. We urge the maintenance of strong university staffs in the Humanities, both as important for the war effort and as essential for the period of postwar rehabilitation. We urge the strengthening of the Humanities in our postwar system of higher education."

When the McGill arts faculty responded with an evident lack of enthusiasm to the idea of offering the summer session again in 1943, James sought support from another source, the students themselves. Early in the new year, he arranged a meeting at which he stated frankly that the meeting had been called in view of a forthcoming NCCU conference on the subject of deferments and course acceleration in the humanities. The students expressed a strong desire for clear directives from the government as to who should be deferred and which courses should be accelerated.

Consequently, when the NCCU met on 9 January 1943, James felt himself primed with an expression of student opinion that at least called for the ambiguities of the current situation to be resolved. Resolution, however, was not easily found. The subject of compulsory national service was a sensitive issue in any Canadian forum, but for the NCCU the issue was made even more difficult by the predominance of arts registrations in French-Canadian educational institutions – the results of the 1942 plebiscite vote had indicated that the majority of French Canadians were against conscription.[8]

The participants at the meeting, therefore, had to be very careful about what they said. According to Gwendoline Pilkington, a failure to be forthright about the reason for the meeting, and the subsequent lack of an adequate record of what took place, gave an air of mystery to the proceedings that some people were quick to interpret as attempted deceit.[9] One of the most prominent of the humanists, Watson Kirkconnell, at that time professor of English at MacMaster, cast James and R.C. Wallace of Queen's in the role of the villains of the piece.[10]

James was certainly an active participant, particularly as he felt he was speaking on behalf of the students themselves. In addition, he had, of course, been discussing these matters with his colleague on the Committee on Reconstruction, R.C. Wallace, who, as Frederick Gibson makes clear in his history of Queen's University, was as keen as James in this matter (both, Gibson notes, were British born).[11] On his own campus Wallace had acted even more severely than James, by executing the letter of the law that students who failed examinations would lose their deferment. James recorded the proceedings of the meeting in his journal.

Meeting of the National Conference of Canadian Universities. The proceedings opened by a very good speech from Mr. Macnamara [of the National Selective Service], immediately after which R.C. Wallace proposed that the Universities Conference should recommend to the government that all students in Arts and other non-technical subjects be deferred for at least two years after senior matriculation provide they had not attained the age of 20 before beginning Second Year. Malcolm Wallace [Principal of University College, Toronto] spoke strongly in favour of this and I followed.

This proposal was undoubtedly intended to be seen as a moderate one. The opposition was not, however, in the mood to be reasonable. They were reacting not to the terms of the motion but to what they believed was the intention of the Wallace–James party, that is, "to close the liberal arts faculties down." The opponents to the motion took the floor and, when the vote was taken, soundly defeated it. James' account of the debate concludes, "We finally passed a resolution saying that we agreed wholeheartedly to do what the government called upon us to do – and if they wanted us to do anything else we hoped they would inform us." These sarcastic sentences reflect James' sense of disillusionment. He himself felt deeply and sincerely the urgency of the wartime situation, yet he had failed to win others, either at McGill or in the university world in general, to share his concern. But his failure resulted in part from unfamiliarity with the complications of Canadian politics, a point made by Frederick Gibson in his closing comment.

It was an anticlimactic conclusion to one of the most potentially dramatic episodes in the history of Canadian universities. The "crisis" of 1943, if such it was, resulted not from national manpower needs but from a series of miscalculations which, in retrospect, seem a comedy of errors. Wallace and James, in their zeal to advance the war effort and disarm critics of the universities, had wholly misjudged the attitude of the government and of their fellow university presidents. The prime minister, far from desiring to raid the universities for additional manpower, was anxiously reflecting in the autumn of 1942 that the expansion of the armed forces had already gone too far. And nothing could have been less likely to win the approval of the Mackenzie King government, still staggering from the effects of the 1941–42 conscription crisis, than any proposal which would have obliged them to intervene in the provincial field of education and to do so in a manner which would have stripped the universities and colleges, including the classical colleges of Quebec, of their students and professors.[12]

Gibson adds, by way of solace, that Wallace and James could at least now say to critics of the universities that they were doing all that the government asked of them.

But that is not the whole story. At the beginning of 1943, the government itself was still deeply confused as to what its manpower needs truly were, and the academic leaders could not be blamed for the national uncertainties. "In regard to recruiting the year [1943] was one of ups and downs, of confusion and contradiction. In the first six months, the RCAF was faced with an aircrew procurement crisis of serious proportions; in the second half of the year, it had to deal with an embarrassingly large surplus of recruits."[13] In January 1943, therefore, James and Wallace were not misjudging the manpower needs as unrealistically as Gibson suggests. Moreover, those who opposed the Wallace–James initiative did so not on the basis of superior understanding of the national situation but in defence of particular interests of their own.

However, according to Watson Kirkconnell, a positive result of this affair was that the humanists once roused and banded together, remained united and founded the Humanities Research Council of Canada – a consequence that James, had he realized he would be credited with responsibility for this act, would have heartily approved.[14]

In these larger schemes, such as his plans for accelerated courses, or a national limitation of non-essential university courses, or even the work of the Committee on Reconstruction itself, James had either failed or achieved only partial success. But in his management of the university and in his more general public appearances, he was creating both the appearance and the substance of success, and was gaining good opinions from the majority of those who observed him. On campus there were still a few who, to use his own phrase, "hated his guts" – mostly, it would seem, because of bruised egos or of disturbed sloth; he had certainly been a disturber of their peace. But the majority of his colleagues were coming to recognize his competence and to appreciate his firm and just rule; these qualities were winning him, if not love, at least respect and admiration. Others, who viewed him at a somewhat greater distance, thought of him very well indeed. On 10 April 1942, for example, at the annual dinner of the University of Pennsylvania Club of New York, James received the William Guggenheim Honour Cup, awarded annually to the graduate who had brought most honour to the university during the year. To be recognized in this way by his former colleagues and fellow alumni, when he had been active for nearly three years in a foreign country, far removed from their own interests and notice, was a compliment to be cherished, an assurance that he was not entirely forgotten in the circles where he had formerly achieved so much.

Another assurance that there were those who observed and appreciated his doings came in a more tangible form, which was, in truth, even more welcome. In June that same year, the Executive Committee of the Board of Governors agreed to new financial arrangements that would greatly increase James' income and free him completely from his growing burden of debt. In a hand-written diary note, James recorded the detail.

Monday, 1 June [1942]

In terms of the Greek tragedy, I must watch my step because things are going too well. Last year's operations of the University have produced a surplus so that I can grant most of the budget requests, and give a few salary increases that were not even requested ...

McConnell has given the house at 1200 Pine Avenue as a Principal's residence – and both Irene and I are delighted with it. (In fact we wish that we could move in tomorrow!) ... McConnell indeed has been most friendly of late and today he told me that he had been able to arrange with [the Income Tax authorities] that I should get – *tax-free* – an entertainment allowance of $7,500 p.a. ...

By way of celebration, Bay and I went to see *Pull Together Canada* – a revue that is staged to build up public morale. We enjoyed the whole thing tremendously: the cast was good and the show admirably produced – while the moral (without an "e") came close to home.

The actions of the Executive Committee constituted substantial recognition. James' debt to the university of $5,000 (more than a year's salary for many of his colleagues) was cancelled. The tax-free addition of $4,000 annually to his entertainment allowance and the provision of a rent-free, furnished residence simultaneously reduced his expenditures and increased his income. By his leadership in the university and by his energy and initiative in public affairs, Frank Cyril James had shown that he deserved the rewards that were coming his way. But whether domestic and personal peace was ever to be among them was becoming more and more doubtful. When belittling his own achievements and competence in university affairs earlier in the spring of 1942 he had written:

The same lack of ability, understanding and patience is evident at home. When I wrote to Sir Edward about my chaotic finances he immediately said that I ought to take the McConnell house (to be owned and operated by the University) and have my [entertainment] allowance increased ... That should be simple enough to accept, but Bay and I have been arguing about the house ever since to the ruin of both our dispositions, without reaching a stage where the thing could be discussed sensibly!

Presumably his remark about the "moral" of the revue *Pull Together Canada* coming close to home meant that he knew the remedy even in this matter was in their own hands.

CHAPTER SEVEN

Preparing for Peace

In September 1943, Cyril James was beginning his fifth year at McGill. One matter of particular importance that had to be decided was the choosing of a new chancellor. Edward Beatty had held the office for so long and with such magisterial authority that no one quite knew how to replace him.

The obvious nominee was John Wilson McConnell, a successful businessman who had already demonstrated outstanding leadership abilities, as well as a high degree of generosity toward McGill. But a small group of governors led by George McDonald were resolutely opposed to his election. While they presented their concern as a desire to see a person of academic rather than commercial distinction representing the university in its highest office, there was also a well-known antipathy to McConnell himself. His success in commercial activities, which had given him his power in corporate and political circles, generated in some other businessmen envy and resentment. The majority of the board, however, were convinced that to offend him by not offering him the position of chancellor would be a foolish mistake. If he continued to think favourably of McGill, his present generosity toward the university was likely to become even more bountiful. In addition, he could influence the giving of other commercial magnates and through them their corporations. From that point of view alone he would make a very good chancellor.

But the interests supporting the contrary view were also powerful. McDonald had allied himself with Beatty to make it impossible for A.E. Morgan, the principal before Lewis Douglas, to continue in office more than two years, and he still had considerable influence in the financial circles of Montreal and also in the Graduates' Society. His opposition and that of one or two other governors to McConnell's election was no secret in the inner conclaves of either the business or the university elite.

As a result, the position remained vacant for several months while the quiet struggle went on. As vice-chancellor, James chaired the numerous committee meetings dealing with this thorny matter, and was not only fully aware of all that was said and done, but was also in an influential position with regard to the result. Mrs McMurray, recognizing this, wrote the principal a typical memorandum, telling him bluntly to "make sure" the committee nominated McConnell, because he had already served on the boards of both the Montreal General and the Royal Victoria Hospitals, and would re-direct his generosity toward them if he felt snubbed by the university. James had the wisdom to keep that paper discreetly hidden with his personal diary.

As it turned out, Mrs McMurray was wrong on this occasion. The nominating committee did ask McConnell to allow them to place his name before the board, and on his declining to accept nomination, they returned a second time to urge him to change his mind. James also spoke with McConnell alone. But McConnell remained steadfast in his decision; he knew that the vote had not been unanimous, and he had his own susceptibilities in the matter. (Mrs McMurray had described him in her memorandum as "a proud man.") However, his pride, if that is what it should be called, was of a commendable variety; he did not allow this matter of the chancellorship to lessen his interest in McGill. In fact, after this incident he increased the scope of his giving, so that he, and the McConnell Foundation established by his heirs, have proved by far the richest source of the university's benefactions, surpassing even those of Lord Strathcona and Sir William Macdonald. Even though he refused to be named chancellor, McConnell remained for the next decade the power behind the throne.

Faced with McConnell's refusal to stand for election, the governor's nominating committee decided that Morris Watson Wilson should be named. Wilson was an extremely able businessman, who had risen from the rank of office boy at age fourteen in the Merchants' Bank of Halifax to president of the Royal Bank of Canada at age fifty-one. He had been closely associated with Beatty's efforts to organize North American help for the British air force, taking a leading part in the organization of the transatlantic air ferry service.[1] Wilson was therefore no mean successor to Beatty.

The final comment from James on the choosing of a new chancellor was written on Monday, 10 January 1944, after a lapse from diary and journal-keeping that had left the final episode of the story unrecorded.

This diary seems to have gone to pieces during the last three months of the past year, when so much was happening that ought to have been recorded. The long Chancellorship row alone was worth a book. Now that Morris Wilson has been installed in office, that George McDonald seems likely to resign, and that McConnell has already passed the $5 million mark [in raising endowment funds] – there ought to be a note of rejoicing here [at this point in the resumed record].

This is a hand-written entry, added to his dictated journal, and, as so often, James confided to his diary what he could not say aloud to any other person.

But somehow today has been rotten – and I came home tonight with a feeling of irritation and uselessness. I just don't measure up to this job. I bungle simple discussions with students about exams; I bungle more elaborate discussions with Deans – and somehow I find myself getting less and less popular ... and I think it is due to the fact that I can get along more easily with my inferiors or my superiors than I can with my equals.

In actual fact the "bungled" moments were very few in comparison with the long hours he spent this same month, competently discussing the intricate legal details of the Morgan Woods acquisition at Ste Anne de Bellevue, the needs of the humanities in American education with the Rockefeller Foundation directors, the state of Protestant education in Quebec with the Teacher Training Committee, a possible scheme for McGill to train Chinese physicians with Wilder Penfield, director of the Montreal Neurological Institute and Hospital, or the role of the National Research Council in the encouragement of research in small business – he did not think it had one and said so bluntly. There appeared to be no subject he could not discuss with the experts, from psychiatry with Ewen Cameron to the newly invented electron-microscope with David Keys. But the informal discussions with students or the small-talk with colleagues before and after business meetings – these were what he "bungled." The comment that he could not establish easy relationships with his peers was an accurate and significant piece of self-knowledge. One perceptive colleague once described James as "wistful." Although it seems an odd choice of word, behind the perfection in the public role there was indeed a man who wanted to be friendly and popular, but who had somehow been shut off from the opportunities of natural affection. But if this trait briefly revealed itself to a few close observers, it was generally obscured by admiration for his apparently effortless dispatch of the university's business, from circumventing the pretensions of the secretary of the Graduate Society who wanted a place of honour in the convocation processions) to finding a solution to the problems presented to cancer research "because of [Professor of Surgery Edward] Archibald's pig-headedness, and high reputation among many potential benefactors of the university."

The "long Chancellorship row," in fact, left Cyril James in a remarkable position. The role of the principal at McGill had always been monarchical. The University Charter of 1821 named the institution, nominated a number of high-ranking dignitaries (such as the governor-general and bishop of Quebec) to be its governors, and further ordained that there should be a principal, who, for the term of his office, would also be a governor. Consequently, since busy office-holders such as the governor-general or the bishop often could not attend board meetings, the principal frequently found himself and an acquiescent chief magistrate of Montreal (his connection with McGill College being purely *ex officio*) the only governors available to transact business. Any student or professor appealing a ruling from the principal to the Board of Governors was likely to meet the same face under a different hat. When the charter was revised in 1852 to make the commercial magnates of Montreal who made up the Board of the Royal Institution for the Advancement of Learning also simultaneously the Board of Governors of the University of McGill College, the principal's place on the board was left intact. This new board revised the statutes, creating an academic senate and naming the principal as chairman. It was he who would report the Senate's actions to his fellow governors, which meant that the principal was still the only means of access to the governing body.

From 1855 to 1919, there were only two holders of the principalship, both outstanding, prestigious personalities: Sir William Dawson and Sir William Peterson. Neither man was challengeable in his exercise of benevolent autocracy. Their successor, the World War I hero Sir Arthur Currie, had continued in the same tradition. But as his health deteriorated and the reins began to slip from his hands, the decision was made to revise the statutes, in order to introduce some mild curbs on the principal's ill-defined but near omnipotence. The process took place during the short term of Currie's successor, A.E. Morgan. However, the next appointee, Lewis Douglas, declared the changes inadvisable and, expecting to be in office many years, protected his position by engineering a further revision that restored and spelled out the principal's autocracy. The outbreak of World War II precipitated both his departure and the sudden appointment of Cyril James, who thus inherited an almost unfettered authority.[2]

While Edward Beatty was in office, the fact that the principal was answerable to the board had had considerable meaning. But with the one natural leader, J.W. McConnell, declining to take office, and with his own growing ability to manage the board by his mastery of its complex business, James was able to assume almost sole control of the university in every aspect of its affairs. It speaks well for his character that, in accordance with the oath he had sworn to himself at the time of his installation, he used his position for more than twenty years to advance not his own interests but those he deemed the best interests of the university.

It should be pointed out that James' one-man rule of the university was not incongruous with the contemporary style of Quebec society, which, in the 1940s, and continuing even into the 1950s and early 1960s, did not follow what are considered normal democratic patterns.[3] The paternalistic Roman Church, not yet having experienced the Second Vatican Council, sought to protect both religion and culture by tight control of educational and social structures. At the same time, Premier Maurice Duplessis ran the province as a personal fiefdom, in which the democratic processes served only as a façade. Church and State were cut to one pattern. A small minority – men such as Frank Scott and women such as Thérèse Casgrain – protested the political despotism, but the majority accepted it placidly. Consequently, even at McGill, it was not until well into James' second decade that mild protests began to be heard among professors regarding the lack of democracy in university governance.

James himself was quick to resent any curbs, however slight, that might be placed on his freedom of administrative action. For his first two years in office, Beatty had been inactive as chancellor because of illness, and other members of the board seldom visited the university. Somewhat unreasonably, James was irked when Morris Wilson and one or two other governors began to appear even infrequently on campus to take part in some of the committee-work.

30 January 1944

Sometimes I grow a little worried about my fitness for my job – more with Morris Wilson than with Sir Edward ... When Sir Edward was here *I* ran the University with his guidance and advice – but Morris is more active and the Chancellorship discussions have stirred up many Governors to greater activity. Realistically I think that the presence of governors on Senate, on Selection Committees [for full professorships] and on other mixed committees complicates the job of the principal, since it puts him in the position of having to oppose a coalition of Governors and Faculty in public. This could not happen under the American or the English system of University administration and, if we are to preserve our special brand of mixed administration at McGill, I think that we should return to the fundamental principle that the principal is the sole normal channel of communication between Faculty and Governors – eliminating all these mixtures and clearly defining the functions of the separate bodies. I must put that in my academic testament, when the time comes, for the benefit of my successors.

The last remark is, of course, facetious, but what precedes reveals how strongly James held to the idea of autocratic powers. He did briefly consider the notion of working with colleagues who would exercise delegated authority – this upon a visit to his former university, where he observed a tendency to multiply administrators – but he rationalized on this possibility also.

Even if one admits that the rapid enlargement of the hierarchy at Pennsylvania seems absurd at a time when the student population is less than it was before the war – there are still two basic questions to answer. How far can one wisely go in delegating administrative responsibility to others? What are the characteristics of a good university president?

Although McGill is but half the size of Penn, I am conscious of the fact that I cannot do all that I should like to do, simply because the day is not long enough – yet I am healthy and fairly energetic. Two or three first class assistants would be a tremendous boon to me and to the University – but faculties seem not to like administrators per se, and Deans seldom escape from local loyalties to their own faculty.

James was assisted, one might even say "aided and abetted," in this notion that he alone could perform effectively on campus by David Landsborough Thomson, the dean of graduate studies from 1942 and vice-principal for the later years of James' term of office. A man of unusual personality, Thomson was a biochemist, who kept well abreast of developments in his discipline and knew everyone else's work but conducted no research of his own. He was a brilliant teacher, a provocative lecturer, a witty conversationalist, a lover of good company, but in no sense a practical man. As dean of the graduate faculty, he took the chair at all PhD oral examinations and joined easily and pertinently in the discussion of the thesis. He once remarked that he disliked examinations in pure mathematics because there only the candidate and the director of the thesis knew what they were talking about. He had a ready opinion on most subjects that arose in Senate and the gift of putting into appropriate words the consensus that was emerging from discussion. But he seldom attempted to initiate; he was content with the structures and patterns he had inherited. He was also content to be James' official deputy, performing routine tasks in his absence but never in any way challenging or trespassing upon the principal's unique authority. Although James had described himself as "fairly energetic," he was in fact intensely energetic; David Thomson on the other hand was the shrewd, well-informed observer; the two men understood one another and suited one another extremely well.

Inevitably, the longer James stayed in office the more natural his dominance seemed. His familiarity with every facet of the institutional business, his careful attention to detail at the meetings of all the faculties, and his clear grasp of the agenda of every meeting he attended (he still made a point of doing his homework very thoroughly) came to be taken for granted.

In addition, James was given ample opportunity to build up, through his admirably-phrased addresses, polished after-dinner speeches, and other addresses, the James persona, the public person. One such occasion was a special convocation that conferred only two degrees. In 1942, when the contribution of the United States to the Allied war effort was beginning to produce great benefits and to promise even more, Cyril James had proposed that McGill should offer President Roosevelt an honorary degree. Senate gladly concurred, but Roosevelt, while expressing appreciation, replied that he could not make the journey to Montreal to receive the award. Two years later, James learned early in September that Canada was to provide, for the second time, a meeting place in Quebec City for Roosevelt and Winston Churchill. James immediately proposed to the governor-general, the Earl of Athlone (who was *ex officio* the university's Visitor), that both Roosevelt and Churchill should travel to McGill at the end of the conference to be honoured by the university. But an additional journey to Montreal could not be included in the conference planning. James then telephone the governor-general's aide to suggest that if the mountains could not come to the prophets, the prophets would be prepared to come to the mountains: McGill would hold a special convocation in Quebec City. James provides a full account of the subsequent events in a diary note, hand written late at night on 16 September 1944.

Up to yesterday nothing had happened and, while I was talking to McConnell yesterday, I happened to see a picture of Churchill on his desk and absentmindedly expressed the wish that McConnell would persuade him to accept a degree. J.W. (who knew nothing of the previous developments) was greatly interested and, after I had described the situation, said that he would call Mackenzie King at lunchtime.

Having no great hopes that M.K. would bestir himself on behalf of McGill, I was much surprised at 4.10 p.m. when J.W. called to say that a convocation had been arranged at the Citadel for three o'clock tomorrow afternoon.

Members of the Senate had to be telephoned to obtain their agreement; the diplomas to be grossed and signed; a private car secured on the morning train to Quebec. It was seven P.M. before James could leave for home to prepare the presentations.

The latter task was not easy. I was appalled at the thought of speaking before the two most famous orators in the world – and perturbed by the task of delicately balancing the things that I said about each ... This morning I got up at six and worked on the three[4] speeches before breakfast – but most of the presentation speeches were later revised in the train and I was still writing the final script of the Churchill one as we pulled into Quebec ...

While the rest of the party took up their places at the northern end of the sunlit terrace, Wilson and I went in to greet Churchill and Roosevelt. Athlone and Princess Alice were with them. Everybody seemed to be in excellent spirits especially M.K. but I was shocked to see how ill Roosevelt looked ... Athlone opened the affair (adding spontaneously to my speech) and it proceeded according to the plan ... There were no more hitches, and the whole thing was over in little more than half an hour – so that there was a chance to chat informally before the press conference at 3.45. In addition to the honorary graduates (who were both so delighted that Roosevelt wants to keep his gown and Churchill wants a copy of the presentation speech) there were Mrs. Churchill, Anthony Eden, Lord Leathers and more than 150 newspaper men – but no general audience had been allowed to attend.[5]

The words James found to say for Roosevelt were:

Mr. Chancellor,

I have the honour to present to you one who, long a friend of Canada, has attained imperishable stature throughout the length and breadth of this North American Continent.

More than a decade ago, he courageously tackled the problems of those millions, throughout the United States, who were the victims of depression, and by the inspiration of his leadership was a source of hope.

His humanitarianism now embraces unnumbered millions throughout the world. The vast production programme of the United States during the early months of this war owed much to his vision. The processes of lend-lease, by which equipment was supplied to the hard-pressed democracies in their hour of greatest need, was an expression of his confident courage. In that tragic hour, when the outposts of the United States were treacherously assailed by a vindictive enemy, that courage did not falter. The industrial and scientific resources of a great nation, which he mobilized with undreamed-of speed, have forged the weapons by which the armies of the United Nations are today marching forward to victory.

Mr. Chancellor, by authority of Senate and in the name of all Canadians, I present to you Franklin Delano Roosevelt, President of the United States, in order that you may confer on him the degree of Doctor of Laws, *honoris causa*.[6]

The even greater task, at least for a Canadian, was to find words not inappropriate when applied to Winston Churchill. James' final version, polished and repolished in the Quebec train, may not have been faultless, but who else could have done so well?

Mr. Chancellor,

I have the honour to present to you one who needs no words to attest his greatness.

The medals that he wears proclaim his military service. The books that he has written are treasured alike by historians and all students of our sweet English tongue. As a Minister of the Crown, his services to the British Commonwealth are unsurpassed.

He is of that company of immortals who have rallied England in the great climacterics of her history. His vision foretold the present war and, in that dark hour when France had fallen and the bastions of Britain were threatened, his splendid words expressed the unconquerable spirit of his people. Those words can never be forgotten. They embodied the shining courage by which he evoked from the men and women of that island fortress the supreme efforts of the last four years. They inspired a faith as flaming as his own.

Mr. Chancellor, by authority of the Senate and in the name of all the people of Canada, I present to you Winston Spencer Churchill, one of the greatest of Englishmen, in order that you may confer on him the degree of Doctor of Laws, *honoris causa*.

Cyril James conceived the idea of this dramatic convocation, he knew the right people to approach, he made sure that all the players were provided with their parts, he found the appropriate words for giants of international renown, he played his own role splendidly, and in all this he supplied a distinctively Canadian contribution to an historic international occasion. It is doubtful any one else could have done that.

Another significant day followed in less than a month on the bicentennial of James McGill's birthdate, 6 October 1744. The university celebrated the 1944 Founder's Day Convocation with festive ceremonies appropriate to a bicentennial. To begin, a small procession of municipal and university dignitaries made their way from the office of the mayor of Montreal to James McGill's house in Bonsecours Market, where a plaque marking the bicentennial was unveiled. Speeches recalled James McGill and his civic achievements: the mayor spoke in English and French, the Chancellor followed in English, the principal of McGill took up the theme in French, and finally the rector of l'Université de Montréal concluded the ceremony with a generous tribute "à un grand montréalais."

In the afternoon, the guest of honour was again General A.G.L. McNaughton. A new plaque had been cut for the founder's tomb, and Colonel H.D. Rolland, supported by a guard of honour mounted by the Grenadier Guards, presented it to the university of behalf of the regiment and the Graduates' Society.[7] Then followed the colourful ceremonies of the convocation in the Currie Memorial Gymnasium, suitably decorated and filled to overflowing with graduands, students, faculty, and friends.

The evening began with a dinner at the Mount Royal Hotel, the highlight being a half-hour segment of broadcast time on nation-wide radio. Cyril James did not stay for the dancing, but his final verdict was the "the whole day has been unusually successful." It was yet another occasion on which the McGill principal was seen at his impressive best.

Despite the heavy load of his office, James found time to read widely. His diary notes, written generally on Sundays, often name, sometimes with brief comments, the books he had been reading during the week; they are seldom novels but often biographies, memoirs, or essays. The letters of T.E. Lawrence ("much more revealing than *The Seven Pillars of Wisdom*"); a biography of Wellington; some D.H. Lawrence (a novel re-read but "still sawdust and vinegar"); the *Holmes–Pollock Letters;*[8] Robert Swanson's *Rhymes of a Lumberjack* ("reminiscent of Robert Service but not as good"); Konrad Heiden's *Der Führer* (Hitler "looms out of this book more clearly than from *Mein Kampf* as an extraordinary person"); it is a mixed bag that indicates wide-ranging interests, and enquiring mind.

In consonance with those broad interests, James took personal notice of the work of the various faculties of the university and did not hesitate to prod the deans concerning departmental goals and programs, especially with regard to preparations for the post-war opportunities.

January 10, 1944

Meeting with all the deans ... to discuss the question of internal academic organization and personnel, with a view to postwar rehabilitation. There was a good deal of rather desultory discussion on the subject of personnel and plans, with many of the deans tending to think that this was simply another suggestion about ways of spending money or requesting money. It was however finally agreed that each dean should obtain from each department chairman a carefully worked out statement of the needs of that department and what it expected to do in teaching and research during the next five or six years, together with an equally specific statement of the type of person who was needed to fill the existing gaps in the teaching staff. I suggested that it would also be useful to have as an appendix specific suggestions as to the names of people who might be appointed if and when such appointments were authorized by the Board of Governors since these suggestions would constitute a preliminary document for such selection committees as might be set up.

James was greatly assisted in the spring of 1944 by J.W. McConnell's magnificent effort to raise funds to renew McGill's endowment and re-equip the university to meet postwar developments. By exercising his commercial influence, McConnell raised a little less than $7 million, a sum equivalent to many times that figure in today's values. James and his office acted as the back-up team, with James keeping careful hand-written lists of pledges, donations paid, and amounts outstanding. As he put these lists into his private papers, he reflected that the question now was whether he "could be as wise at spending them as McConnell had been in collecting." Some of those who contributed might have balked at the word "wise"; they might have preferred "astute," or even "ruthless."

Whatever the word, James felt he now had the resources to

permit the university not only to award much-needed if modest salary increases, make new appointments, and replace equipment, but also to venture into new teaching fields. What turned his mind to geography is not entirely clear.[9] Regarded as a synthetic science occupying middle ground somewhere between geology, meteorology, anthropology, and history, geography had been recognized as a university-level discipline only in the years between the two world wars. As early as January of 1944, James had been thinking and talking with advisers about the possibilities of new developments, and, for some reason of his own, geography was the one that appealed to him most. It is significant that for advice and guidance he looked first to his American friends, rather than to colleagues in the university.

Saturday, January 8

Spent most of the morning with J.H. Willitts at the Rockefeller Foundation talking over various National Bureau and Economic matters in addition to McGill affairs. In regard to the possible development of Geography at McGill Joe showed me a letter that had just come in from [Carl] Sauer [professor of Geography, University of California] containing the names of those whom he suggested as candidates. As an obiter dictum I said it seemed to me that if [the right man] came to McGill he might be able, cooperating with [J.E.] Gill and [J.J.] O'Neill [both of Geology] to evolve a very valuable research programme concerned with the further investigation of Arctic phenomena which were looming large in both meteorological and economic discussion at present. Joe was very much interested in this casual remark and told me that Raleigh Parkin[10] had recently written a very enthusiastic letter about the need for investigation of the Arctic, recommending Trevor Lloyd as the ideal person to carry out such a study. Unfortunately he had enclosed two of Lloyd's papers and after consideration of the papers the Rockefeller made a grant of $10,000 to the Canadian Social Sciences Research Council on the express understanding that Innis[11] would carry out the preliminary investigations.[12] Innis is already engaged on this on a full time basis during the present year and will undoubtedly make a good report so that the general idea which I had suggested at random might conceivably come along very appropriately as a second stage in the investigation.

"Suggested at random" – the idea was indeed to prove a seminal one. But before the geography department could be established, James had to gather further advice and then try his ideas out on his colleagues at McGill. By the end of March matters had progressed to the point of creating a professorial selection committee.

The first appointment in geography was made that summer in the person of George Kimble, formerly a lecturer at several English universities on the history of exploration and currently serving the British Admiralty as a climatologist. Kimble quickly named another climatologist, F. Kenneth Hare, who was serving in the Royal Air Force, as his assistant.[13] Following their demobilization in September 1945, the department began both teaching and research. But even before these plans could take effect, James' interest and widespread inquiries began to produce results. He was approached by a group of geographers and like-minded individuals who had secured funds from the Rockefeller Foundation to found the Arctic Institute of North America and who thought Montreal would be an excellent location for the office and library. The institute wished to remain independent but associated with an academic community. James responded that he could not assist financially but he could provide rent-free accommodation. The offer was accepted and the deep involvement of McGill in northern studies began. When thirty years later the Arctic Institute moved to Calgary, the McGill Centre for Northern Studies continued the university's Arctic commitment without a break. The geography department was to undertake many other ventures, but northern research, as James had foreseen, was its first and natural expansion.

The way in which James was quick to welcome new fields of activity is further illustrated by the first instance of McGill's involvement in the Caribbean, another area that became a major interest of the university in the postwar decades. A visitor who called to see him at the end of May 1944 made an interesting proposal, to which James responded positively but with modifications of his own. He saw another opportunity to broaden the sphere of McGill's influence.

Sir James Irvine[14], and the members of his West Indian Education Committee, arrived in Montreal this morning and came to the office for a chat. They told me that they had decided to set up a university in Trinidad – but were eager to have it under the tutelage of some established institution during its early years.

In regard to medicine, they hoped that McGill would assume that responsibility, and perhaps conduct the examinations. As an alternative I suggested that the students might do pre-medical work in the Arts Faculty at Trinidad, come to Montreal for two years pre-clinical work and then return to Trinidad for clinical work and internship under an arrangement where McGill would supply professors of Surgery, Medicine, Obstetrics and Pathology. These would be McGill professors – rotating on three year terms with their opposite numbers in Montreal – and all would be on a full term salary basis. Irvine seemed to be attracted by this idea,which would give the students a McGill medicine degree – and felt that the U.K. would be willing to finance such a scheme.

Obviously James was willing to adapt and improvise in order to accommodate the extension of McGill's influence. In that regard, he was a true successor to his predecessors Dawson and Peterson, who had conceived and built up a Canada-wide network of schools and colleges, affiliated with the university and following its curricula. McGill had helped establish the University of British Columbia before World War I, and now, after World War II, it would be ready to help establish the University of the West Indies.

And there were even more exciting possibilities presenting themselves. J.S. Foster of the physics department, who had been a post-graduate student of Nils Bohr in the late 1920s, had, in the decade before the war, planned to introduce the study of particle physics at McGill by building a cyclotron – the first in Canada. The Board of Governors had approved a site, the National Research Council had allotted funds, and some preliminary work had been undertaken. The war had necessarily interrupted these activities but early in September 1944, Otto Maass, the professor of chemistry who was himself much involved in war work, came to the principal's office with confidential information: Foster, who was on leave conducting research on radar, would probably be ready soon to return to McGill to pick up his particle physics interests. Moreover, the Canadian government had supported a secret research effort, located in the as-yet unoccupied buildings of the new Université de Montréal, with large sums of money – as much a eight million dollars from federal funds. The United Kingdom contribution had been of the order of two billion dollars! Maass was convinced that, when it could be disclosed after the war, this secret work, "in nuclear physics" would be of great peacetime significance. McGill should be ready, he said, to inherit the work being undertaken on the other side of the mountain and support Foster strongly on his return.

James readily agreed, and when Foster returned, he was given facilities and space. With the help of the National Research Council, the McGill cyclotron was built, and the university pioneered for Canada the strange new world of particle physics. But neither James nor Maass realized while they were talking together of "inheriting the work" at l'Université de Montréal that it was part of something called "the Manhattan project," or that in only nine months it would create at Hiroshima a reverberation that would be heard not only around the world but also in the conscience of mankind. This development was, in fact, part of the consequence of Ernest Rutherford's work on the McGill campus forty years earlier, but certainly not something McGill would be able, or would wish, to inherit alone. It did, however, make sense in 1944 to give Foster as much opportunity as possible.

Still other intriguing possibilities were coming up. James went to Ottawa that fall to discuss with Air Vice-Marshal Ferrier the creation at McGill of a chair in aeronautics. Hans Selye had received a large grant to establish a laboratory for histological research, and Wilder Penfield had ambitious plans for the Neurological Institute. There was even a visit from the president of the Dressmakers' Guild of New York to discuss the establishment of a School of Dress Design, Montreal being a major production centre for the ladies' garment industry. James suggested the delegation should visit Macdonald College, and asked for a memorandum of their proposals, together with their suggestions for the necessary financing. The second half of 1944 was certainly a time of innovative thinking. Some of these proposals, like that of the School for Dress Design, came to nothing more; others, like the proposals in histology and neurology, led quickly to important developments; others again, like the proposed cooperation in the Caribbean and the plans for work in aeronautics came to fruition only in James' later years; but all were received positively and given careful consideration. James was committed not merely to the physical and financial administration of the university, but most strongly to its social and intellectual advancement.

The government was also concerned about educational opportunities, particularly for veterans. Brigadier-General H.F. McDonald, chairman of the federal government's Advisory Committee on Rehabilitation and Demobilization, was concerned not to repeat the mistakes of World War I: in 1919, academic standards had been dangerously disregarded and educational opportunities for veterans had been narrowly restricted; this time those opportunities would be made readily available. President Cody of Toronto, and Principals Wallace of Queen's and James of McGill had been invited in the fall of 1942 to advise McDonald's committee, so James knew what government plans were being made for the veterans and had some idea what the numbers were likely to be. But he had considerable difficulty in getting Dean Macmillan and the Faculty of Arts and Science to make realistic preparations. Dean Macmillan, who came in December of that year to see James about several items, referred to a committee that the arts faculty had set up on the admission of veterans (who at that time were very few) as an unimportant, rather routine matter. James disagreed: the committee should give a strong lead, or the faculties would content themselves with generalities; there should be a clear statement on the matter of service activities counting toward qualification for admission and also a statement regarding the need for continued acceleration of courses, "because these men would not want to waste time sitting around in the summer." He went on to suggest courses designed especially to the veterans' needs.

I was not suggesting that we needed simply to telescope our present course and admit people into second year instead of first year, but that we should institute an entirely new scheme of courses which recognized that the students' practical experience was a tremendously valuable thing and around that practical experience to try to build up for him a cultural and scientific knowledge which would give him a rounded education. No problem in our whole educational system was more serious or more difficult than this one ... Macmillan said he had not fully realized all of those implications, but felt that this obviously was a field in which McGill University ought to provide leadership for the country and that he would take the matter up with the Senate Committee.

There is a distinctly admonishing tone to James' suggestions; it is clear that a good deal of the time he was impatient with his colleagues, having to urge them on to more strenuous efforts. In this, he appears not to have been very successful; six months later, in May 1943, the dean came in with an unsatisfactory report.

Macmillan came in ... to tell me that the meeting of the B.A. Advisory Committee the other day had been exceedingly turbulent. Adair and Dawson, sometimes abetted by Darbelnet, had opposed strongly any special concessions to men going on active service and even more strongly any special privileges to those who returned from active service to the University. They insisted that the whole attitude of the University was wrong and that our publicity was conveying the idea that this was an armed camp rather than an academic institution.

E.R. Adair was a history professor who had caused an outcry in the fall of 1939 by declaring in a public lecture that Britain had no reason to involve herself in Poland's affairs, and that if she had done so, Canada had no obligation to follow suit; Carl Dawson was a pioneer sociologist who had previously shown a marked lack of enthusiasm for the war-effort. Darbelnet was the professor of French.

Apparently interpreting their readiness to speak out so openly on this occasion as indicative of a poor spirit in the faculty generally, James exhorted Macmillan to set clearer academic aims and objectives – in a word to exercise more effective leadership. It is noticeable in both these interviews that although Macmillan was the considerably older and more experienced man – he had been teaching at McGill for more than thirty years, nearly twenty of them as full professor, and had also served as a federal cabinet minster – there was no doubt as to who was lecturing whom. James had achieved a complete ascendancy over his senior staff.

Of the importance of the issue at hand, James had no doubt: the end of the war would see great numbers of demobilized men and women returning from the forces armed with the government bursaries that had been promised as early as October 1941. True, when James had first spoken to Macmillan on the subject, there had been only twenty-four veterans enrolled in universities in all of Canada, and the following year still only seventy-three, but with the coming of peace the trickle would become a flood.

The few veterans to be found in Canadian universities before the summer of 1944 were men discharged because of disabilities. But in the fall of that year, when it was discovered that air-crew training schemes had been too successful and that there was a surplus of men in relation to equipment, some air-crew members were permitted to return to their studies subject to immediate recall. The universities immediately felt the pressure. By January 1945, two thousand such students were registered; by the end of the year, with the war successfully concluded, the number had risen to 14,500. Two years later it had reached 37,000. This was some two thousand more than the total student university population in the whole of Canada in 1939. Veteran men and women who would not normally have contemplated post-secondary education gladly seized the opportunity offered to them by the federal bursaries. Universities found themselves faced with doubled enrolments and immense problems ... shortages of classrooms, laboratories, books, equipment of all kinds, and especially teachers at all levels and in all disciplines.

Some universities were, of course, more popular than others, and since McGill was a prestige university and had joined in the common pledge that no duly qualified veteran would be denied a place, its resources came under tremendous pressure. For a principal such as Cyril James, the question was not whether McGill could or would carry the load, but simply how. But before an answer could be formulated there was a prior problem to be addressed and solved.

Since a student's fees covered only a part of the cost of the education, each veteran admitted by McGill would constitute an additional burden on the endowment. Provincial institutions, such as the University of Toronto or l'Université de Montréal, could expect provincial funds to cover the balance of costs but as a private university, McGill would have to meet them from its own resources. There was also the further consideration that James, as we have seen, had raised with his colleagues: veterans would require special academic programs tailored to their needs, and these would generate additional expenditures.

Fortunately James had not been alone in foreseeing these difficulties. His colleagues in the NCCU had been warned by their committee on postwar problems that catering to the needs of the veterans, both academically and physically, would be more expensive than providing for the needs of civilian students.[15] It was not enough that the veteran should receive a bursary that would cover fees and living expenses. The institutions would also need assistance, preferably by way of a *per capitum* grant from the federal government. The university heads readily grasped the point and, in November 1944, asked the president of the association, J.S. Thomson of Saskatchewan, to approach the federal authorities. After what Thomson described as "a most successful session of collective bargaining" (the universities asked for $200 per student, the government representatives offered $100, and they compromised on $150, the universities' original target) history was made when Prime Minister Mackenzie King announced that federal assistance would be given to all Canadian universities accepting veteran registrations.[16] With this assurance of a federal grant and with the splendid support of J.W. McConnell's successful fund-raising, James was ready, in January 1945, to cope with the incoming crowds. He underlined the importance of the occasion by formally meeting the 200 veteran registrants on the Arts Building steps. Many were still in uniform. At the May registration there were four hundred more. In the spring of 1939 the total student registration figure had been 3,275. By the spring of 1945 this figure had risen significantly to 3,905, and by the fall of that year it had jumped to 6,370 – an increase almost as large as the total pre-war student body. The principal's prophecies were being more than fulfilled.

One important aspect of these figures, as James was quick to notice, was that not all of the increase was due to the return of the veterans. Despite a raising of entrance requirements, nearly five hundred more "civilians" registered in September 1945 than in 1939. The war had shaken up Canadian society; a larger percentage of the college-age population was seeking a university education. As James commented in his annual report, this meant that a considerable part of the unprecedented growth would not disappear when the veterans wave had passed through. McGill, having agonized for so long over accelerated courses, now found itself caught up in a program of accelerated expansion. The major postwar preoccupation of the university and, even more, of its principal, was how to keep up with the pace.

James had long ago come to appreciate the value of his secretary, even if she could at times be somewhat trying. Mrs McMurray acted as a filter, retaining a great deal of the flow of smaller matters that sought the principal's attention, either to deal with them herself in the principal's name or to re-direct them to other offices, such as that of the bursar, or the registrar, or one of the faculty deans. Even so, a great deal of small stuff slipped through. And there were, of course, accidents. On one occasion, a newly arrived assistant professor was told by a mischievous colleague that the principal had telephoned asking that he come to see him immediately. The young man combed his hair, straightened his tie (ties were then *de rigueur*), and presented himself to Mrs McMurray. She said, "You haven't an appointment, but I suppose the principal has called without telling me. He does that sometimes – he's free now, you had better go in." Arriving in the inner sanctum, the young man said, "You wanted to see me, sir!" James glanced at his engagement pad and, realizing that something was amiss, responded, "Then why don't you sit down, tell me your name and what you do." Encouraged to talk about his work and his interests, the assistant professor afterward recalled the conversation as a very pleasurable experience. But that young man was fortunate. Many a full professor without an appointment failed to get past the redoubtable Mrs Mac.

One typewritten, uninitialed, but easily identifiable page in James' private diary reveals Mrs McMurray at her sardonic, pro-principalian best. One day in December 1944 when the principal was absent, Professor C.L. Huskins came to the office seeking Mrs McMurray. Huskins was a competent but fussy professor of genetics, who had required special handling once or twice before. Mrs Mac dutifully left the principal an account of what transpired.

Huskins came in to "consult me for my personal advice." He had a letter from University of Wisconsin at Madison inviting him down there at their expense to see whether he might like to take a job there. He went on and on in typical Huskins fashion, but the point emerged to be this: He would like the principal on [the strength of] this letter to assure him that he would have a future in the biological sciences [at McGill] to his heart's liking and that money would be put into his department.

I talked to him like a Dutch aunt and I told him that no principal could at this moment assure him of any such bright future; that his future was bound up with everyone else's and that we had a postwar depression era just around the corner, that I was sure if you were here today and he could consult you, you would tell him as I did – well, go down to Wisconsin and see what it is and whether they do make you an offer or whether you are just on a list of people being interviewed. I said that in my experience every principal was only too delighted for any of his staff to receive an offer from a first class institution, it gave everybody a lift up that our staff were of that calibre and it was only when such offers died away that there was cause to worry.

He stated that he would not take $10,000 at Wisconsin in preference to staying here, his wife had a nice job here now and his girls were ready for McGill.

I said well, it won't hurt you to go and see about it as they have asked you to go, and that if he came back with an offer in his hand of $10,000 then it would be time to discuss the matter seriously with the principal.

It is doubtful the principal could have given the unsettled professor better or different advice. In fact, when, after his return, Huskins reappeared in the office, James counselled him in much the same terms Mrs McMurray had, and after much hesitation, Huskins did accept the position at Wisconsin.

During the last two years of the war, James' diary notes have only a little to say about his domestic affairs. In February 1944 he remarks how much he and Irene are enjoying living at 1200 Pine Avenue; never before has he felt such an affection for a dwelling-place. In the fall he managed to sell the property he had previously bought on Peel Street but only by taking a heavy loss – he bought at $15,000 and sold at $11,500; he would not likely have much nostalgia for that home. There is, however, no more talk of personal financial troubles, so presumably the salary adjustments of 1943 served their purpose. Indeed, in the summer of 1944, when the staff generally received their much-needed salary increases and Morris Wilson suggested the principal should be included in the list to be submitted to the board, James replied it would not be necessary, at least for the present year.

In the dearth of personal references in the diary, one small group of entries is exceptional. Alone of his colleagues, Muriel Roscoe begins to appear in a clearly more friendly relationship. From earlier references to "Miss Roscoe" or "Dr. Roscoe," the entries move to dinner parties, where among the guests are "Irene and I and Muriel Roscoe." On one occasion he is able to snatch time in his study while entertaining house-guests because "Muriel" has taken them off driving. In July 1944, in the course of the usual weekend diary note, he says of the Sunday: "another empty day – a little gardening and reading, much loafing and listening to radio-guesses regarding what is going on in Germany ... Muriel dropped in for a couple of hours this evening. She is coming to Chester next month!" The opening remark refers presumably to an absence of university business on the day of rest (he did read the British White Paper *Employment Policy* in the afternoon), but even so it is hardly a flattering comment after a friend's visit. But that is fully made good by an unusual entry in which Muriel Roscoe has clearly become one of a happy holiday party. For once, Cyril James seems fully to have enjoyed a vacation.

[Wednesday, August 30, 1944]
The rest of August might be summarized by applying to an individual the adage that happy nations have no history. We have spent the month with Viva Bengtsen [?] at Chester, Nova Scotia, where the heat wave that afflicted all of this continent was a welcome blessing to holidaymakers ... the first three weeks of the month the weather was so warm that bathing was a real joy. That is a record for Chester! Muriel Roscoe was there most of this time – and one or two others came and went – but we made up a pleasant family party that picnicked and sailed and swam so that the month went all too quickly. The only day on which we interrupted the pleasant arrangement was the Wednesday when MVR and our two selves went into Halifax by bus to lunch with Dr. Chipman and – much as we all like him – we were glad to get back.

This is indeed an unusual entry. Once he returned to Montreal, however, the old pattern reasserted itself. All through the following winter, 1944–5, Cyril James worked tirelessly at the business of administering his university – if not quite leaving no stone unturned, no avenue unexplored, then certainly no duty shirked, no promising lead neglected.

Cyril James, in fact, suffered from the defects, but was also endued with the virtues, of a single-minded commitment to a high ideal. On the first day of January 1945, for example, he happened to be alone in his home high on Mount Royal. His study looked out over the great city of Montreal, a scene he often surveyed while he was musing. On this occasion he had found two old letters, one from Edward Beatty written in 1940, the other written a year later in decidedly fulsome terms by an elderly lady, a friend of the "McGill family," about his role as principal. They suited his New Year mood and started him writing.

1 January 1945

These two letters by their date might seem to belong to an earlier page of this record, but I found them perchance this morning and re-read them. They belong here. The writers are both dead but the memory lingers as a challenge. Sir Edward in the early stages of his last illness paying high compliment and talking of learning a new subject: Mrs. Miller at the end of a long life handing on the torch.

Somehow, as I look at myself against the light of these two letters, I think that there is more for me to do than I have yet attempted. Last year, to be sure, was a banner year at McGill – seven million dollars of new endowments, higher salaries, a grand Chancellor firmly in office, the Quebec Convocation, the Bicentennial [of James McGill's birthday] – a very successful year. But I sometimes realise that I have fallen into the habit of thinking of these things as accomplishments rather than new opportunities. The real task still remains: the making and maintenance of McGill as one of the really great Universities of the world – and that not for itself but in order that we may offer to each generation of students the best possible education for the tasks that will confront them. I must get additional staff, and I pray that I may be given the power of judgment to choose the right people, but I must also do more myself. I must try to curb my irritation and cocksureness, to study more deeply the problems that are not mere discussions for today but the foundations of many tomorrows – and I must do all this with a due consideration for the thoughts and feelings of others (Irene pre-eminent among them) so that I may not by degenerating into a priggish intellectual snob become useless for my job.

It is diary notes such as this that prevent one from dismissing James as merely a brilliant public performer. There was also a private person of great integrity. He was aware of his shortcomings and often resolved not to make the same mistakes in future. If in this resolve he was not always able to achieve success, that ranks him with the rest of us. But he was sincerely devoted to what he conceived to be his high calling, and on this New Year's day he was renewing once more the vows he had taken at his installation five years earlier. These high minded intentions could not have made Cyril James an easy person to live with, despite his penitent resolutions. Even his niece Doreen has confessed that she found "Uncle Frank" a difficult person to get to know.

So concerned was James with making sure he used the university's new resources wisely and made the right new appointments that he not only consulted widely with friends and influential people in the United States, but also decided in the spring of 1945 to visit England again to canvass opinions there. Thanks to Morris Wilson's good standing with the RCAF, he was given a place on a transatlantic flight leaving 5 March. Already great improvements had been made in flying conditions: proper seats were provided and oxygen was not required; but even in a heated cabin, at 10,000 ft, it was very cold. Some sixteen hours after leaving Montreal, James arrived safely at Prestwick in Scotland, where once again he took the train to London.

No sooner had he secured a room at the National Liberal Club than there was a loud explosion and the building shook under the impact of a German V2 rocket-bomb that had fallen nearby. The first few entries of his London diary record each time one of these horrors fell, but after a day or two, he seems to have become inured to them like other Londoners. But they were a constant reminder to all in the south of England that the war was by no means ended.

This was a very different visit from his previous one; this time James did not have entrée to the offices of cabinet ministers and senior civil servants. But as principal of McGill he was well-received in academic circles, and he had long talks with influential people in and around the universities of London, Oxford, and Cambridge. He received a flood of advice and collected scores of names, few of which have any significance today. Of those that do – men such as Oliver Franks and Lionel Robbins – James had to recognize they were even then beyond any inducement he could offer. Although the tangible result of these conversations for the university was small, the visit undoubtedly enhanced McGill's reputation and James' own standing in academic circles in Britain. It also further broadened his understanding of developments in the United Kingdom. He visited many McGill men and women in the armed services, and he spoke to a meeting of two hundred McGill graduates at a luncheon, again organized by Sir Harry Brittain in a

London hotel. As an exercise in university public relations, the journey to England could be judged worthwhile.

There were other bonuses, too. James visited Canada House several times, talking at length with Vincent Massey, still the high commissioner in London. In this way, he heard of an embryo idea that was to have long gestation, but was eventually to prove extremely important. It concerned something Massey called "the Canada Council," which was apparently first conceived along the lines of the British Council.

James wanted to enlist Massey's support in the proposal that McGill rather than London University should be named by the Commonwealth Office as the sponsor of the medical faculty of the proposed University of the West Indies. He pushed the idea vigorously with the academic authorities in London. But in his annual report for 1944–5, James recorded with regret that despite McGill's best efforts, the Imperial government had decided that such arrangements with colonial territories should be concentrated in the care of London University. McGill's active involvement in the life of the West Indies and of its newly established university would have to be placed on hold for a few more years.

Another matter on which James spent a great deal of time while in London was the proposal to create "a khaki university" in the Canadian Forces. An institution of this kind had been set up at the end of World War I which had constituted a great advance in armed services educational programming but, from the universities' point of view, had suffered from severe defects. James was anxious to ensure that this time the educational courses available to men and women awaiting demobilization were compatible with Canadian university requirements. On Saturday, 24 March he was in York to visit Canadian airforce crews. "After talking with the station education officer and inspecting his quarters, I addressed an army forum of more than 200 RCAF personnel, a splendid group which fired more than an hour of questioning at me." In the end, the decision to repatriate and demobilize the Canadian forces as expeditiously as possible put an end to the idea of a "khaki university" and resulted in veterans arriving at the university gates more quickly, and in larger numbers. The decision solved problems in Britain, but created more in Canada.

While visiting the airfields in the north, James was again given a rare insight into the realities of service life.

Less official, but no less interesting, was my experience of operations. At Leeming I was in the control tower when the squadron came back from

Hanover – and realised the intensity of waiting. The red flares of a plane with wounded aboard; the clearing of the runways for the plane that had had two engines knocked out; the long minutes of waiting when there is still one plane that has not reported – all these are familiar from the movies, but they have to be experienced to be understood. One does not realise also that, although planes land at intervals of one minute, that involves a whole hour for sixty planes which are flying around waiting to land! I also attended the interrogation of the crews – splendid lads but rather weary and deep-eyed – and nearly ended my journey when a Lancaster, loaded with bombs, crashed on the take-off to catch fire and explode.

When we returned to York, around 11.0[0] o/c, to retire for the night, I felt utterly worn out, but very proud.

There were also relatives to be seen in London, and not purely for social reasons. Irene's niece Doreen, who had enrolled as a first-year student at Acadia University in Nova Scotia, in September 1944, was not happy in a small rural town after city-life in London and Montreal. She was homesick and wanted to return to England and her family. However, her parents had drifted apart during the war years, for no obvious reason, and her home-coming after five years of absence would not be well-timed. James decided he would have to see the parents while in London, in order to convince them to reconcile their differences for the girl's sake. So in between his conversations with academic authorities on bright young men in the social sciences, and with service personnel on postwar education for veterans, James was also visiting the London suburbs, having tea with one in-law and then a drink with the other, trying to persuade them to resume their partnership. Finally an extended family party was arranged, which both parents attended and so met up again. Everyone behaved as if no separation had taken place. James observed in his diary that it was a precarious reconciliation, but hoped it would hold for Doreen's sake – she was by then on a ship crossing the Atlantic on her way home. The incident gives a rare glimpse of James in family relationships. It also reveals that if he was neglectful in the day-to-day details of personal relationships, James could nevertheless go to a great deal of trouble when he could see there was a job to be done.

During this London visit, James refers several times to the pleasure of experiencing once again the beauty of an English spring. From his window at the National Liberal Club, where he had a small but comfortable room, he could see a bed of daffodils coming bravely into bloom, and he also enjoyed several walks in London parks. But all too soon it was time for him to return to Montreal, which was where, as he told one newspaper reporter, "he wanted to be when the war ended." He knew that longed-for day would usher in for him a period of new challenges.

Bur first he had to make the journey home. He had come across so speedily and comfortably that he hoped he might be given a seat on a west-bound transatlantic flight, and was delighted to discover his standing with the RAF was apparently still that of a Very Important Person. A place was found for him on a plane leaving Prestwick at 10:10 A.M. on Saturday 7 April, bound for Newfoundland and Montreal. All seemed set for a routine flight.

But because of strong westerly winds, the plane was diverted from Gander to the Azores, and about halfway across the ocean, the top of the propeller of the inner port engine broke off, tearing through the cabin roof just above the heads of the pilot and co-pilot. The aircraft went into a steep dive, but the pilot managed to regain control and to keep the plane on course more slowly until it arrived in the Azores, eight hours after take-off. Here the eight passengers were told they would have to remain on the island until a new engine arrived, possibly in a week's time. A particular embarrassment was that American money was the only currency acceptable in the Azores and no facilities existed for changing either British pounds or Canadian dollars. After some thirty hours of disorganized living at the airport, the group was put on an American flight bound for New York.

This was an Atlantic Transport Command plane, carrying a large number of wounded. The civilian passengers were assigned to the cargo bay, where there were no seats and where the metal floor was fitted with staples and ringbolts, which made lying down extremely uncomfortable. Ten hours later, when they put down in Bermuda for a long re-fuelling stop, it was announced that the plane would not be going to New York but to Miami. No one in Bermuda having had any foreknowledge of the civilian passengers and no suggestions being made for their further transport westward, the passengers decided to continue with the ATC plane. After another five and a half hours' flying time they arrived in Miami, where they were met by representatives of the American women's auxiliary services, the WAVES and WAACS, who shepherded them through the quarantine, customs, and immigration barriers and obtained hotel accommodation from them. After their long hours in the ATC cargo hold, this was luxury indeed. Morris Wilson in Montreal cabled James some American funds, and another Montreal influence secured him a seat on an Eastern Airlines night-flight

to New York, which meant he was able to leave Miami at ten
P.M., expecting to arrive at La Guardia early the next day.

But it was not to be. The eastern seaboard was wreathed in fog
and the plane was diverted to Raleigh, North Carolina. There they
waited on the ground a long time, took off again, landed again
at Washington, and arrived over New York at one P.M. But the
fog was still disrupting airtravel, and the plane had to circle, so
it was three P.M. before James reached the terminal. He discovered
here that the only reservation available to him was a seat on the
Colonial Air Lines plane leaving at eleven P.M. for Montreal. Not
feeling very secure with this arrangement, James also reserved an
upper berth on the night train. The fog closed in again, cancelling
the Colonial Air Lines flight, so he joined the train, finally arriving
in Montreal at 8:30 A.M. on Thursday, 12 April. What was to have
been a ten-hour journey had taken five days. James recorded it
all meticulously, without complaint or ill-humour.

After breakfast, a shave and bath he went down to the office,
which was decked out in flowers "by courtesy of the East Wing"
(i.e., the administrative office staff). He stayed only until lunch-time,
took the afternoon off to see "the family" at Notre Dame de Grâce,
and went to bed early. After such a journey, he surely needed to
stay put in one place, like Livingstone's bearers, "to let his soul
catch up with him."

When the European war finally ended in April 1945, James at
first felt curiously deflated, and was surprised to find how little
urge he had to go out and celebrate the victory. He judged that
he had contributed little personally to the war effort, and he knew
that for him the major tasks lay not behind but ahead. The end
of the Japanese war the following August found him on vacation
again in Chester, Nova Scotia, and he did not record any reaction
to that event or even to the new and horrifying weapon that had
hastened it. (He was not writing a day-to-day diary at the time.)
As for the holiday itself, he later described it as short but very
pleasant (it "added to the usual pleasures a long weekend at Deep
Cove with Cyrus Eaton.")[17] But another comment suggests that
James would not be particularly keen to go back to Chester a
third time: two domestic seaside holidays had proved enough.
Irene drove back at a leisurely pace with Muriel Roscoe, but Cyril
hastened on ahead, travelling on a very crowded train. He was
anxious to get back to the university: the postwar problems, foreseen and discussed for so long, were now upon him.

The installation, 12 January 1940. Lord Tweedsmuir,
Chancellor Beatty, the principal-elect

The Founder's Day Convocation, 1940. T.H. Matthews, J.W. McConnell,
W.W. Chipman, W. Molson, the principal

Convocation, Quebec City, 16 September 1944. J.W. McConnell,
Churchill, Roosevelt, Athlone, Chancellor Wilson, Principal James

The principal welcomes returning veterans. January 1945

Impromptu party, 1947. Lismer's sketches on walls

Lismer's sketch of Mrs Mac 'coping.'

Visiting the Arctic Institute of North America, 1948

The principal, 1948

CHAPTER EIGHT

Instant College and
Personal Relationships

After the vacation in August 1945, James returned to Montreal ready to take up the challenge of running a university in a postwar world. He contemplated it with his usual misgivings.

Sunday, 2 September

This coming session will be a very difficult one, and at the moment I am doubtful of my own competence. It will be my first peace-time experience of University administration – and the single concentration of aims that characterised the war-years will be replaced by the problems of leadership and changing ideals in a difficult world. I shall have to make a large number of appointments and although I imagine that this is the most important part of my job I am doubtful of my ability to do it well.

There will also be the great variety of problems arising out of the large registration of ex-servicemen – problems of staff, of schedules, of space and of residences. In a word, I shall no longer be presiding over an established organisation, but must face the task of gradually creating a new and larger organisation! At the moment I can only see vague outlines and problems for which I have no clear solution!

This entry proved to be a remarkably accurate prognosis. The early days of September brought the usual mixture of important and ephemeral events, following close one upon the other, making it difficult to distinguish the significant from the trivial. He dealt on the telephone with an adjustment to the *per diem* rates chargeable at the Montreal Neurological Hospital; Mrs C.S. McEwen came in to discuss the $50,000 remaining in the Ajax Fund (a women's hospitality program for sailors) and its proposed use for scholarships and fellowships for naval veterans; a tiresome problem which would not go away that concerned providing the Morgan family with firewood from the Ste-Anne-de-Bellevue Arboretum; Dean Meakins came in to report that Hans Selye, the brilliant but unpredictable *prima donna* of histology, had been enticed away to the new Université de Montréal by the promise of unlimited research facilities, and that it was a great loss, but not without compensatory aspects; Registrar T.H. Matthews reported day by day an everincreasing enrolment; the federal government, which was paying the promised $150 per annum for each veteran, was now saying that if it was found that the veterans were not costing the universities that much, the *per capitum* would be reduced, a tedious complication of accounting; and the usual parent was coming in to demand explanation for his son's "inexplicable" failure in last year's examinations.

Out of this kaleidoscope of events and persons one subject emerged as far overshadowing the others in importance and in demands. It began innocently enough. On the Wednesday of his first week back in the office, James had a lunch-time conversation with Group Captain Low of the War Assets Corporation.

5 September 1945

He told me that if the Univ. were to get what they wanted from the War Assets Corp. it would be essential that they have somebody who at 24 hours notice could go out and inspect the material that we wished to acquire. He also felt it important that the Univ. should offer to purchase for cash the articles that they wanted, particularly in view of the special grant which the Dom. Govt. had given for veteran students, although they could haggle about price if they wanted. I told him that in agreement with this suggestion the Governors had set up a special fund of $125,000 with which he was familiar.

He also pointed out that there was a good deal of material, such as corvettes, gun carriers, aeroplanes, etc, which could be obtained free of charge on permanent loan by the universities. The government never again expected to see material lent in this fashion and the universities if they used imagination could obtain a lot of what they wanted by dismantling this equipment at a cost no greater than that of transportation. I promised to pass this idea on to Bladon and Macfarlane so that we could explore it further.

Leigh Bladon was professor of mining engineering, whom James had found very useful in such matters, and P.W. Macfarlane was the superintendent of buildings and grounds. There is an element of humour in this glimpse of a solemn tête-à-tête at the University

Club between "the man from WAC" and the principal of McGill, the two men mentally (papers not being allowed in the club dining room) combing the lists of corvettes, planes, guns, and military supplies that could be had simply for the asking, and James trying to think what might be useful where: surely, there must be a department in some faculty that could find good use for a tank, not new but fully reconditioned?

But, in fact, a serious purpose lay behind the principal's meeting with Low. The registration build-up had begun to hurt; the numbers were even greater than James had foreseen and were continuing to grow. The situation had become such that new, unprecedented steps had to be taken. The solution, he had come to believe, was not to be found in hastily assembled prefabricated lecture-rooms and laboratories.[1] What was needed was nothing short of "instant college," a ready-made satellite campus, and James had an idea as to how it could be achieved.

I asked Low if he could help us in regard to finding a place close to Montreal where we could set up a separate university such as first year engineering with its own class rooms, instructors and residence accommodation. In view of the fact that the rapid demobilization may bring several thousand people to us next year this seems to be the only practicable method of approach. He later telephoned to say that the establishment at St. Hubert seemed to fill the bill and I arranged for Macfarlane and Bladon to go with Low and look at the property on Friday. I suggested that we should also look at CWAC [Canadian Women's Army Corps] barracks and ANA [Army, Navy and Airforce] house as residences for students actually studying on the campus.

The journal breaks off with this 5 September entry and does not resume until the end of the month, when it tells the story of quick decisions and even faster action.

Saturday, 29 September
The past weeks have been hectic and interesting – they should have been recorded in detail but I have had neither the time nor the energy to dictate ... Even at this moment I do not know exactly what our enrolment is for the coming session, but I know that it is higher than ever before and still growing – since students from the armed services will be admitted until October 15th. This has meant a revolutionary rearrangement of the whole time-table (which Adair tried to attack in the Arts Faculty meeting yesterday but received little support and was sidetracked by Macmillan who emphasized the splendid work that the Time Table Committee had

done to meet the emergency). It has also meant a rapid expansion of the physical facilities of Macdonald College where we have taken over, and are using, all additional buildings and facilities that were constructed by the CWAC.

Most revolutionary of all, it has led to the creation of a temporary college – an experiment that is I think unique among Canadian Universities at the moment. Early in September I asked Bladon and Macfarlane, in conjunction with Low of War Assets, to explore the possibility of McGill getting additional buildings. It soon became apparent that no adequate buildings were available in Montreal and, after surveying the various possibilities in the surrounding area, we decided that if we could take over the buildings of No. 13 Elementary Flight Training School at St. John's,[2] we could operate it as a unit in which first year B. Sc and first year B. Eng (*males only*) could live and carry on their studies.

On September 11th I asked the Air Ministry for the use of these buildings – and began a series of discussions with the Deans and Group Chairmen as to the desirability of adopting such a plan. All agreed that it was necessary: some thought it a splendid idea.

On September 17th I learned from Ottawa that we could have the use of the buildings – but would have to make arrangements with War Assets for the use of the equipment – so I asked Bladon and Macfarlane to follow up this matter, which they are still doing. Because of the fact that our needs outran the procedure of the Government, the RCAF people agreed that we should simply take over all the stuff that we need, sign for it, and leave until some later date the precise discussion of terms and conditions. When we found that the available equipment was inadequate, and RCAF had no other stores available, I telephoned Douglas Abbott [the Minister of Defence] who put me in touch with the Master General of Ordnance, and the latter immediately sent from the Army depots in Montreal, Ottawa and Toronto the stuff that we needed. Nobody could have had greater cooperation, and without that aid the project could not have come to birth.

After full preliminary discussions by the Board of Governors, we announced the project in the press on Tuesday Sept. 18th – announcing also that A.H.S. Gillson would be Vice-Principal of the College ... On Tuesday Sept 25th – one week later, we formally took over the buildings, and on Thursday evening, Sept 27th, the first group of students moved into the residences and had dinner in the dining hall that night.

Tremendous credit is due to Macfarlane, Bladon and Gillson[3] – and I am hopeful that the whole thing may prove a great success. I remember vividly the unsatisfactory results of postwar congestion at LSE and Wharton after the last war, and hope that his experiment may at least reduce that discomfort.

This was Cyril James at his imaginative best. He found a solution that only he, because of his familiarity with the authorities, could have conjured up. Taking Low at his word, he asked not for airplanes or guncarriers but beds, blankets, sheets, cooking pots, plates, mugs, cutlery, benches, tables, chairs, blackboards, bunsen-burners, and household supplies. He had little difficulty stating his case. McGill student numbers were growing beyond all expectation. By the end of the 1945–6 session, the total number of students registered in regular day-session degree and diploma courses at McGill had risen to 6,746, an increase in one year of 205 percent. Further, as James pointed out in his 1945–6 annual report:

Even in previous Annual Reports of normal years it had been suggested that an expansion of our residential facilities was highly desirable, but during the past session the problem has assumed the greatest urgency. The ability of many veterans to enter the University was dependent upon the availability of residential accommodation, and in a large number of cases proper housing had to be found for a wife and children as well as for the student himself. If the University had refused to accept the responsibility for discovering or developing residences for its students the fundamental purpose of the Dominion Government's rehabilitation plan would have been defeated and the offer to veterans of an opportunity to attain a university degree would have been an empty gesture.

This meant that the "instant college" had to be a residential one, with bachelors' and married quarters.

In spite of the wholehearted cooperation of the Dominion Government in accelerating the transfer of buildings and equipment, a great deal of work had to be quickly done in order to transform an air force station into a college. Some of the buildings were renovated as residences for single students, and others (with one or two-room apartments) were put into shape for married students. Special diets for young children, hot plates for the preparation of babies' feeding bottles, and laundry facilities for young mothers, were among the novel problems of academic administration that were encountered; while the Student Health Service found itself confronted (for the first time in our history) with family responsibilities.

By the end of the first month of the new session, twenty-five days after the first mention of the idea of Group Captain Low, 600 students had taken up residence in "Sir William Dawson College." In January, with the number rising to 950, the contiguous No. 9

Repair Depot of the RCAF was also taken into use. The management of the dining halls was contracted out to Industrial Foods Limited, but the business of getting the buildings ready as family apartments, bachelor dormitories, dining halls, lecture rooms, drafting rooms, laboratories, recreation rooms, and so on devolved on McGill staff, particularly P.W. Macfarlane, the superintendent of buildings and grounds. Macfarlane employed local contractors as much as possible to undertake specific tasks, but the direction of the operation from Montreal, in which Cyril James was much involved, must have been full of problems. Only the fact that the Douglas Abbott referred to in James' 29 September entry was not only the minister of defence but also a McGill graduate made the complex operation possible.

The library was a particular challenge, but obviously not one that could be evaded. An undergraduate collection housed in the Arts Building, known as the Carnegie Collection, was moved bodily from the one campus to the other, and this core was then supplemented with new purchases and with a transfer of books from the university's main collection, the Redpath Library.

Those who lived through these hectic events commented in retrospect on the sense of commitment and unanimity of purpose that characterized all who were involved. Timetables were ingeniously contrived so that professors could lecture on campus at McGill and then hurry into their cars, cross the river by the Victoria Bridge, and drive the twenty-five miles to St John's to repeat the operation there, as often as not returning to Montreal to meet senior classes in the afternoon. In winter weather it was not always a simple journey. A good deal of the teaching was done by graduate students and junior staff specially recruited for the Dawson campus. In September 1947, the total registration at Dawson had reached its maximum of 1,687; and by 1950, when the main wave of veterans had passed through the university's programs and the St John's operation was closed down, an estimated 5,600 students, mostly veterans but also a considerable number of civilians, had received part of their education through the facilities of the auxiliary campus.

Dawson College did not stand alone. Many other innovations and provisions were made to help cope with the veterans' incursion. New timetables and curricula increased the efficiency of classroom and laboratory use on the Montreal campus. At Macdonald College, temporary housing for married students was erected at a cost of $225,000 (the prefabricated buildings, which lasted for thirty years, were familiarly known as Diaper Dell), and at Lachine another RCAF station was taken over for additional married quarters and renamed "the McGill Peterson Residences." By the spring of 1947, McGill was providing living accommodation for 3,215 persons, of whom 233 were married students with families. The amount of detailed planning and negotiation that these operations involved – the greater part going through the principal's office – was enormous. In execution James received a great deal of help from colleagues, academic and non-academic alike, but the overall plan and its financing were his sole responsibility.

Many members of the McGill staff have looked back on the Dawson College operation with a sense of surprise that they carried uncomplaining the heavy teaching load and other inconveniences for so long, but in almost every case the reminiscences have more than a touch of nostalgia. Professor Cecil Solin, the example, who became one of McGill's most respected teachers of mathematics, recalled his experiences at St John's with considerable affection.

Since it was a large Air Force School ... there was plenty of classroom space, which was comfortable and well-suited to teaching. The Science department set up adequate facilities for courses in physics, chemistry and biology. The hours were long and I can recall lecturing as much as twenty to twenty five hours in a five-day week, often repeating the same lecture a couple of times to different groups ... Many of the students realized they had a wonderful opportunity of getting an education under DVA benefits and took full advantage of it ... by and large, they worked hard when they worked and played hard when they played ... Without reservation they were the best group of students I have had as a group in my thirty five years at McGill ... in all it was a truly wonderful educational and social experience, and although it was nice to come back to the Montreal campus, I believe students and faculty alike missed it ... Friendships made then are just as firm today.[4]

Two of the students, V.M. Jolivet and D.H. Kennedy, wrote a history of Dawson College that ended with a summary of the advantages and disadvantages of spending part of one's university career at St John's.

Perhaps the greatest advantage of Dawson was the formation of the "Dawson Spirit". This intangible thing might be called "esprit de corps", and it existed in all things going on at Dawson ... Academically, standings at Dawson were on the whole better than at McGill University. This was probably due to the isolation of Dawson and the ever-present aid available from other students. In extra-curricular activities and sports, exceedingly large participation was obtained, partly because Dawson was a residential college ... a disadvantage was the loss of certain activities which are available to Montreal students, such as concerts, plays, etc. Also, the lack of feminine companionship was found hard after long periods in Dawson. All told, the advantages of Dawson far outweighed its disadvantages.[5]

So said the students in 1950, and so obviously thought the more than one hundred graduates who reassembled at McGill on 28 November 1980 to celebrate the thirtieth anniversary of the closing of an institution they remembered with pleasure and gratitude. W.H. Hatcher, professor of chemistry and vice-principal of the college at the time of its closing, called Dawson "McGill's most daring and successful experiment in one hundred years. " According to Cyril James, some of the students gave the college a more derisory title – "Dawson City" – but they said it with affection and pride.

McGill's success in dealing with the postwar increase of registrations marked a turning point in James' relations with his staff. His previous call to be prepared for postwar crises had, in the absence of hard evidence, largely gone unheeded; what activity had taken place had been the result of his own planning and persistent prodding. But the return of the veterans constituted for every one at McGill a present and challenging situation, which was of such a nature that James had to call on deans, departmental chairmen, and faculty committees to find their own *ad hoc* solutions. Consequently he became the leader of a common effort to which the whole community was strongly committed. As he said in his review of the St John's operation, "Every member of staff who taught at Dawson College made a contribution"; but this could also have been said of the professors who taught double-sized classes at McGill or Macdonald, repeated lectures to different sections of the same class, and grappled with twice the amount of marking, always the most unwelcome chore of academic life. It could also have been said of the students, who suffered (without complaining too loudly) from crowded classrooms, a lack of seating in the library, and a shortage of textbooks that made dependence on lectures all the more necessary. The fact that the principal shared in the teaching (he regularly participated in Economics 100) and that his lectures were always stimulating also increased his stature on campus. One of his earlier students, Michael Townsend, B Comm '47, has left a vivid impression of James' lecturing performance.

... to find ourselves exposed to a man of his intellect and almost musical grasp of the English language was indeed an experience. I recognize now that the material, being very simple economics, was almost too highly polished but nonetheless his classes were looked forward to by all of us. Dr. James would unhesitatingly interrupt the flow of his discourse to answer our questions or discuss points with us, and then just as unhesitatingly would pick up exactly where he had left off.

He always moved rather quickly, with his black gown billowing out behind his rather tall, spare form, and would enter the class, not so much with a bustle as with a flourish, with a smile that was not curt but not too invitingly warm, and launch into his material. He usually finished with the bell and left with the same flourish, undoubtedly to return to the helm of the ship of state. As very junior passengers on that ship, I can assure you that many of us were duly and lastingly impressed by his participation at that time in things academic.[6]

The change of relationship between James and the McGill community is exemplified in a letter he received in January 1947.

Dear Principal James:

It was with some surprise, but considerable pleasure, that we read in your recent Annual Report certain generous remarks concerning our work in connection with Sir William Dawson College.

When Dawson College was first established it became a privilege and a challenging adventure to have any part in its operation and, throughout its intense history, this adventure has become more and more apparent.

The growth of its manifold operations has taught each of us many things, but, most important of all, it has intensified our knowledge of each other, so that in after years when our present close association in the University's work may be loosened, we shall have the pleasure of knowing that the added strength we have each derived from the other is being used to follow your leadership in the service of the University.

With kindest regards, we are, Sir,

Yours sincerely,

P.W. Macfarlane

A.H.S. Gillson

Carleton Craig[7]

Although a formal letter, it testifies to the growing acceptance of James on campus and the admiration of those who worked with him. There were, and always would be, some members of the academic staff at McGill who could not forget their earlier resentments – particularly some members of the Department of Economics, who still thought of him as a junior colleague jumped into authority over them. But after the Dawson College experience, the McGill community in general began more and more to take pride in the principal who was giving such strong leadership.

This shift came not only to the McGill faculty, but also to James; during those years of war, Cyril James had also changed. He had come to feel a pride in McGill and Montreal. As 1946 drew to an end he made a Sunday evening hand-written diary entry.

Sunday, 3 November, 1946

This record grows intermittent. The days when much is happening go unrecorded: ... the 125th Anniversary Convocation and Hetherington's visit,[8] the Special Laboratories! ... At the moment I find it hard to make plans and decide what I want to do. Sometimes, when I am in good spirits and things at McGill go reasonably well, I think about the possibility of staying here for the rest of my life. I play with the idea, if God gives me years, of emulating the record of Sir William Dawson;[9] I dream dreams of McGill's future and I think of the quiet peace of this house as the source of plans and achievements. The other day Frank Scott said that never in his experience had he known McGill to be as intellectually alive – and, even though he may have meant alive to C.C.F. gospels[10] I took heart at this comment and was on top of the world.

Then, as usual, he begins to doubt his own abilities, becoming somewhat maudlin as he compares himself unfavourably to university principals and presidents he knew. But in the midst of his self-deprecation, he makes a serious comment. Sometimes, he says, he wants "to run into a corner and hide – to become a professor again (but even then I doubt my competence when I listen to Keirstead, Higgins or Boulding [professors in the economics department] and realize that I have stood still intellectually during those past seven years in which they have forged ahead!)." This last remark does ring true. The university administrator vows when he takes office that he will keep up his teaching or his research, or at least his professional reading, but the vow can almost never be kept. James stayed with teaching Economics 100, the introductory class, for twenty years, but it did not require much fresh reading. The constant pressures on the principal of a large multiversity, such as McGill was fast becoming, do not allow many leisurely evenings for quiet reflection, or undisturbed mornings for intense thought. On the other hand, an intelligent principal such as James, who listens attentively to his deans and chairmen, can gain a liberal education that is without price. He is initiated into the issues at stake in the preference of candidate A rather then B for a chair in law; he grasps the point as to why so much of the university's resources must be poured into J.S. Foster's cyclotron; as a member of the Quebec Provincial Protestant Education Committee he gains an insider's view of Canadian history and politics; he learns why geography has come of age in a postwar world; he begins to understand why Osler's great dictum, that clinical practice and medical research must go hand in hand, has to be rediscovered in every new generation; and he begins to see why all the flowers have gone from the gardens of botany. James may not have kept pace with the latest debates in economics, but he was now intimately aware of the questions at issue in a score of disciplines, of which in 1939 he had only the vaguest notions. He had paid a price, certainly, but in return he had received such a depth of perception, and on such a broad front, that his general understanding was maturing into something more nearly approaching wisdom.

Monday, November 11, 1946
Over the weekend I was at Chalk River ... to inspect the atomic energy installation. Much of the process I do not clearly understand in spite of the explanations, but the immediate power and the future possibilities are at once apparent. There is also food for thought in the fact that the average age of the team there is 29 – and one feels old in the company of these bright young men.

But men who begin to feel old also begin to feel insecure. This is particularly true in the academic world. Although university administrators are accorded immense power and commensurate moral authority, they know full well they have practically no means of enforcement. If a challenge is so radical as to flout all moral authority, university administrators can only fall back on the civil authority, and to do that is in itself an admission of defeat. James seemed to have a premonition of the student uprisings that were to come a full twenty years later.

Up to now I have been lucky – lucky in my Chancellors, lucky in my staff, lucky in the absence of serious student troubles – but I know in my heart the fear that some day a storm will break out that I cannot ride.

Although he had been gone five years before the most serious trouble began, he knew its powers were there on campus, lying dormant, and in his depressed moments the fear that it might strike during his time haunted him. "Uneasy lies the head that wears a crown," especially if that head houses an intelligence as sharp as that of Cyril James. So while in the experiences of Dawson College and the expansions of the postwar years he entered into a new and closer relationship with his colleagues in the university, he never took them or his own position for granted.

James had changed in another way too. While retaining his high regard for the United States and his appreciation of Americans and their way of life, which he had first learned at the University of Pennsylvania and Valley Forge, he had also renewed his emotional ties with England. In June 1946, Irene having gone ahead to England, James was left alone in his study overlooking the city. He settled down to listen to that transatlantic miracle, the broadcast from London of the Victory Day celebrations. A Londoner whose street-memories were bred into the bone, he had seen the city in the days of its agony and now, sitting by the radio, looking out over Montreal, he could imagine it in all its glory. Broadcasters painted for him the word-pictures of the splendid pageant.

Saturday, 8 June

This is V. day in London, and tonight as I sat beside the radio I could not repress the tears. The broadcast began with that same military march that, night after night during the darkest periods of the war, began the regular broadcast of radio news-reel. Quite frankly I thought that the descriptions left much to be desired from the viewpoint of good broadcasting – but a single sentence could tell so much to the imagination that was waiting to conjure up a memory. That lone Hurricane flying up the Mall[11] over the ranks of the RAF to recall the Battle of Britain, and the battered canteen behind the Civil Defence Workers to recall its impact during long days and nights of bombing – the massed bands of the Highland regiments whose pipes evoke the memory of so many millions of gallant men down all the years – the great splendour of fireworks and searchlights in a city that has been darkened for so long – the sirens of the tugs as the King's barge came up the river (and where else in the world would they allow people to crowd on the bridges to see him?) – the spontaneous chorus of the crowds joining in God Save the King as the bands played the Royal Salute for his landing, the voice of the man in the street, who has done so much and suffered so much, that seemed to drown out the great salute of 45 guns! One does not mind skill in broadcasting on such a day. All the memory of bombed and battered London is here in my mind as background ... Somehow the whole thing makes me feel very humble and a little sad! I came from the stock but I think that I have not lived up to it – and I feel a hurting desire to be able to do more than I am doing, in order that some future generation of these people may not have to take the day's delight of a Victory Parade in payment for so many years of misery and sadness. A thought like this plays havoc with any concept of the Economic Man – and gives a sudden vision of what the world might be if only that great power of good-will could be harnessed to some decent spark of idealism. Sometimes I wish I knew more about how to think – so that I could follow through some of these ideas that such a moment can engender.

These hopes, tears, hurting desire – these are the emotions of an idealist, a sincere and basically humble man, and they explain in great part why James could commit himself so fully to the tasks he believed life had allotted him. Ironically, when the broadcast was finished, and he telephoned across the Atlantic to share the moment with Irene in Britain, she had seen nothing of the celebrations, "for which I am sorry, but she is well, and so are the family."

James said he had been lucky with his chancellors. Certainly his relationship with Beatty had been most fortunate (James had known how to please an aged and dying giant), and the new chancellor, Morris Wilson, and his wife Leone had behaved very kindly to both Cyril and Irene. As James wrote of him, "Morris Wilson liked people." But hardly had the university entered the new year of 1946 when a severe blow fell. Dr Chipman informed the principal confidentially that Wilson was suffering from an aneurism of the aorta and should undertake a good deal less, and rest a great deal more.

Tuesday, 29 January, 1946
I had a long talk with Brow [the Wilson family physician] at lunch, and he told me that Morris and Leone have both known the full facts of the situation since last summer when Morris went down to see a heart specialist at Philadelphia. With full knowledge of what they were doing (although, I think, with an inner hope that the diagnosis might be wrong!) Morris and Leone have decided that nobody should know about his condition – especially his friends and the people at the Bank. He insists that he wants to "die with his boots on" and not to be labelled an invalid.

Wilson was not to have his wish fulfilled. He became ill shortly after James wrote, and remained an invalid until he died in May. James had been too busy to keep his typed journal going, but for this event, deeply moved, he made a hand-written diary entry.

Morris Wilson died last night! ... Morris deserved better than this ! Like Beatty, he had worked hard and given all that he had throughout his life – and we had hoped that there would be long days to reap the fruits in peace and friendliness.

Wilson was an admirable and likeable person, but his loss as a friend did not affect James as deeply as had the loss of Edward Beatty, nor was his passing from the university scene as significant for James' career as Beatty's had been. James' relationship with the Board of Governors was now securely established, and he made no great effort to control the choice of successor. The sub-committee appointed to nominate a new chancellor deliberated through the winter of 1946–7, and at the end of April, almost a year after Wilson's death, James recorded laconically: "A busy week. Tyndale appointed Chancellor (to everybody's delight as far as I have heard) Dobell appointed Comptroller – and Collip resigned to go to Western." The inclusion of other appointments and resignations along with the chancellor's election indicates that James regarded the choice of Associate Chief Justice Orville Tyndale as an event of no great consequence; indeed, Tyndale was to prove competent and cooperative but not a driving force in university affairs. Although chancellors over the next decade were to be distinguished and decorative, there was no doubt in anyone's mind that the man at the university's helm was the vice-chancellor.

The loss of J.B. Collip, however, was notable. The foremost biochemist in Canada, he had been the colleague of Banting and Best at Toronto when they were engaged in the investigation of insulin. It was he who devised the ethanolic method for its puri-fication so that it could be made available to human patients; the process was patented in the name of Banting, Best, and Collip. At McGill he had directed the Institute of Endocrinology, further enhancing his reputation with a steady stream of papers on the biochemistry of animal hormones. Along with three other McGill men – Otto Maass, J.S. Foster and J.H. Ross – he had received the Medal of Freedom from the United States for contributions to wartime research – only nine such medals were awarded to Cana-dians. Collip's departure to become dean of medicine at the University of Western Ontario therefore represented the loss of an outstanding scientist. The men and women whom James was now appointing in considerable numbers across a wide range of departments were youngsters who had as yet to make a name. The difficulty of building an academic staff of quality was one of James' constant and anxious preoccupations.

Another of his persistent concerns was reflected in the appointment of Sydney Dobell as comptroller. James was constantly reviewing the administrative functioning of the university and the efficiency of his own office. One difficulty, he recognized, lay in Mrs McMurray's domineering character, and at least on one occasion he contemplated moving her to some other office in the university: "She irritates me." But he never did, until she reached retirement age, because for all her annoying ways, he benefited greatly from her apparently limitless capacity for work, her personal efficiency, and her fierce, Scottish loyalty.

James accomplished one part of his personal program – the renovation of the administrative offices – in the 1947–8 academic year. Housed in the historic "East Wing" erected in 1843, the offices had remained fairly undisturbed, even during the reconstruction of the Arts Building in 1925. But the increased university business for the principal, the registrar, the bursar, the secretary to the Board of Governors, and all their administrative staff required more efficient use of the available space. The interior of the old building was therefore to be drastically remodelled; in particular, some of the walls of the principal's office were scheduled for demolition. To celebrate the memories that the old room housed – James had identified it as Sir William Dawson's study, dating back to at least 1855 – he threw an impromptu party at five o'clock the evening before the builders moved in.

Among the haphazard collection of guests invited into the sanctum sanctorum, already stripped of most of its furnishings, was the young painter Arthur Lismer, already teaching at McGill. Lismer looked at the blank walls, pulled out his charcoal stick, and proceeded to draw irreverent pictures of the principals who from this room had exercised their rule. A young classics professor, Paul McCullagh, had the good sense to produce a camera to capture the cartoons, which after the weekend would disappear forever under the workman's pick. The cartoon of Sir Arthur Currie shows him bestriding the battlefield in his general's uniform and his principal's cap and gown; Arthur Morgan appears only as a portrait being unceremoniously bundled off by a workman; Lewis Douglas, who became wartime director of Allied Shipping, is hilariously depicted as a small boy playing with boats in his bath; the malicious cartoon of Mrs McMurray shows her coping in the principal's absence – professors dropped in the wastepaper basket, a student (?) impaled on a billspike, a visitation of colourful overseas delegates waiting at the door. But even the ebullient Lismer at a party could not depict Cyril James as other than a presiding genius, extremely neat and tidy in appearance, ruling from a desk (which is in fact the marble mantlepiece) surmounted by the McGill coat of arms. The impression of "correctitude" could not have been more effectively conveyed.

To celebrate the history that disappeared in this reconstruction, James asked the Board of Governors to rename the East Wing "Dawson Hall"; accordingly the name was carved into the stone lintel. Few people today realize that the building was ever known by any other.

Absorbed as he was in university administration in the postwar years, Cyril James had little time to give to family matters, particularly to his father. Although he and Irene's parents had been in Montreal for almost five years, Frank James senior had not been happy. At one point, to his son's annoyance, he had taken a job as a night watchman on a Montreal wharf, and as soon as the European war ended he made preparations to return for England, leaving on 15 June 1945. His son recorded the fact with the bald comment: "I never did know the name of the ship," which sounds as though he was not involved in the arrangements in any way or even there to see him off. Clearly the bond between himself and his father had not been strengthened during the five years that Frank senior had lived in Montreal. Six weeks later Irene's parents also sailed for Britain and for the first time in five years, Cyril and Irene had no family responsibilities this side of the Atlantic. James commented on this fact in a diary entry, dated 4 August, after an hiatus of nearly three months. He wrote, it seems, with a certain sense of relief.

It is a few days more than five years since Mum and the two Dads landed in Montreal; a few weeks longer since Doreen's arrival. As I look back, it seems like a lifetime and, since their presence here is almost synchronous with my Principalship, the two have been blended into a pattern of life that must now be changed quite considerably. I am still glad that we asked them, very glad indeed. Doreen has had a chance that she would not otherwise have had, and her letters suggest that she is already reaping some advantage from it in her work at the Admiralty. That extra advantage of training should help her a great deal, not only in the distant future, but in the months of the present that are made difficult by the renewed (and final) break between [her parents]. As to the old folks, they of course are no longer at the beginning of life so that experience is just experience and not an asset. Yet I am inclined to think that they will find some happiness in their Canadian memories during the years that lie ahead – and I am profoundly glad that they were saved from this experience of the war in London. Indeed, If it were not for the shadow cast by the [marriage break-up],[12] I think that this summer of the war's end in Europe and the family repatriation would be an occasion of great rejoicing.

It is the comment of one who had done his duty, and is glad he has done it, but is also relieved it is over.

The sense of separation from his father was finalized just a few months later when in November James received news of his father's death. At an armistice service later in the month, he thought particularly of his father, and with affection. He was pleased that the hymns included some that his father loved and had often sung. Over the years, James had been a considerate and thoughtful son to both his parents.

With his younger brother Douglas, Cyril's relations were also cordial but not close. The seven-year gap between Frank and Digs, as they were known in the family, seemed to have been emphasized by the middle brother Mervyn's death in 1918, followed by Frank's departure for the United States only three years later, which left the sibling relationship friendly but detached. Douglas had an honourable war record as an officer in the British Army, and was afterwards engaged in the Colonial Service in West Africa. They met on coincidental visits to England at least once after the war and got on well together, but with their careers unfolding in different parts of the world, the brothers did not have much in common.

It was with his niece Doreen that the more permanent relationship developed. Early in 1949, when he heard she had been hospitalized in London, James immediately wrote her that he would be responsible for all her medical expenses. When he was visiting in England that summer, he went to see her in hospital where he learned that she expected to be released in a couple months,[13] but that, as she had had to give up her job at the Admiralty, she would unfortunately be dependent on her parents. In one of his many sincere and kindly gestures, "Uncle Frank" told her that when she did return home, he would make her a small monthly allowance to give her a degree of independence. This was all the more generous at a time when he was confiding to his diary that he had run an overdraft with his bank the previous month and saw no chance of setting the matter right in the current month. It is the first time for five years that he refers to financial anxieties.

The strange contradictions in James' nature, whereby a basically good and kind person appeared so often to be inhibited by a shyness or reticence from expressing his emotions freely, are well illustrated in the ten-year correspondence that he began with Doreen at this time. During her long convalescence he wrote her almost weekly and continued the practice after she had recovered. The letters always began "Cara Dorinda mia," a little family whimsicality that had become an affectionate habit. One wonders if Doreen did not take the place of the child James and Irene had lost years before, back in the Philadelphia days. Yet the content of the letters, written so faithfully, lack just those personal touches that normally characterize family correspondence, especially between elder and younger. Chatty reminiscences, evidences of fatherly interest in what the young girl was doing, bits and pieces about daily life at 1200 Pine Avenue, these are missing. At times the content of his letters was almost indistinguishable from his journal entries; they detailed where he was, whom he met, what engagements he was fulfilling, the matters preoccupying his mind at the moment. Even in this personal correspondence with a young niece, always written by hand, he could not unbend to indulge in small talk – and yet his quick response to her medical needs, his persistence in writing to her, even at the busiest times, and his small reproaches if she was irregular in her replies, are evidence of his deep affection for her.

James took great interest in Doreen's engagement to be married, and he helped the young couple financially in the purchase of a house. After her marriage he continued the correspondence, from home or from wherever he was travelling, and kept this up until he retired to Amersham, sufficiently near to her home in Chalfont St Peter to allow telephone calls and frequent visits to replace the need for correspondence.

Cyril's relations with Irene appear to have reached an uneasy compromise. She returned from England in the fall of 1946 to be told that she required a surgical procedure. With Cyril's concurrence, she elected to go to Abington near Philadelphia, where the James had been friendly with the surgeon Sumner Cross and his wife Nan. Irene was familiar with Sumner's hospital, and believed herself to be in good hands. A rumour had circulated in Montreal that she was suffering from cancer, and Dr Chipman, who, as a gynaecologist understood the situation, remarked: "I am glad she is going to Abington – this is a gossipy community." Nevertheless, the picture of Irene, facing a major surgical operation, going off alone to friends in Philadelphia rather than accepting the excellent services available in Montreal, where she would have had the presence of her husband near at hand, makes its own comment.

It must not be forgotten, however, that we see the marriage relationship only through Cyril's eyes. We do not have Irene's version. Although Cyril writes respectfully of her at all times, and in general behaves very dutifully towards her, there is no doubt that for him even more than for most men the obligations of his career came first. In an age of single-income families, when the husband was literally the breadwinner, that was almost universally accepted and understood. But from Irene's point of view, the situation could not have been easy. She had considerable justification for her general preference of Philadelphia, New York, or London over her home in Montreal, where she had no friends, and where her husband was preoccupied with work.

There is however one vignette from the intermittent diary notes of these years that shows that at times Cyril and Irene could be relaxed together, and could both be happy in the same circumstance.

Monday, 21 April 1947

But without losing myself in introspection, I want to record the sheer joy of staying with the Masseys at Batterwood House during the past weekend. It has taken a long while to get to know them – and I am half amazed that we ever succeeded when I remember the gaucherie of my visit to London in 1942 – but I do not think that either Irene or I have ever enjoyed a weekend more. It is not only the beauty of the house and its peace – each of the Masseys is a real character of great strength, and it is fascinating to see in the privilege of their home the way in which mutual admiration and affection have welded characters that might have provided intense antagonism or the utter submission of one party. Their enjoyment of living – and the spontaneous nature of their welcome were added reasons for our pleasure and contributed to make these days memorable.

That Cyril should enjoy himself in the urbane Massey setting is perhaps not surprising; that Irene should also be relaxed and happy in that milieu is surely a tribute to her hostess.

CHAPTER NINE

Wider Horizons

The postwar years were a time of great expansion for McGill not only in student numbers but also in physical capacities. Geography, as we have seen, was started as a new department, Psychiatry set forward in conjunction with the Royal Victoria Hospital, the Neurological Hospital was (as usual) waiting to expand, Psychology under Donald Hebb had launched on a new, exciting course, the Arctic Institute had been given space on the McGill campus, the Cyclotron and Radiation laboratories were given their own new buildings, and the physical sciences and engineering faculties were crowded as never before. A diary entry for the first weekend of 1947 reveals James' busy agenda for the year.

Saturday, 4 January, 1947
During the past few days of clearing up the arrears of work and reviewing our present position, I have talked with the architects about the possibilities of our building programme, and the probable developments in the building industry. There is a lot to do – Administration, Physics, Chemistry, Engineering, Donner, Swimming Pool and lots of smaller jobs so that it looks like a busy year.

Two expansions of McGill at this time deserve mention because they represented the broadening of mental horizons as well as the addition of new programs and buildings, in which Cyril James' participation was significant. The first is the creation of a theological faculty and the second the establishment of a medical research facility, both in 1948. Unfortunately, the initiatives are each given only brief notice in the journal. Often the only mention by James of quite major projects is in the university's annual reports, where the information is of necessity meagre.

This is certainly the case with regard to the creation of the new faculty, but fortunately other records exist. Since the late nineteenth century four independent theological colleges had benefited from association with the university while at the same time remaining free from academic control. These colleges were encouraged, particularly by William Birks, a prominent Montreal merchant and a strong United Church layman, to teach cooperatively the academic subjects of a theological education, while remaining separate for doctrinal and liturgical instruction. Birks and a fellow businessman named John Ross raised a considerable sum of money to build and endow a home for this joint effort, on land adjoining the campus. A handsome building, well-crafted inside and out, it was named Divinity Hall. As Birks and Ross were both governors of McGill, the question was raised: Why not take the building and its endowment into the university's care, and recognize the academic enterprise as McGill's theological faculty? Harvard, Yale, Oxford, Paris – all have theological faculties; why not McGill?

The idea of a theological faculty at McGill had been raised and rejected before: first in Sir William Peterson's day and then in Sir Arthur Currie's time. It lay fallow through the 1930s, but during World War II the proponents hoped that in might fare better. H. Keith Markell, historian of the faculty, wrote in 1979: "What was required to get a concrete proposal for a Theological Faculty on the launching pad ... was a combination of the irrepressible W.M. Birks and a University Principal who was not merely politely sympathetic toward such a faculty but enthusiastically in favour of it. The latter ingredient was supplied by the arrival at McGill as principal of F. Cyril James."[1] The proposal to establish a faculty of divinity was put before the University Senate in May 1940, six months after James took office.

Considerable sentiment, however, was voiced against the motion, principally by David Thomson, soon to be dean of graduate studies and research, and by C.S. Le Mesurier, dean of law. McGill had deliberately chosen to become a secular university in the nineteenth century, they argued, and it would be anachronistic to acquire a faculty of theology in the twentieth. The debate dragged on for some years, the proposal being strongly promoted by Birks, and certainly favoured by James although somewhat passively. The efforts he made were probably by showing approval in committee and by quiet persuasion. According to Birks, James secured the final approval by getting the proposal remitted by the Faculty of Arts and Science to a smaller body called the Council of the Faculty, whose membership was well stacked in favour of the proposal. The chairman, Dean A.H.S. Gillson, was well-known as a committed layman of the Anglican Cathedral congregation, and the faculty's member-at-large, Professor R.D. MacLennan, chairman of the philosophy department, was himself a Presbyterian minister. There were also present the four group chairmen who were *ex officio* voting members. The principals of the Anglican and United Church colleges (which both strongly supported the scheme) were present as "consultants." If James was assured of the voting sympathies of the four group chairmen (as it would seem he had good reason to be) he could also be assured of a vote of approval from this particular body. So when, early in 1948, the item appeared on the Senate agenda once more, it was supported by a unanimous recommendation to approve from the Faculty of Arts and Science. The arguments for either side were re-presented, and, at the end of the day, the proposal for a faculty of divinity won handsomely.

Whatever role James played in the background of these events, he certainly gave the new faculty, once it was established, every encouragement. The arrangement for filling the new appointments was that the colleges would nominate but the university would appoint, so that James could and did interest himself closely in gathering the new team. He had a hand in two appointments in particular. The first was of J.S. Thomson, president of the University of Saskatchewan, with whom James had worked closely in a number of matters concerning the National Conference of Canadian Universities. Widely known as the head of the Canadian Broadcasting Corporation during the war, Thomson was also greatly respected as a theologian, having been professor at Pine Hill Divinity School in Halifax before being called to Saskatchewan. Aware that Thomson was ready to move, James easily persuaded the colleges and the Board of Governors to appoint Thomson as the new dean of divinity and also persuaded Thomson to accept the appointment. This masterstroke gave the new faculty prestige and stature from the beginning. Thomson served for nine years as dean of divinity, before leaving to be installed as moderator of the United Church of Canada.

The other appointment probably owed less to James' initiative, but once made it engaged his deep interest. The chair of comparative study of religion had attracted from India a young specialist in Islamics, Wilfred Cantwell Smith. Smith not only brought his own erudition to the campus but also established, with James' encouragement and some modest financial help, the McGill Institute of Islamic Studies, which speedily became an academic enterprise of world-wide repute. It was a remarkable venture; in those days

Islam was a dormant, negligible element in world affairs, and none could foresee its imminent reawakening on a global scale. In these developments in the field of religion, James saw the university extending its frontiers to embrace subjects for which he had a natural broadminded inclination. The faculty continued in this liberal tradition, turning away from the narrow dogmatism that David Thomson and his colleagues had feared. Consequently, two decades after its inauguration the enterprise changed its name to the Faculty of Religious Studies and expanded its horizons to include not only Christian and Muslim but also Jewish, Hindu, Buddhist, and world-wide concerns. This development suited James' vision for McGill very well.

The other major new venture was of a very different character. Through his association with the Rockefeller Foundation and the Carnegie Trust, James had become aware of the less-widely advertised Donner Foundation, established by William Donner, an American steel merchant, who, like Carnegie, had not only amassed a great fortune but was prepared to be generous with it. But even more than Carnegie, Donner took a personal interest in the objects of his benevolence. One of his unusual ideas ran counter to the McGill tradition that medical research and clinical services should be kept in close relationship. Donner wanted a medical science centre where surgeons could devote their whole time to research, undisturbed by clinical obligations, and he was willing to pay for it. James realized that such a building would relieve a great deal of the pressure on space and services in the hospitals, and would supplement rather than conflict with the McGill tradition. He cultivated Donner assiduously, visiting him in Florida, both listening to the industrialist's ideas and spelling out the way in which McGill could put them into practice. The result was a grant of $250,000 (a respectable amount at that time) to provide for the Donner Medical Research Building and its equipment. The groups accommodated in the building included psychologists and biochemists, but the major group worked in the Max Lauterman Laboratories for Experimental Surgery. Surgeons in those days had not been as active in research as physicians, and in providing a quiet retreat form the pressures of the operating theatres and clinics – a building where surgical procedures could first be tried out on animals before being attempted on humans – McGill was breaking new ground. Excellent results in such procedures as bone-transplants and open-heart surgery were soon achieved. Although James is known to have been very active in securing the Donner donation, there is no mention of it in his diaries, and the reference to the erection of the building in the 1948 annual report is austerely brief. Yet the expansiveness of the McGill outlook in the postwar years is well illustrated by the questing activities that the Donner Building was designed to house.

The postwar years also saw James consolidating his position as firmly outside the university as within. A particular pleasure for him was an invitation early in 1947 to apply for membership of the Athenaeum Club in London. The invitation, from the president and committee of the club, was privately conveyed by his friend Sir Hector Hetherington, principal of Glasgow University. He was duly elected in April of that year. In April the following year he was elected a Fellow of the Royal Society of Canada, no doubt for his earlier contributions to the discipline of economics, and in July 1948 he received the honorary degree of LL D from his first *alma mater*, London University, no doubt both for his scholarship and for his eminence in university administration. In December he received the Croix du Chevalier de la Légion d'honneur at the hands of the French Ambassador "for services to France during the war." That citation must have surprised him somewhat, but it was only courteous to accept gracefully. The year 1948 also saw him elected president of the National Conference of Canadian Universities (1948–50), and, at the Oxford meeting of the Association of Universities of the British Commonwealth, elected chairman of AUBC's Executive Council, a choice that recognized the part he had played in the renewal of that organization during his visits to England in the period of postwar malaise.

James arranged for the June 1949 three-day meeting of the Executive Council of the AUBC to be held at Cyrus Eaton's Nova Scotian retreat, Deep Cove, the first time that activities of the association had been located outside the United Kingdom. It contributed greatly to the success of the meeting that it took place in such beautiful and spacious accommodations. The agenda concerned itself with such matters as the exchange of scholars and scientists, the advertising of vacant appointments, and the provision of scholarships among the various commonwealth partners. The discussions and conclusions were thought to have been so constructive that before the adjournment the council passed a special vote of thanks to its chairman, Dr F. Cyril James, for the leadership he had exercised throughout its deliberations.

A consequence of this meeting was an invitation for James to visit India in December in order to attend an India-America Relations Conference, as well as to attend a university convocation in

Pakistan, at which he would as a matter of courtesy receive an honorary degree from the University of Lahore. The India-American Conference had been arranged by the American Institute of Pacific Relations and the India Council of World Affairs. Why James was invited is not clear; it was not a particularly academic occasion; possibly the reason was that India had fallen into the trap of considering Canada to be more or less part of the United States. Whatever the reason, James was happy to accept. The time was only two years after the granting of independence, and the agony of the partition that had wracked the subcontinent was still being felt. As a Canadian, it would be extremely easy to put a foot wrong, either with his Hindu hosts in Delhi or with his Muslim hosts in Lahore, or indeed with angered mobs on either side, who might well not bother about nice distinctions between member-countries of the Commonwealth, even if they knew of them. James was determined to do his best for the kind of international relationships he believed in and for the associations he represented, and of course also determined to see as much as possible of the fabled lands he was being given the opportunity to visit.

Because he had met up with his brother in England the previous summer and had found it an enjoyable experience, he decided to add a side trip into Africa on the way home, to see for himself where Douglas was living and working. Perhaps in part to justify the African detour, he would also take the opportunity to visit the owner of a diamond mine in Tanganyika, J.H. Williamson, one of McGill's most interesting (and it was believed most wealthy) graduates.

James kept fairly detailed diary records of his travels, and if some of the entries are no more than any other traveller might produce, seeing for the first time the Taj Mahal or the Egyptian pyramids, they at least show that as a tourist Cyril James did his homework (in London he acquired Murray's *Guide to India and Pakistan*) and they also reveal that he had his full share of sensitivity to history and beauty. With the conference itself, however, he was not greatly impressed. On the second day he wrote in his diary:

Our sessions were somewhat more interesting today because we actually settled down to an expression of our opinions about foreign policy. I took fairly full notes – and looking them over I feel (as I did toward the end of the sessions) that a lot to time was spent saying little.

Between the sessions of the conference James took the opportunity to see what he could of the city, and of course there were also the formal luncheons and dinners, which were truly impressive affairs.

A small group of us was entertained to lunch by the Prime Minister – Pandit Nehru – whose official residence (the old Commander-in-Chief's house) is a magnificent palace, with servitors in scarlet livery and turbans. Dr. Ambedkar [a member of Cabinet and leader of the "Untouchables"] was among the guests – and although I did not have much chance for private conversation with either, I was fascinated by the contrast of two men who work so well together. Not only caste and tradition [are in contrast but also] task and method of approach. But each is charming and profoundly interesting in his own way.

Even more splendid was the Governor-General's Reception tonight. Britain, in the construction of New Delhi, certainly bequeathed to India the most magnificent group of public buildings that I have seen in any country. Government House is a perfect setting for pomp and ceremony – and although these are far below Vice-Regal days the occasion was still impressive. Bengal Lancers in scarlet coats and turbans all the way up each side of the stairs and stationed at each pillar around the reception hall; servitors in scarlet and gold; the great marble hall – it was an occasion to be remembered!

For James, with his lingering sense of boyhood nostalgia for the days of empire, such ceremonial magnificence would be especially attractive. Once he decided no one was going to say anything profound on the subject of US–India relations, he became less conscientious about attending the sessions of the conference and spent part of each day seeing the many sights of Delhi and absorbing the atmosphere of India. The high point of this experience, as for most visitors to India, was a weekend visit with a companion to Agra and Fatehpur Sikri.

The Taj Mahal, which we visited this afternoon, is even lovelier than my expectations. It is magnificent from a distance and equally splendid when one inspects the detail of the lattice marble screens; loveliest of all, perhaps, when one crosses the river in a little ferry boat, propelled by a youthful Charon, and sees the white marble tomb rising between the two towers of red sandstone. Certainly Muntaz-i-Mahal, for whom Shah Jahan created it 300 years ago, is the luckiest of womankind in her earthly immortality … To me the most impressive memories are the glorious little mosque of white marble in which lies the body of the Saint, Sheikh Salim Chisti, in an exquisite tomb of mother-of-pearl; the great splendour of the Victory

Gate up which one marches on great steps that force the visitor to bend the knee ... and the great tomb of Akbar ... as I stood in the vault, and heard the call of the guardian *Allah Akbar!* echoing around the vault, my imagination captured something of long ago and the memory of human greatness.

The visit to Lahore for the convocation, although not a long one, evidently impressed him; he gave a full account of his experiences there. Although he remembered it mostly as a university occasion, he was not insensitive to the emotional undertones that were still vibrating.

After Convocation there was a large lunch under awnings on the lawn and the Vice-Chancellor (Malik, whom I met at Oxford) told me a little of the impact of partition: the student body cut in half; 70% of the teaching staff leaving to go to India; income greatly reduced. But all those whom I met paid great tribute to Malik's energy and wisdom in these trying times and the place seems to be picking up rapidly. All through my conversations with these people I was constantly conscious of the continuing tension between India and Pakistan – in which Kashmir is only one of the factors, although perhaps the most important at the moment.

At the Forman Christian College, he was glad to find that many of the staff remembered with affection the young colleague he had recently appointed to the McGill chair of the Comparative Study of Religion, Wilfred Smith. Their ready endorsement confirmed his own satisfaction with that appointment.

After his return to Delhi, James was provide with one last memorable experience of the Indian countryside.

Wednesday, December 21

In the Canadian [High Commission] car ... I set out after breakfast to drive to Aligarh – 80 miles of narrow road with a blinding dust whenever the wheel left the macadam – trains of camel carts and ox carts – tongas, monkeys scampering about the road – men and women walking endlessly – and the manifest life of the villages through which we passed, each with its road barrier at which a tax is collected!

Arriving at 11:30 we had coffee at the home of Hyder Sahib – the acting Vice-Chancellor of the great Moslem University of Aligarh – and then made a long tour of the buildings, especially those in the fields of science and engineering for which Aligarh is famous. Found that Wasid[2] – who got his Ph.D from McGill last May – is on the staff, and was also impressed by the professor of physics, who is a student of Compton's. Some good research is being done here as at Lahore but there is a paucity of equipment and I have a strong feeling (in which Hyder agrees with me) that India needs craftsmen and foremen more than it needs research scientists ... luncheon had to end on schedule so that we might accept the invitation of the student president (resplendent in a green gown) to address the student society. It was a good meeting, all in the hands of the students and held in their own hall, and afterwards we were deluged with requests for autographs, and with questions that betrayed a great ignorance of America, and as well as a strong suspicion of communist propaganda ... [We left] at 5:15 to drive back over the same road made eerie by dust and darkness, so that the dung-fires beside the road were a kind of fairy lights – and the many trains of camel or bullock carts a ghostly memory made real only because of the choking dust.

When James came to sum up the significance of the conference he found he was not able to give it very high marks. But he realized that he himself had learned a great deal outside the conference.

We have heard a diversity of viewpoints and met interesting people, but somehow the formal meetings and the great receptions are to me the least rewarding part of the visit. The real knowledge that I have gained comes from private chats, from visits such as that to Aligarh, from observation of the streets ...

Having some time to spare before he left Delhi, he took the opportunity to wander for three hours on his own down the Chandni Chowk, absorbing all the sights, smells, and sounds of the greatest bazaar-street in India. He observed the evidences of acute poverty on every side, and the houses of obviously well-to-do people with their own carriages and horses, all cheek-by-jowl with the hovels of the poor. He saw the little shops of the brass workers and the iron-founders, the silversmiths and goldsmiths, the ivory workers and the jewellers, and he observed the great open square of the Jama Masjid, India's largest mosque. But his appreciation of India was more than that of simply the tourist. He enjoyed meeting the students at Aligarh, one of the few times when he had personal contacts with young people, and learned a great deal from his conversations with both Indian and Pakistani academics.

His visit ended on Christmas Day when he boarded the 2:15 plane for Karachi with three other passengers. The aircraft was bedecked with Christmas decorations, but James remarked that it was a doleful affair and that he hoped he would never have to pass Christmas Day in a similar fashion again. He left the plane at Cairo, spending two days sightseeing in Egypt before starting off on his visit to his brother in Kenya.

This side-trip to Africa proved more adventurous than Cyril James expected. The first part of the journey was straightforward enough. It took him from Alexandria to Nairobi by flyingboat. It was a plane of the Solent class, having two decks and travelling "very comfortably." The other passengers, mostly British immigrants to Kenya, included many children – the families little knew that the days of the white man in East Africa were already numbered. James was once more impressed by the aridity of so much of the earth's land surface: he looked down on the "great deserts of central Africa, and rough hills at the foot of distant mountains" and realized more vividly than before the importance of the natural lakes, and of the decision to build the great reservoir at Assouan. At this time, the dam holding back the Nile waters was relatively modest – the Assouan High Dam was still in the future – but already the artificial lake stretching back into Nubia was significant enough to impress itself strongly upon his memory. The flyingboat's route followed the Nile south to Khartoum and then inclined southeast to Nairobi, where fourteen hours after leaving its Mediterranean moorings the craft touched down on Lake Naivasha. The subsequent sixty-five-mile drive through the Great Rift valley gave James the opportunity to observe, on the one side, the history-recording canyon walls, and on the other the Stone Age living-sites, where some of mankind's earliest-known ancestors had lived and hunted and manufactured their primitive tools.

Emerging from the gorge, James saw "red soil reminiscent of Devon and a countryside that – apart from the mountains – might have been the west of England, with flowers and flowering trees in profusion! I can understand why the folk in England are enthusiastic about Kenya." While waiting in Nairobi for his brother to make contact with him, he identified in the hotel and nearby gardens fifteen varieties of flowers already known to him, and many more unknown. But he also spent several frustrating hours on the telephone and in the telegraph office trying to reach either Douglas or Williamson, his later host in Tanganyika. "Two things stand out in my mind about Kenya," he recorded in his diary, "– the profusion of fruits and flowers, on the one hand, and the difficulty of communications on the other."

The following day, however, Douglas and his wife Florence arrived by Land Rover to take James back with them to their home in Kongwa. From there Williamson's private plane would pick James up to fly him to the diamond mine at Mwadui in Shinyanga territory. On Saturday, 31 December the three set out to drive the five-hundred miles across Kenya to Kongwa.

We started out from the hotel and were soon out in the open country where I saw and photographed a great variety of game: giraffes (many), gazelle, Thompson's gazelle (small, with brilliant yellow and black marking), buffalo, impala, baboon, zebra, dit-chit (? – a small deer not much larger than a hare), leopard – one that was almost too close for comfort since we had no gun. I saw blue cranes, pink flamingo, storks and vultures, as well as many smaller birds that I could not recognize. The drive was hot and dusty – so dusty that I was almost red when we reached the hotel at Arusha around 9.15 and the water in which I washed my hair became mud!

The first part of the journey successfully behind them, the travellers became mindful of the fact that it was after all New Year's Eve and joined a party in progress in the bar. "The mood being on us, Digs and I danced every single dance with Flo – so that we went merrily to bed at 1.15 a.m. Quite a celebration – and none of us very sober."

But the next day showed the other face of travel in Africa.

Early in the afternoon we began to encounter "the rains"! In Africa – or at least in this part of Africa – rain is unusual and when it comes it turns the roads into a kind of clay that seems to have the consistency of butter. We skidded and slid – so that driving was hard and the rate of progress diminished. Then, about 83 miles from Dodomar, we came upon a causeway over which several feet of water was pouring in flood! We had to stop – and we stopped for more than two hours before the flood had fallen to a level that made it possible for the Land Rover to push through the water and get across. By this time it was almost dark – and the darkness added to the hazard of the roads – so that we finally reached Dodomar around 10.30 p.m. The kitchen and the bar at the hotel were both closed by that time but we thought ourselves lucky to find beds – and as soon as I got into mine I fell asleep! I should add as a footnote to the record of a weary day that the rain seems to bring out thousands of insects – scorpions, beetles, flying ants, and mosquitoes – so that tonight (for the first time since I reached Africa) I was glad indeed of the mosquito net!

The next day, over breakfast, the party discussed the possibilities before them; they were told it might take them ten hours or two days to reach Kongwa.

Digs decided to try and get the wireless folk at Dodoma airfield to get into touch with Williamson's plane – which they were able to do and the plane landed at Dodoma instead of Kongwa – a magnificently equipped T.H. Dove that was a great contrast to the spartan simplicity of the Land Rover that has, I feel at this moment, raised permanent corns on all our bottoms!

The pilots – two ex-BOAC captains! – agreed readily to my suggestion that they should take Flo and Digs to Kongwa – so that we left the Land Rover to the native chauffeur and set out on a *35 minute* trip. I saw Kongwa from the air and – for about half an hour – on the ground ... Such is travel in Africa, and I know of no greater triumph for the aeroplane!

James learned the hard way that on African roads one travels hopefully and philosophically.

The flight from Kongwa to Mwadui, also roughly five-hundred miles, took only ninety minutes.

Williamson was on the airstrip to meet me. We drove up to his house – a really luxurious bungalow – for lunch and after that we spent the afternoon going around the mines. His claim is about six miles square – for which he pays a rental to the government and also a royalty on the diamonds produced. (And it should be added that he also pays income tax and super tax on his own residual income at a total rate of 19 shillings in the pound – so that most of the $1 M per month which he is supposed to be making goes to the government) ... We went on to look at the hospital that he has built, the trees that he has planted and the Club for the staff where we had a drink and I met several of them. In the two years since Williamson really started to develop the property he has built up a community that now exceeds 3500 people inside the double ring of barbed wire – but somehow he still impresses me as a shy, lonely man.

That evening the two men "sat around and talked of McGill in the days when [Williamson] was a Douglas Fellow and tutor," and James was surprised to find that Williamson not only read the *McGill News* but also subscribed to the *McGill Daily*, in order to supplement the university news in the *Montreal Star*. James records that he "carefully refrained" from asking Williamson for any benefit for the university, but did invite him to visit Montreal the following October for the opening of the new Physical Sciences

Centre. James decided that if Williamson agreed to come he would nominate him for an honorary degree, but no firm arrangements were proposed, and in the afternoon James boarded the private plane and was flown back to Nairobi.

At 3.30 I left Mwadui in his private plane and landed in Nairobi soon after 5.0[0]. Owing to Williamson I once again got a room at the Norfolk Hotel – some other chap pushed out, I suppose – and had a chance to really unpack my bags in order to repack them for the flight home. David Neville [a McGill graduate living in Nairobi] came along at 7.30 and took me to dinner at the *Flamingo Room* in the Arnold Hotel. Food, service, wine and music were really excellent, and I noticed that all the diners except ourselves were in evening dress. Civilized Africa at its best!

The journey home from Nairobi was uneventful. He was routed via London, where he sandwiched in a McGill Graduates' Society meeting, and arrived back in Montreal at 3:40 A.M. on Sunday, 8 January. On Monday, 9 January at 10 A.M., he was back in his office, giving a long interview about his travels and the America–India Conference to the Montreal newspapers.

Not surprisingly, he saw the problems of India and Pakistan primarily in economic terms. He referred several times to the immense disruption caused when a vast area was abruptly divided in two, "which had been for untold centuries one country, geographically, economically, culturally." (Bangladesh at this time was still East Pakistan.) Whether the mixed populations that found themselves in "India" and "Pakistan" were ever as cognizant of the unity of the sub-continent as their imperial administrators thought they were may well be questioned. But the economic and academic disruptions that claimed James' attention were real enough, and since the partition was so recent, he also could not ignore the tragic effect on human lives; it was present at every occasion, on every street, in every conversation. In his typed summary of all that he had seen and learned in India and Africa, James wrote with his usual care and provided many statistics; but when talking to the Montreal reporters, his language was less polished and his personal concern more evident.

I give just one little vignette that I saw, up near Amritzar. I saw a woman in a silk sari, which suggests that she came from a reasonably good middle class family, somewhere around 35, carrying a baby, with two other children, both dressed in silk, all filthy dirty, and the woman was pushing in front of her, hand over hand, a bedroll of about five ft. long by three ft in diameter, just lifting one end, turning it over, raising it, picking it up and down again, along a dusty road. She had come at least 22 miles from the nearest village and she had further than that to go before she came to any town, and she had travelled all that distance like that, and you have in that, a sort of single picture of the kind of thing that is still going on, to the extent of hundreds of thousands of people, just picking up and leaving everything they had.[3]

In this visit to India and Pakistan, James crossed mental boundaries as well as physical, and his personal horizons were greatly expanded. In a short time he learned a great deal concerning history, religion, culture, and the human condition. While in India he lived in Western-style luxury, and frankly enjoyed it, but he made himself aware of, and felt deeply for, the poverty and suffering around him. In Africa, on the other hand, he seemed untouched by the poverty. He lived both at the luxury level of the administrators and briefly at the more realistic level of those who, like his brother Douglas, actually worked the country. But even that standard of living was far removed from the teeming life of the villages. But the strange feature of James' Kenyan travel journal is the absence of human beings from his landscape. Anyone who has driven African roads is familiar with the colourfully bedecked and piously bemottoed trucks, crowded with cheerful passengers and precarious packages, wheezing and coughing painfully to the top of the next grade, and lurching even more dangerously down the other side. The traveller is equally familiar with the roadside walkers, with their bundles on their heads and their babies on their backs. James saw game and flowers and a diamond mine, but never once does he mention a black man, woman, or child. He makes one reference to "the native chauffeur" of the Land Rover – presumably a black – and that is all. He comments on the intrusion of Indian entrepreneurs into the commercial life of Kenya, and mentions the strong resentment felt by white settlers against the Asian immigrants who were beating them at their own game. But the native people, the Africans, he apparently did not see. Having breathed African dust, and battled with African mud, and experienced all too closely African insects, he returns thankfully to the Norfolk Hotel, enjoyes the food, the wine, the music, approves the evening-dress of the diners, and comments "civilized Africa at its best!"

This was perhaps not simply due to insensitivity. James was a remarkable illustration of a person who can respond readily to one culture that is not his own and be left quite unmoved by another. Those who administered the great missionary movements out of Britain or North America knew very well that there were "the Latin American people" just as there were "the China people." James was obviously not "an Africa person." But India, for all its unfamiliarity, was not something alien to him. As a boy, he had had ideas of joining the Indian Civil Police. Given different circumstances, he could possibly have been one of those many Englishmen who found their destiny in India; he might very well have become one of "the India people."

The year 1950, into which James' India–Africa travels had carried him, was destined to be one of much more travel. As chairman of the executive of the AUBC, he had good reason to visit the universities of the Commonwealth, and his journey to India and Pakistan had whetted an appetite that not even the buffetings of his safari in Africa could lessen. He returned home in January, but in February was flying again, this time to Jamaica to attend the installation of Princess Alice, the Countess of Athlone, as chancellor of the new University of the West Indies. This enabled James to renew many personal acquaintances – he had first met Princess Alice herself as the wife of Canada's governor general – and further prepared the way for McGill to develop particular ties with the Caribbean area, which he continued to believe would one day prove a very desirable development. He returned after a week in the tropical sunshine to endure the tail-end of Montreal's winter, but hardly had the short Canadian spring blossomed into full summer when he was off again. He appeared in a photograph in the *Montreal Star* of 28 June standing at the bottom of the steps leading up to a plane door, with a caption that informed readers that he was "Off on a Round-the-World-Trip." Dr James, the accompanying paragraph read, "will attend a Commonwealth universities' conference in New Zealand. His flight schedule, covering more than 35,000 miles includes Vancouver, Honolulu, Fiji, Sydney, Auckland, Singapore, Calcutta, Karachi, Cairo, Rome and London."

These journeys of Cyril James in 1950 are a remarkable illustration of the rapid development of air travel in the immediate postwar years. In 1942, flying across the Atlantic by way of Gander and Prestwick had been an adventurous if not heroic undertaking. Eight years later he was flying to India, Africa, the Caribbean, and across the southern seas to Australia and New Zealand on regularly scheduled airline flights. In less than a decade, the airplane had proved itself one of the most powerful forces drawing the whole world together into one community, and James was fortunate enough to be one of the early travellers able to benefit from the new mobility.

His journal had become so intermittent by this time that it is only continued by the travel diaries he kept as he journeyed, and by the menu cards, hotel bills, and memorabilia papers he collected from airlines and tourist companies. He kept a full diary of his visits to both Australia and New Zealand, but it is for the most part a factual record of the places seen and the people met, with little personal comment. The trip broadened his knowledge of aircraft and of the world's surface; he received an impression of the Australian continent and of the New Zealand islands, as any tourist might, and he visited three universities in both countries. But his comments on cities and academic institutions are neither very original nor revealing. His main impression of Australia was that it was cold! In every hotel, club or home, he deplores the lack of central heating. He was driven to buying, in succession, woollen underwear, fleece-lined slippers, a warm cardigan, and a hot-water bottle for his bed.

July 26, 1950

This is a strange country – and since I feel tired today, I have been thinking. The discomfort is solely due to the fact that Australian houses lack what we consider good plumbing and heating! The natural climate is superb because here at mid-winter – roses, camelias, asilias and many other flowers are in bloom. I find myself wondering how much of the failure to develop Australia rapidly is due to the aridity of the entire region and the lack of water and fuel – and how much to the human factor of lack of initiative and a desire to escape work? I should think, for instance, that Australia would be hard at work studying the peacetime uses of atomic energy – nobody could use it more effectively – but so far as I know they are doing nothing!

Australia was an educative experience for James, as it must be for even the dullest of visitors, but it did not engage his mind or quicken his imagination as India had done.

New Zealand offered him romantic landscapes and seascapes, the unique experience of visiting the thermal springs areas, and a brush, through the Maori exhibits, with an older civilization and a completely other way of life. The only business achieved by the committee in its antipodean deliberations appears to have been to decide the location of the 1953 meeting of the AUBC. The majority wanted it to be held in Cambridge, England; but James lobbied hard to secure the 1958 meeting for Canada.

Tuesday, August 1st, 1950, Wairakei

... It would also be necessary for us in Canada to raise $120,000 to $150,000 to cover the costs of the delegates after landing. We discussed the matter at great length yesterday and had several private conferences in the evening – after which I proposed that the 1953 congress be in U.K. and the 1958 congress (if we live that long because the Korean news is bad!) be held in Canada. I think it is vital that this congress be a success and hope that Canada will play [its part] – but I do wish that Sidney Smith had been there!

He knew that he had unilaterally committed the Canadian Association to an expensive undertaking but believed the enhancement of Canada's commonwealth role would justify the costs – and hoped his NCCU colleagues would think the same.

The committee finished its business in two days of discussions at the beginning of August, but the members then continued with visits to the universities of Dunedin, Canterbury, and Wellington; it was not until Wednesday, 23 August that James set out on the return journey. He flew almost continuously via Sydney, Darwin, Singapore (where he stayed overnight), Calcutta, Karachi, Cairo, and Rome to London, where he arrived four days later, to spend a week with Irene in her parents' home before setting off on the last leg to Montreal.

The main value of these journeys for James was the establishment of world-wide contacts in the academic community. But with the many references in the travel diaries to "chatting with this one," "had a long talk with another," "was very agreeably entertained in the home of a third," one wonders if the long succession of new names and faces did not become wearisome. Yet James seems to have developed (as he did during the "tour de force " for the Bankers' association before the war) a great tolerance for this kind of experience.

On the other hand, those he met in this way did not always register too deeply with him. A story is told in the University Club that once in the early years of his residence in Montreal a member and James entered the smoking room, where the member remarked, "Look, there is So and So. Do you know him?" "No," said James, "I don't think I do." "Oh, you should know So and So. Come and be introduced." The introductions were made and after polite conversation the two parties moved to their separate tables. The man who had been introduced to James said to his friend, "That is extraordinary. I have just been introduced to Dr James and he obviously didn't know me, so I said nothing. But actually we shared a cabin for a week on a ship crossing to England, three years ago." While travelling, James seemed to gain a more lasting impression of scenery, flowers, and buildings than of people. He could meet twenty, thirty, or more in a day, hundreds in the course of a long trip, greet them courteously, often write their names accurately into his travel-log, then let them drop out of memory unless their paths crossed again. Even then, there were perhaps just too many to recall them all. He enjoyed people while he was with them, but the only person he ever appears to miss while she was absent (and then only occasionally) is Irene. Despite their apparent incompatibility, his attachment to her seems never to have weakened.

The ten years James had now spent at McGill had brought him rich benefits of experience. There were seldom situations he could not now handle, no men or women he could not meet with easy confidence, few tasks he could not face with assured competence. He still knew that he had to work hard to be successful – he continued to do his homework before committee meetings, carefully prepared his lectures and speeches, and took trouble over the detail of events such as dinners or convocations. Although he had travelled much abroad, he did not become careless or neglectful at home. He still kept the details of administration at McGill meticulously in his own hands.

He became perhaps more conservative in his middle age. For all his early years at the London School of Economics, he had become less enthusiastic now about central planning than he had been in the days of the Committee on Reconstruction, although he still saw the need for both governmental guidelines and personal initiatives. James had a pretty fair assessment of himself – he recognized that he was essentially a liberal of the old school, but he also realized that the old liberalism had serious shortcomings. In September 1946, when he opened a conference on atomic physics at McGill, just a year after Hiroshima and Nagasaki, the occasion prompted a sober train of thought.

I opened the Canadian Conference on Atomic Physics this afternoon – in the building where Rutherford began his work some 48 years ago – and this morning I read the last issue of the *New Yorker* which is entirely given up to an account of the atomic bomb at Hiroshima in terms of a few who experienced it and survived. By way of contrast (I am not sure though [that it is by way of contrast]) I have just been reading Bready's *England Before and After Wesley*, in which he points out the fact that

England's strength in the early 19th century was due to a deepened sense of personal religion – and I found myself wondering what deep force will be evoked to act upon the human mind and spirit in our generation. Economics is not enough, although we should do well to remember economic facts and history; evangelism by radio does not seem a hopeful prospect – and I still find myself groping for something that will be more constructive for world peace, and yet as moving to the individual as the devotion which autocratic states inspired in Germany, Italy, and Russia. Liberalism and *laissez-faire* have lost the fire they had in the hearts of Bright, Cobden and Gladstone – but I still think that there is imbedded in their philosophy a larger measure of truth than the modern planners seem to think. The idea is not new to me. I have been getting some of my old lectures and papers ready for the binders – chiefly those from 1924–1931 – and I am forced to conclude that I am pretty consistent on that theme. Unfortunately consistency is not a test of either wisdom or truth.

The colleague who once described James as "wistful" was close to the truth in more respects than one. James was not only wistful in the realm of human relationships; he had also lost the guiding light of religion, and recognized it as a loss. He could still respond to an effective presentation of religious conviction in other men, on the rare occasions he encountered it; on his Australia–New Zealand tour, for example, he had gone with the rest of the academic party to the cathedral service in Auckland where he heard one of their number, Charles Raven, the Cambridge biologist and theologian, preach the sermon:

Sunday, August 6, 1950
This morning I went to the Cathedral to hear Raven preach a magnificent sermon – without a single note – on "Life enriched through life laid down". I cannot attempt to paraphrase it, but to me it was much more than a new revelation of Raven. It was one of the clearest statements of Christianity as a religion designed to enrich and enlarge life – to make us alive to a wider range or experience.

But it was not a dimension he had the time or the will to explore, even if there were moments when he was wistful for something he knew to be lacking in his own personal philosophy. He had work to do and a career to pursue that constantly brought him new challenges and new opportunities. He had now been in Montreal for a decade, and he was ready to begin a second decade, which he confidently expected to be equally demanding and equally rewarding.

CHAPTER TEN

Irresistible Logic and Immovable Opposition

The major topic in Canadian academic circles at the beginning of the 1950s was the looming crisis created by the passing of the veterans. Their coming in 1945 had confronted all universities with large financial problems but none more than McGill. With the cooperation of the federal government, these had been solved. Now, as the holders of grants graduated, the flow of government *per capita* grants began to dwindle. But the expenditures they had generated did not. Buildings, equipment, programs, additional faculty appointments all continued and indeed had to be maintained because the places vacated by veterans were being taken in increasing numbers by new generations of high-school graduates, a larger percentage of whom was choosing post-secondary education. The loss of federal income at such a time constituted as great a threat to the universities as had the lack of it in 1945.

At the time of Confederation in 1867, education had been one of the areas of jurisdiction reserved for the provinces. Although McGill University had petitioned the government of the United Kingdom to recognize university-level education as a federal responsibility, the request had been denied. Yet now, almost a century later, the wisdom and the justice of the petition was being painfully illustrated. The provinces could not supply the new needs of their universities; nor was it equitable that they should. The Maritime universities in particular, received many students from other provinces. Toronto and McGill, both of which were members of the American Association of Universities, received many foreign students, especially for graduate studies and research. The situation plainly called for a national policy to meet a national need. As President N.A.M. MacKenzie of UBC put it in a 1950 article:

The nub of the matter was ... that Canadian universities simply could not educate students without substantial increases in funding. Because of the Canadian tax system, with that powerful income tax lever controlled in Ottawa, the logical, and in some ways the only, source of additional funds had to be the federal government.[1]

No one saw this more clearly than the principal of the university that stood in greatest peril. McGill was unique in that it had begun as a state-supported institution but had been disowned and left to fend for itself. Although it was a royal foundation and had a royal charter and title ("the Royal Institution for the Advancement of Learning"), it had never received crown grants or government subsidies. The likelihood of the francophone and Duplessis-dominated government of Quebec coming to the rescue of the Royal Institution was minimal. But if a Canadian policy was evolved to meet a nation-wide need, McGill would benefit equally with all other Canadian universities. Cyril James had every reason to be urgent in seeking a solution to the problem.

The generosity of private donors, on which the university had traditionally relied, had been splendidly exemplified in the 1940s, first in 1944 when J.W. McConnell had raised more than seven million dollars, after "persuading his friends" to contribute to his quietly organized fund-raising campaign, and then in 1948 when McGill's "first public campaign," led by another governor, Blair Gordon, had secured more than eight million dollars.[2] These were large sums, even by today's standard. But the expenses of education were increasing so much that private and corporate benevolence could no longer meet the costs. Only a public purse was deep enough, and the executive heads of universities were in no doubt that that purse had to be the federal one. The presidents and principals of Canadian universities had been meeting to discuss their common concerns since the days of World War I. During World War II, the National Conference of Canadian Universities had by default become the spokesman for the academic consensus, and then had inevitably moved from that stance to one of a pressure group, urging the universities' needs upon the government, with Cyril James as one of the most active members in encouraging this postwar evolution.

The historian of the NCCU, Gwendoline Pilkington, gives Cyril James full due as one of the leaders in the further developments of the 1950s. He was president of the conference in 1948–50, and both before and after his term in the chair he exercised a potent role in its affairs. At the NCCU's June 1948 meeting, a small com-

mittee of eight executive heads was formed and charged with
gaining the sympathetic concern of the federal government for the
plight of the institutions. In November, James was appointed chairman of a finance sub-committee, which was entrusted with "the
widest possible terms of reference to discuss with appropriate
Ministers the financial problems of Canadian universities."[3] This
committee gathered for its first meeting at McGill in January 1949
to lay plans for a nation-wide campaign to alert Canadians to the
distressed conditions of academia. The committee members estimated the annual cost of the aid needed by the universities to be
$4 million, with another $3.2 million for scholarships and programs.

A brief was drafted covering all of these areas, with Dr. James contributing
an introduction in which he made a fervent appeal to Ottawa to give
the universities the support they needed, especially as the DVA grants
would cease in 1951. He offered evidence as to how Ottawa had provided
aid to scientific research and to the training of veterans "without violating
in any way the established provisions of the BNA Act". In the same way,
[he argued] the financial problems of the universities could be alleviated.[4]

Two months later, James and members of his committee were
given an appointment with Prime Minister Louis St Laurent and
Douglas Abbott, by this time the minister of finance. The essence
of the NCCU brief was presented and met with a positive reception;
the committee was much encouraged when St Laurent referred to
their figures as "a modest request." However, the prime minister
stated that no action could be forthcoming until he had the report
of the royal commission he had appointed on the support of the
Arts, Letters, and Sciences in Canada, the so-called Massey Commission.

It therefore became important to impress the members of that
commission with the content of the NCCU brief. The NCCU Finance
Committee secured a hearing before the commissioners at which
James took responsibility for outlining the universities' operational
plight; R.C. Wallace of Queen's spelt out the need to cover the
overhead costs of research; and other members spoke to the training
of students for such fields as national health and welfare, science
and technology, agriculture and forestry. Of course, the fact that
James was a personal acquaintance of the chairman of the commission, Vincent Massey and that members of the committee were
well-acquainted with most of the other members of the commission
made everybody's task all the easier.[5] An air of optimism prevailed.

However, while the universities waited for the commission to report and for the government to respond, international affairs took a decided turn for the worse. In the early months of 1950, tension between the Communist and Western blocks increased steadily in Korea. War broke out in June. St Laurent reminded the NCCU committee that Canada had again to divert for military use funds that might have been made available for other purposes, including education. He suggested, however, the NCCU might do well to launch their own publicity campaign to inform the public of the universities' dire need; governments, he reminded them, could only financially support projects that had widespread, popular approval. It was, he said, the public not the government that needed to be persuaded.

James immediately urged his academic colleagues to take up the prime minister's challenge. He wrote in February to Sidney Smith, president of the University of Toronto, that St Laurent's views "made a great deal of sense," but that trying to persuade the public to react favourably on this issue would not be an easy matter. The major problem was to win general consent for the novel idea that the federal government should be the one to come to the universities' rescue, seeing that education was a field reserved to the provinces. The federal government had certainly done so with regard to the stresses created on campuses by the influx of postwar veterans, but there it had a clear involvement. What James and his committee were arguing now was that the federal government should acknowledge a responsibility for civilian education in peace-time. At the annual conference of the NCCU in June 1950, he made this matter the main thrust of his presidential speech, arguing that the universities are "an invaluable asset to the nation" and that "in every sense of the word, the universities of Canada are already national institutions," and that "the idea that provincial governments have exclusive responsibility for university education within their borders ... is an anachronism in the middle of the twentieth century." He also made the point, which most people were ready to accept, that the provincial governments could not afford the costs of the new, sophisticated facilities required to keep universities abreast of expanding knowledge and research. He strongly discounted any fears that the federal government, if it gave financial aid, might be tempted to encroach on the autonomy of the universities, and he also expressed his own confidence that there were no constitutional barriers that might prevent federal assistance. In this way he expounded the irresistible logic implied in the inescapable question: to whom else should the universities turn?

The impact of the modern age has forced upon us, in practice, a realization that University education is a national problem ... We live in an age when government takes so large a portion of individual income in taxes that the generosity of the potential benefactor is sharply restricted. And since most of the tax revenues accrue to the national government – in proportion to whose receipts the needs of the Universities seem strangely small – it is to the government of Canada that we must turn.[6]

Soon after the conference he wrote once more to St Laurent, spelling out those "strangely small" figures; the total annual grant that he and his committee were now seeking for institutional support and educational programs combined was $12,842,000. Viewed in isolation, the figure looked not strangely small but forbiddingly large. But James never hesitated to think in bold terms when the occasion called from them, though he was well aware of St Laurent's difficulties. He was also mindful of the prime minister's warning: it is the Canadian people who must be convinced of the justification for additional calls upon the public purse.

Consonant with that reminder, the Finance Committee decided to set up a publicity sub-committee, and under the members' direction the universities' plea was voiced by academic leaders across the country at every opportunity: at university convocations, at Canadian Club and similar speaking engagements, and at Learned Society meetings and professional conferences. Early in 1951, James took it one step further: hiring a public relations company to conduct an information campaign on the universities' behalf. This was something that could not be charged to ordinary NCCU budgets; accordingly, James asked each university president for a donation of $100 to finance the campaign. McGill, Toronto, and UBC would take care of any remaining charges. James may have thought it ominous that the only two institutions that failed to respond to his appeal were located in his own province of Quebec.

The report of the Massey Commission was placed in the government's hands during the summer of 1950. It was expected that it would be tabled in the House of Commons in the spring of 1951 and that the government's response to it would be made known at the same time. This matter was therefore planned as the major item on the agenda of the 1951 NCCU Annual Conference, scheduled for 31 May and 1 June. At the last moment, when it was learned that the report would not be tabled in the House until three P.M., Friday, 1 June, just as the conference was due to conclude, an additional session was hastily called to consider the report and the government's response to it. Pilkington summarizes the information conveyed that afternoon to the anxious academics.

To everyone's delight, the Commission's views were favourable beyond anyone's most sanguine hopes. The report argued that the universities "serve the national cause in so many ways, direct and indirect, that theirs must be regarded as the finest of contributions to national strength and unity". The Commissioners had found that the institutions had been starved for resources and were "facing a financial crisis so grave as to threaten their future usefulness". They were victims of "the twin spectres of falling revenues and rising costs". Hence, among the most urgent recommendations were those asking for direct grants to universities based on the student population of each institution, for a Government-funded national scholarship plan, and for the establishment of a Council for the encouragement of the Arts, Letters, Humanities, and Social Sciences, also to be supported by the Government.[7]

Perhaps even more important was the nature of the government's response. The main recommendations of the Massey Report were endorsed, some for immediate implementation, others as part of a longer-term program. Those concerning the scholarships and bursaries, as well as the founding of what came to be called "the Canada Council," were not implemented until 1956, but the recommendation proposing payments of direct grants to universities was accepted for implementation as soon as possible. The "irresistible logic" had prevailed.

James' own satisfaction at this outcome must have been considerable. While the other members of his small committee had worked hard and loyally, the leadership and driving energy had come from him all the way through. In the work of this committee, he had made a contribution to academic life in Canada that would be, he believed, of inestimable and lasting benefit. His belief has been justified. While the mode of the federal contribution would change, and payments in later years would be made through the provincial governments, rather than independently of them, the fact that higher education is recognized in Canada as a matter of national and not merely regional concern, and should be a charge upon the national treasury, resulted in large measure from the campaign that Cyril James as chairman of the NCCU Finance Committee brilliantly organized in the years 1949–51.

For his own university the victory had a degree of importance greater than for any other. McGill, which had never received statutory government grants, would for the first time be recognized as a university "tout comme les autres." From now on, McGill would receive grants not by special vote, or at a politician's whim, but by statutory measure. The injustice of a hundred and thirty years had at last been corrected.

Nor were the tangible dollars to be overlooked. In pleading the plight of the universities generally, James had been painfully aware of the unhappy situation in his own institution. Noting, as he had, in the university's annual report for 1949–50, that the year had ended with a deficit of $284,700, he warmly welcomed the prospect of the $500,000 he calculated for McGill, especially as that sum would be a recurrent item, year by year. It would, he decided, be used not just to meet the deficit; some of the new money would be put toward awarding modest salary increases, which were greatly overdue, and not only for the academic staff. "When we turn to the non-teaching staff," he said, "the secretaries, technicians and others who contribute so much to the work of the University, we find that more than half of them are receiving annual wages of less than $1,550."[8] It is understandable therefore that everyone at McGill – governors, academic staff, and non-academic staff alike – joined in welcoming his achievement. Any lingering doubts that James was not really a McGill person dissipated in the warmth of euphoria.

But his old nemesis was to return to haunt him: a failure to circumvent the sensitivity of federal–provincial relations. The trouble began as early as August of that same year, when Marcel Faribault, secretary-general of l'Université de Montréal, wrote to the NCCU contesting its legal right to speak or act on behalf of all Canadian universities and declaring federal grants to universities to be unconstitutional. The rectors of the three major francophone universities, Laval, Montreal, and Ottawa, hastened to assure the authorities that they favoured the grants scheme, "provided that the provincial government had no objection." This brought Duplessis onto the scene. In a letter to St Laurent dated 17 November 1951, he bluntly asserted that the federal government had no right to tax Quebec citizens to raise funds to give grants to universities; if the Government of Canada had funds available to support education it should return them to the province, which would dispose of them as the provincial government saw fit. However, in a second letter dated 30 November he wrote, "We don't like it, but we accept for this year."

In January 1952, the federal government duly made available for all Canadian universities $7,100,000. This compared favourably with James' first estimate for institutional needs of $4.2 million.

Research needs and scholarship provision would be considered later. McGill itself received $615,270, which was also more than James had expected, and in the university's annual report for 1951–2 he wrote, justifiably, "This entry in the financial statements is of historic importance." He also pointed out that for the first time since the end of the war, when the return of the veterans had begun to distort the normal patterns of financing, revenues (albeit by a modest $17,325) had exceeded expenditures.

But amid this general satisfaction, the reluctant acquiescence of Duplessis "for this year" hung heavy in the air. The blow fell in November 1952, when the premier announced to the newspapers that Quebec had refused to accept the federal grants for 1952–3 "and for every future year."

This put James in an extremely difficult position. The board had raised salaries modestly in 1951 and, with the Committee of Deans, had been working out a further series of much-needed increases to take effect in the year 1953–4. James had been counting on the federal funds to permit the new expenditures. Furthermore, he and others, especially the more "activist" members of the academic staff, believed that McGill was legally free to accept funds from whatever source offered them. But the vindictive spite of Duplessis was legendary, and his powers were immense. The governors individually had many business interests in the province of Quebec, interests that could be severely harmed by retributory taxes. It was commonly believed that Duplessis had passed the word around that if the McGill governors accepted the federal funds, punitive taxes would be slapped on mining and forestry operations in the province, and particularly on newsprint. J.W. McConnell, the university's senior governor and its most generous supporter, was also the owner of *The Montreal Star* and therefore especially vulnerable.

James went to see Prime Minister St Laurent to discuss this impasse. According to his notes of the interview, the prime minister speculated that Duplessis wanted to pose as St George protecting Quebec from the English-speaking dragons. It would be bad psychology for McGill to accept Ottawa's money if Laval did not; McGill would be regarded as an English-speaking outpost of Ottawa in Montreal. But the federal government would certainly pay the funds directly to any Quebec university that requested them. St Laurent expressed disappointment that leading English-speaking citizens of Quebec, such as McConnell and John Bassett, had not protested Duplessis's action. The prime minister added that he was thinking of creating the proposed Canada Council, which would deal with such things as universities, libraries, scholarships, and the Canadian Broadcasting Corporation. Perhaps this would provide a way around the Duplessis roadblock. Legislation would shortly be introduced and debated, but not passed, in order to raise discussion and test further sentiment. Modification and enactment would then follow. With these vague promises, James left the interview knowing that the politically minded St Laurent was not going to pick a gratuitous fight with the powerful provincial premier: a federal election was looming ahead, within a year or eighteen months.

James then telephoned Msgr Vandry, rector of l'Université Laval, who told him that Archbishop Roy had been consulted (the university was at that time under papal jurisdiction) and that Vandry had been informed that the university would not be allowed to accept the Ottawa grants. If that was the answer from Laval, the answer from l'Université de Montréal (another papal foundation) would be the same. So here was another power not wishing to cross swords with Duplessis. James also enquired as to the plans of Bishop's University, Quebec's other anglophone institution.[9] The reply was that Bishop's, a small liberal-arts college, was nicely endowed and operating with a comfortable surplus, and that the size of their grant from Ottawa was not large enough for its cessation to cause much concern. It was painfully obvious that if McGill wanted to oppose Duplessis it would have to do so alone.

McConnell was, of course, easily accessible to James, and the principal must already have known that the senior governor would not readily risk giving offence to Duplessis. Shortly after the St Laurent interview, at a private dinner party, James was able to talk directly the other "leading English citizen" St Laurent had named, John Bassett, president and managing editor of *The Gazette*, Montreal's other major English-language newspaper. Bassett, James wrote in his diary, thought it best "to humour Duplessis, rather than to fight him." In any case, Bassett was sure that the alliance of Duplessis and Drew, the federal Conservative leader, would defeat the Liberals in the coming election, and "he saw no future to Federal grants for any universities." On the other hand, he assured James that he always had the interests of McGill at heart, and he hoped that McGill would honour Bishop's on its centenary this year (he was the chancellor of that institution), as well as the coming 175th anniversary of *The Gazette*! The evening must have offered, whatever the menu, only cold comfort to at least one of the dinner guests.

James then decided to take the members of the academic staff into his confidence. Early in February 1953, he called a general staff meeting at which he conveyed the factual background, succinctly but clearly. He emphasized the point that it was out of the federal government's postwar experience of providing for returning veterans that the idea of federal aid for Canada's universities was born. He touched on the political complications attendant on the coming election, and the fact that no other university in Quebec was willing to take a stand, and drew the unpleasant conclusion:

There is the background to the present situation in which it is practically impossible – and I think, in the long run, highly undesirable – for McGill to take any action on its own account, without any coadjutors in this province.

He then turned to the McGill situation. The modest increases in salaries instituted in 1951 had been made possible because the governors had privately raised $600,000 in new funding; without the expected federal grant, plans for further increases must now be abandoned.

Budgets therefore will be revised from the figure on which they were drawn up three weeks ago, on the general principle of no reductions in salaries and wages, but equally, practically no increases at the present time, and of postponing everything that is not absolutely imperative for the next fifteen months, reconstructions, new equipment, other things of that kind, in fact everything which we can do without for the next twelve months without inconvenience or serious loss, and reducing as much as we can the current expenditures on materials and supplies and other things where there is any possibility of reduction.

The professors heard the sad story in attentive silence. At the end, one or two queried minor points, but the consensus was clearly a recognition that James and the board had done everything possible. One professor asked whether, since Duplessis had made grants to francophone colleges outside Quebec, some anglophone provinces might be willing to send support to McGill. James replied that it might be possible to put such a query to, for example, Saskatchewan, but he himself would not be very sanguine as to the answer. That raised a laugh, and with that despondent humour the session ended.

From James' point of view, however, all was not lost. The federal government had decided to sequestrate the funds due to the Quebec universities "until such time as they would be in a position to receive them" – leaving the universities to conclude, as one professor put it, referring to Duplessis, "while there's death, there's hope." In addition, the fact that James had played such a constructive part on the national scene had greatly enhanced his reputation in the academic world in general, while his open recognition that the McGill staff were sadly underpaid, and his vigorous efforts to improve the situation, had left his academic and non-academic colleagues with the conviction that he had been on their side and was contending for them. Expressive of this sentiment was a letter written just before the staff assembly by the dean of graduate studies, who was more aware than most of the turn of events.

Dear Dr. James,

I should like with all respect to express my admiration of the courage and cheerfulness with which you are facing this very difficult situation in our university's affairs – a set-back which must be peculiarly disappointing to you in view of your very great share in making the Federal grants possible at all – and the patience with which you listen to suggestions and discussion, much of which is unhelpful or irrelevant.

Sincerely,

David L. Thomson

Although the formality of the relationship between the two men is evident, the personal esteem of the dean for the principal comes through strongly. There were still, of course, individuals who disliked and resented James, but Thomson's letter certainly expressed the major sentiment. Evidence of this came in the spring in an unusual gesture from an unlikely quarter. At the 1953 Annual Awards Banquet of the Student Council, when the outstanding students were recognized for their achievements, the first mention was of a special "Gold Award to F.C. James."

The sequel to this story of funds granted and denied was also not without its ironies. A year later, in February 1954, Duplessis unpredictably announced that the Quebec universities would receive from the province annual grants to make good the losses due to their deprivation of federal funds – he boasted that they would get more from the province than they would have received form the Government of Canada. In fact, McGill received $314,000, which was only about half of what it had been expecting from the federal government.

In making his announcement, however, Duplessis took the opportunity to criticize the McGill principal personally, commenting sourly that "he puts his foot in it regularly enough." For James this incident brought a double benefit. One was the much-needed dollars of his new provincial grant, but the other was a growing partisanship in the English-speaking Quebec constituency on behalf of James as a person. As one correspondent wrote to him: "There can be no greater testimony to one's integrity than to have incurred the wrath of one M. Duplessis. Congratulations!" As for the dollars, after 1954 the provincial grant was moderately increased year by year, making salary increases possible. However, these ameliorating circumstances were by no means the end of James' difficulties arising from federal, provincial, and university relations; the problem of Duplessis's intransigence was to return only two years later in even sharper form.

CHAPTER ELEVEN

Many Distractions

The spring of 1953 brought Cyril James a number of personal preoccupations, which at least served to distract him from his university and political concerns. They were important enough to provoke him into writing a diary note about them, even though journal-keeping was by now a thing of the past.

Thursday, 19 March
This – to put it mildly – is an unusual spring. The large problem of Duplessis and the financial future of McGill seems to have worked an unexpected (and partly coincidental) counterpoise in the Gold Award from the students, the silver cigarette box from the Vermont bankers – and now the invitation to receive honorary degrees at both Cambridge and Glasgow during July, as well as the invitation to a seat in the Abbey at the Coronation, which comes from Ottawa.

The mention of the Gold Award from the students shows how much that unusual gesture meant to him, and the invitations to receive honorary degrees at Glasgow and Cambridge, decidedly more than *pro forma* at this stage of his career, he could interpret as acknowledgments of his personal achievements. As a measure of his national standing, the allotment by the federal government of two of its precious seats at the coronation of Queen Elizabeth to Cyril James and his wife was an outstanding accolade. He had truly made his mark in Canada since he had stepped on the Quebec landing-stage only thirteen years before. But in his own scale of values, an even greater honour came from his former *alma mater*.

That is enough mental disturbances – but yesterday Al Williams [an old Philadelphia colleague] telephoned the final shock in the series: a unanimous invitation from the trustees to succeed Stassen as President of the University of Pennsylvania.

The same honours mean different things to different people, but most men and women value above all else the recognition given at that place and in that institution where once they were young and insignificant. James had arrived at the University of Pennsylvania a student immigrant, ignorant of America, as near penniless as made no odds, without family, friends, or influence. Thirty years later he was being invited – unanimously, he notes – to become the chief person of all. It must have been a moment to savour. Even coronations dimmed beside that.

This was not the first offer of its kind. In 1949, he had been invited to visit Queens' University, Belfast, "to view and be viewed," as the saying goes, and he and Irene had made a brief visit to Northern Ireland. In 1952, he had been offered the vice-chancellorship of Birmingham University in England. But after rather more consideration than he had given Belfast he had declined the offer.

This invitation from Pennsylvania, however, was a different proposition. True, it did not hold out the possibility, as had Birmingham, of a knighthood (Sir Cyril would have sounded very well – he had admitted that in a diary note about the same possibility attaching to the Belfast enquiry) and the basic salary at Penn was lower than at McGill – in the $18,000–$20,000 range. But he already had one bank directorship in Montreal; he could expect other similar appointments in Philadelphia. His relationships with American banking and commerce were cordial and with the large foundations very good, and he had many friends and acquaintances on campus and in Philadelphia. The warmth of the invitation from Philadelphia was clearly genuine and the pressure from prestigious persons intense. Also, he still nurtured his deep appreciation of the United States, which he had gained in his first Philadelphia years and had enhanced with Dr Burk at Valley Forge. But when he considered his British citizenship, his influence in Canada, and the Commonwealth ties, it was hard to believe that even the University of Pennsylvania could offer prospects more alluring. Still, it was a difficult decision.

My mind keeps changing sides. On one side is the fact that I like McGill and feel at home in it even though I am sometimes bored and occasionally frustrated. Part of that feeling may be timidity – the reluctance to change – but it is not entirely that. Inside me there is still a British immigrant that is deeply interested in the AUBC and feels that Canada can contribute to the Commonwealth and the world. There is also the fact that I dislike the idea of quitting in the middle of this squabble over Federal grants. As I look back, I think that [though] I contributed something both to the rejuvenation of the AUBC and to the provision of Federal grants, there is still a good deal to be done on both counts.

On the other side of the fence – perhaps I have contributed all that I can contribute under these heads, am now grown stale, and should let somebody else take over. A new challenge may wake me up as well as provide me with new opportunities – and Penn is one of the oldest Universities in North America. It has a great tradition, but has suffered of late from lack of good administration so that it does not now hold its proper place in the US. But it could – and there is the deepest of all compliments in being asked to go back to a place that learned in seventeen years all of my weaknesses as well as any good points.

He consulted in confidence with one or two who he believed could advise him with an informed understanding of the complex issues involved. Notably, he approached the decision almost entirely from a consideration of service, and not from a regard for his own profit or advancement. In this time of judgment, when issues had to be weighed with great care, the old sense of having dedicated his life to a cause returned, so that the major question became: where can I serve to the greatest profit those ideals in which I believe?

On the other hand, few personal decisions are pure and uncomplicated. It cannot have been entirely out of Cyril's thinking that if he went to Pennsylvania he would lose one considerable personal benefit. At the time of the Birmingham offer, McConnell had informed James that he had set aside in the principal's name a list of securities to the value of $50,000, which would be available to him when he retired from McGill. The modest pension scheme for the staff that James had instituted could not make retirement provision for him consonant with his present income. Such matters had not been discussed when he was appointed, and now McConnell was personally putting things right. It was not a bribe to remain, but it certainly tended to anchor James firmly to the university as long as McGill wanted him to remain. However highminded his motivations, it was a consideration he could not afford to ignore.

Even so, we should recall that he consistently viewed his work at McGill in terms of vocation, and his principal advisers took the same view. Lewis Douglas, who had himself been principal of McGill but was an American and knew the United States well, could write with unique authority; James' friend Hector Hetherington, vice-chancellor of the University of Glasgow, knew what he had achieved in the area of Commonwealth relationships, particularly since James had made Canada and its universities significant as never before in British academic circles. It must have been something of a relief that both men tendered the same advice. Lewis Douglas wrote that McGill gave James the opportunity to play a Commonwealth role, as Pennsylvania could not, while Hetherington advised in a hand-scribbled personal letter:

... if the primary consideration is the weight of your Commonwealth service, I think McGill wins: and I add to that the risk to McGill and Canada that would arise from an early change of direction in this present situation. I'm sure your translation to Penn would not be *sheer* loss to us: and I'm sure it would be a great gain to the University and public life of a powerful neighbour, on whose wisdom our fortunes now to a considerable extent depend. But *on balance* I am clear about the severity of our loss ... You like America and Americans, both of you – as I do, on far less knowledge and experience. But your roots are her: and your sphere of action is in Canada. I think you sh'd hang British: and come to the Coronation.

Blessings on you both – whatever you do: and all affectionate greetings from both of us,

Yours, H. H.

From these comments and a review of James' postwar activities, it is clear he was becoming a notable Commonwealth person. His securing an invitation from Cyrus Eaton for AUBC to hold its executive committee meetings for the first time outside Britain at Deep Cove, NS, and his subsequent travels to India and Pakistan were contributions to the revival of an institution that in the general postwar malaise was in danger of dying; the visits to universities in Australia and New Zealand fall into the same pattern. The growing number of honorary degrees accorded to him by British universities – probably more than to any other Canadian or Commonwealth person (London, Birmingham, Glasgow, and now Cambridge, and soon Edinburgh) – can be seen as a tribute to his outstanding commitment to the Commonwealth ideal. Hetherington hints that the invitation to attend the coronation of Queen Elizabeth may have had its genesis in the same activities, and the membership of the Athenaeum Club may also have originated in the same way.

The strange development was that in this discussion Irene came down eventually for staying at McGill. She pencilled Cyril a rather incoherent letter, presumably from somewhere other than home, though the paper is imprinted "1200 Pine Avenue West, Montreal." James evidently thought it important enough to file with his diary papers. It is not dated, but it must have been written prior to Wednesday, 15 April.

Darling,

I am trying to tell you the answer as I see it. You want to stay here because you believe in the British tradition, and the tremendously important place the British universities have to uphold that tradition. Stick to it – there is no complication where a belief is concerned. Let the "little" ones shout and scheme – your purpose is clear. Put all this confusion out of your mind when you talk to the [Board] on Wednesday and say just what you had in mind ... You *have* been asked [to go to Pennsylvania] (even it there are some who would like to think otherwise) and knowing the truth must give you strength. No man has the ability as you have to leave no doubt as to his sincerity. Don't be reticent on this occasion – show them all you stand for, and what this University means to you ... even if right away you can't floor Duplessis, perhaps it would be well to stay with it, if they need you. Yes, you can't wield the stick Mrs. McMurray spoke of, but perhaps this is the better way.[1] And if it doesn't work (and that I do not for one moment believe) no man can do more than stick to his principles.

Because we have both been tired and worried we have sometimes misunderstood each other – but I'd willingly go to hell with you; and make a good job of it, too! ...

God be with you as I am – although I'll admit He might do a better job.
B[ay]

Clearly, Irene stands in the "my man right or wrong" tradition, but of her admiration for Cyril and her belief in his cause there is no doubt. Her references to criticism and opposition are explained in the record of the Board of Governors meeting, held on Wednesday, 15 April 1953, to which she referred, though her descriptions may be somewhat exaggerated. What emerges as fact is that Irene, possibly because of this opposition and a desire to rush to his defence, came to support the view that James should stay at McGill.

James had pretty well made up his mind to decline the invitation from Pennsylvania when a decision was suddenly forced upon him. The fact that the offer had been made was leaked to the

Philadelphia newspapers, which, taking it for granted that he would accept, printed the news with long articles about him, together with an excruciatingly bad photograph of a bright young man with a heavy moustache. This item was, of course, picked up by the Montreal press, and James felt obliged to make a public statement. But first he asked to meet privately with the Board of Governors. He kept a record of what was said. J.W. McConnell, in the absence of B.C. Gardner, the chancellor, who was in England, opened the meeting as senior governor by saying, "Dr. James has not the slightest hint of the comments I wish to make before calling upon him." He then read a long catalogue of all James achievements in the fourteen years at McGill – the money raised in private funding, the property acquired on and around the campus, the new buildings erected, the old buildings rehabilitated, the new donors attracted to university support. He concluded:

To sum up – in a nutshell, the final results: the Endowment Fund which 14 years ago stood at $18,000,000 has been increased to $37,500,000. The Property Account which, during the same period has increased from $14,800,000 to $22,700,000.

Now, having perhaps embarrassed Dr. James, I shall ask him to explain to the Board the heaviest and most serious problem with which he is now confronted: the details of which he wishes to lay frankly before the Board of Governors. Personally, I think it would be tragic for McGill to allow Dr. James to resign, if he can be retained. I cannot contemplate McGill without Dr. James.[2]

Even as detailed by McConnell it was an astonishing list of achievements. Yet possibly James may have felt much more could have been said: his concern for new appointments, his commitment to increasing salaries, his development of a pension scheme for both the academic and non-academic staff, his foresight with regard to the veterans, his role in the NCCU in the battle for federal grants, his advocacy of McGill in Britain and the Commonwealth, and above all his passion for the enlarging horizons of the mind of man. It is to be hoped that someone among the group of business men who in 1953 constituted the McGill Board of Governors had some thought beyond the bricks and mortar and dollars and cents of the past fourteen years. But even if their ideas remained at that level, the catalogue was more than impressive. It conveyed McConnell's main message: "I cannot contemplate McGill without Dr. James."

After such a beginning to the meeting, James' task was not

difficult. He began by referring briefly to the earlier invitations to assume positions elsewhere, which had been comparatively easy to decline. He then described in some detail the Pennsylvania offer, explaining its particular attraction for him. For this reason he had discussed the matter confidentially with McConnell and other members of the Executive Committee of the Board.

On the basis of those discussions my decision is still to remain at McGill. This also is a great university, for which I have a deep personal affection. You and I have faced many problems together during the course of the past fourteen years – problems arising out of the war, problems associated with the influx of veterans, and the present financial problems created by the decision of the Government of Quebec. Throughout those fourteen years, the McGill family, as a result of the loyalty and hard work of every member of the Board of Governors, and of the teaching staff, has surmounted these difficulties. I am confident that McGill University can surmount its present difficulties, and continue to play an outstanding part in the life of Canada. Even more, I am deeply convinced that it can play an outstanding part in the life of the British Commonwealth of Nations, which I look upon as holding an importance equal to that of the United States in the development of the world and the preservation of peace ...

There is only one question that I should like to put to you. My decision to stay at McGill is contingent upon your desire to have me stay. It has been suggested by a man not a member of this Board but known to many of you that many members of this Board would like to have a new Principal. The suggestion came as a great surprise, since I thought I knew your minds, but I propose to withdraw from this room so that any members of the Board who wish to express an opinion can do so without embarrassment.

We are left with some questions. Who was the man "not a member of the Board" who had told him that some of the governors were wishing for him to go? What was the opposition that Irene had inveighed against so strongly in her letter? Her suggestion that some people were saying that James had not really been invited to Pennsylvania is explained by the formal contradiction of the story in the Philadelphia papers by the chairman of the Pennsylvania trustees. As James said to the governors, no university will admit publicly that it has been turned down. Some individuals unfriendly to James may have picked that denial up and circulated it in Montreal. But in speaking of some governors wanting a change in the principal's office, James is obviously referring to a source of information nearer to home. It had to be someone able to talk to him with some freedom, someone not a governor but so placed as to be able to claim with some plausibility insider-information, and someone possibly not himself wholly committed to the idea of James staying longer at McGill. There was a group influential in the Graduate Society and in Montreal financial circles who were allergic to McConnell, and perhaps this dislike had carried over into a similar lack of enthusiasm for his protégé. The information may have been conveyed under the guise of a friendly warning, but James gives the impression in his phrasing that there had been a certain malice in the communication. Or, of course, James may have been oversensitive on the matter. Either way, he decided to seek a formal vote of the board members, to settle the issue beyond doubt.

When after a short interval James was called back into the Arts Council Chamber, it was to be told that the board had unanimously and warmly expressed their wish that he should stay. We may think that after McConnell's strong introduction of this "private matter," it would have been a bold governor who openly voiced dissent. But James received what he wanted: full backing from McConnell and on the books a recorded unanimous vote of confidence from the board.

That vote was echoed over the next few days in an extraordinary flood of correspondence from all kinds of people, all conveying the same message: "We are greatly relieved and very glad that you are going to stay with us!" Correspondents included graduates, members of the academic staff, members of the board, and distinguished persons outside the university community. "Before I start the activities of the day, I wish to express my personal gratification that you are not leaving," wrote D.P. Mowry, the dean of Dentistry. A significant letter came from Hugh Keenleyside, at that time the director-general of the Technical Assistance Administration of the United Nations Organization in New York. It referred to the two offers, the one from Birmingham and the other from Pennsylvania, and continued:

This note is just to say how happy I am, as a Canadian and on personal grounds, that you resisted these temptations and are to remain at McGill. I only wish that more of our fellow Canadians could learn of the proposals made to you, and of your action in regard to them. I hope that you will accept this note of appreciation from one who has admired your work in and for our country, and who takes pride in your friendship.

Both the major English-language Montreal newspapers joined in the chorus of thanksgiving. *The Montreal Star,* McConnell's paper, gave the news-item a double-column headline: "Dr. and Mrs. James to Attend Coronation for McGill – Principal Refuses Offer to Head University of Pennsylvania." *The Gazette,* which generally viewed McGill's affairs with more objectivity, gave good coverage, stressing James' loyalty to the British Commonwealth, and then spreading itself more generously in an editorial headed: "Good News for McGill University." If James still lacked close friends, he was now surrounded by a large circle of well-wishing and admiring acquaintances.

Sometimes that admiration was of a high order. In the previous fall of 1952, the former chancellor, Associate Chief Justice Orville Tyndale, had died, quite unexpectedly, and shortly thereafter James received a letter that illustrated how this personally lonely man could nevertheless win the affection of a great many of his nearer circle. The letter was from Judge George McKinnon, a colleague of Tyndale in the work of the Quebec Superior Court.

I was sorry not to have seen you after the ceremony at the cemetery, for I wanted to tell you about our last weekend with Orville just before he was stricken.

He talked freely about his tenure of office at McGill, and said that the great thing he got from it was the friendship he formed with you.

He was unstinted in his admiration for you and his appreciation of your many great qualities. His devotion to you was sincere. His association with you meant so much to him. I thought I would like you to know all this, for I am certain your heart has been heavy over Orville's untimely death.

It was indeed affection, or something very like it, that motivated the last, and for Cyril probably the highest, accolade upon his decision to stay at McGill – on 8 May 1953 the members of the Faculty Club held an end-of-term cocktail party in his honour. The Board of Governors by their resolution, the students by their Gold Award, and now finally his academic colleagues were together expressing gratitude for the past and happiness that he was going to continue with them.

The spring of decision and acclaim became the prelude to a summer of pomp and ceremony. The frustrating fact is, however, that apart from two or three scattered notices and a schedule of engagements, James has left no record of what must have been a series of remarkable experiences, from early June to the end of

July. The lack of material regarding the coronation of Queen Elizabeth II is particularly disappointing. A letter, dated Easter 1953,
written by James to his niece, Doreen, gives but a small glimpse
of the preparation for the great event.

Bay is having all sorts of fun with her tiara, and the making of her
coronation dress – but you will have to write and ask her to tell you
the details, because she does it much better than I could. And we both
chuckle about the advice and information that comes from folk who were
there at some earlier coronation – banal things like how to wrap your
sandwiches and the inaccessibility of lavatory accommodation. Really, there
are moments when the whole thing sounds a little like Bank Holiday on
Hampstead Heath and I have a mental picture of noble dukes (as soon
as the Queen retires for lunch) pulling peanuts and oranges out of their
coronets and starting to make up for lost time.

On the day, Irene wore her tiara and a white silk dress while
James wore his vice-chancellor's gown over white-tie and tails.
He received, and was bidden by command of her majesty the
Queen to wear, a medal struck in honour of the occasion. But
what Cyril James, a poor boy from the London suburbs, thought
and felt as he literally (the abbey was very crowded) rubbed
shoulders with the noble and famous remains unknown.

Possibly the many other events that crowded that summer (1953
was an AUBC Congress year) simply gave him no time for comment
and reflection. On 19 June, he was proposing the principal toast
at the alumni society dinner of the Hackney Downs School. On
24 June he attended a McGill Graduates' Society reception, together
with Wilder Penfield and Percy Backus,[3] and on 27 June he helped
(again in academic robes) celebrate the 700th Grosseteste Com-
memoration in Lincoln Cathedral. On 2 and 3 July he was in
Southampton to give support to the university on the occasion of
the installation of its first chancellor, His Grace the Duke of Wellington. The next week there were meetings of executive heads of
universities in Durham, and then from 13–17 July he and Irene
were in Cambridge as guests of Charles Raven for the AUBC
seventh quinquennial congress. At the congress it was confirmed
(as had been proposed in New Zealand) that the next gathering
would be held for the first time outside the United Kingdom –
in Montreal. On the last day the congress gathered in the Senate
House for a convocation of the University of Cambridge at which
James, with eight others, one of whom was HRH the Duchess of
Kent, received the LL D degree. Finally, on 23 July, Cyril and Irene

were guests of the Hetheringtons in Glasgow, where Cyril received yet another LL D. On 2 August they boarded an evening flight at Heathrow, London and landed six hours later at Dorval, Montreal – so swift and uneventful had air-travel become. But what Cyril thought of such an astonishing summer is not known: that we have any record of his movements is due solely to the exemplary Mrs Mac, who typed up for him a detailed itinerary, with added informatory notes.

Later that year, in November, J.W. McConnell sent to James a list of the securities that had been placed in his name, valued at $50,180. McConnell was, as always, as good as his word. When Cyril totted up his own securities, he found that their combined worth was a gratifying $135,300. But he also noted a current overdraft at the Montreal City and District Bank of $22,000. He was living very expensively. All that travel and junketing in England had generated bills that had finally come home for payment.

In these middle years, James' highly pressured lifestyle could not but cause serious repercussions within his domestic situation. He and Irene often endured a tense atmosphere in the home, and she escaped to England as often as she could. He had a housekeeper named Anne who ran the house, and when Irene was away, Cyril seemed content with a bachelor existence. Sometimes there would be a rare period of relaxation, and for both of them a return to happiness. In the summer of 1951, for example, after receiving the honorary degree from Birmingham and spending time at Barnet with Irene, James had flown back to Canada to attend meetings of the NCCU in Ottawa. But returning to Montreal, he felt lonely and depressed and indulged in a sudden impulse.

Thursday, 16 August, 1951
Mrs. McMurray is back from her holidays, and so far as I can judge all of the work in the office is cleaned up – so I am flying to England tomorrow to spend two weeks with Bay as a silver wedding anniversary!

The twenty-fifth anniversary of their marriage was indeed to fall three days later, on 19 August, and in his diary file there is a reply cable: "Wonderful news. Overjoyed. Meet you Heath Row. Love, Bay." This sudden dropping of all responsibilities and flying off for two weeks to spend time with Irene, without any odd duties being tucked into his schedule, is quite uncharacteristic, but was undoubtedly very good for them both, and for their marriage.

Unfortunately, this happiness was never very long lasting. In a slim file that contains only two sheets of diary notes, mostly concerned with financial affairs, a letter from Irene, postmarked Barnet, 2 September 1954, is preserved without comment. Evidently he kept it as too significant to be destroyed, but it is a sad, pathetic item. There had obviously been a time of great tension between them. She appears to have reached the point of saying that she would not return either to Canada or to him. What James replied is unknown, but it was evidently conciliatory. Her return letter begins with a moving glimpse of her in the Barnet home, having received his reply, but lacking the courage to open it. When she had done so, her relief and unhappiness overflowed together onto her pages.

Darling:

I have just read your letter – I was afraid to open it when it arrived yesterday. What a chump I am! But instead of sitting here sweating, wondering how I can possibly put things on paper I am going just to write – it's the only hope I have. Your letter has given me the chance, Frank, to say what I think will help. I *want* to help, but please let me be part of it. Can't you talk to me about your problems? That is the biggest thing of all. Don't you see – I'm asked to turn up at all these formal occasions, but the people I meet are just people. I am interested in human nature, and it would be so much easier if I could talk to you about faculty and what they do and say. As it is, I feel so out of everything. I know there is trouble, but further than that you won't tell me about it … I don't expect after every day for you to come back and give me a running commentary to satisfy my ego, but if I knew more I might help – not to interfere, my darling, but to feel that we were together for the job. I don't dislike McGill, I am proud of it and of you. These last two years life has caught up with me, but *please* remember I have been loyal to you and to your job for so many years. Talk to me a little more – just try it – I am sure it will help … I know the problems, darling, and my heart aches for you. And here you say, quite rightly, "stop blathering and do something!" I will. I am coming back. But *share* your burdens, Frank, with me. I see you dashing about on McGill affairs – if they were mine too I would have something to live for. I say it now, Frank – you and me – and *then* McGill … Of course, our life must be built around our life and work – *our* life and *our* work. I don't want to escape from it. I do want a little bit of life outside it … Let me believe that if I make a decision in the home or outside, that you will back me. Don't let us be ashamed to let all the world know we are all-important to each other, it will put everything and everyone in their proper place. Believe me, trust me – and I shan't let you down.

Irene saw the problem clearly from her side of the argument, and surely deserves our sympathy. If she had been less intelligent, and could have been content with the role of home-keeping, admiring spouse; or if she had been more intelligent and better qualified, so as to be able to say in today's style: "I am going to live my own life with my own interests"; or if she had had children to demand her attention; or if Cyril had been more accommodating, less insecure, and more able to talk about his work to her rather than to his diary; if ... but as it was, they were held together by the bonds of marriage and by the social etiquette of their generation, and, at times, by a genuine affection for each other; yet they were also constantly frustrated by a severe incompatibility of temperament and situation. In a later generation, they probably would have separated; as it was, they patched up their relationship from time to time, and carried on in a not very satisfactory fashion.

Although he had problems making friends with his peers, Cyril could win the warm regard of older men and women. The friendship originating from their Philadelphia days with the surgeon Sumner Cross and his wife Nan endured well over the years. When at the end of March 1955, Nan wrote saying that her husband had suffered a stroke and shared with them her concern that loss of income and financial strains compounded her anxieties, Cyril responded not only with consolation but also very practically with a substantial cheque. Possibly he felt that he owed Sumner professional fees in respect of Irene's surgery and that this was the proper time to acknowledge the debt. Even so, it was a quixotic action, although not out of character. Nan wrote again in April.

My dear Irene and Cyril,

Your letter has just come. I wish you could read the thoughts in my heart – there are no words. Your friendship which grows more precious every year has been one of our greatest treasures. Our visit last May seemed to fill our cup of blessing to overflowing. I treasured every moment, especially as Sumner felt sure we could come again ... Your unbelievable and *loving* generosity will lighten my anxiety ... I have a 5-year calendar which I have used as a diary to record noteworthy events ever since we have lived in [this house] and under 28 June 1934 I have written "Cyril and I made a shrine for the garden." It is still in place, a constant reminder of our tea parties together. We accept with deep gratitude your *wonderful* check ...

My love to you both,

Nan

That is the letter of one who had found both Cyril and Irene to be special friends.

But Cyril at least was aware of his own deficiencies in personal relationships. Referring to some of his anxieties about the university in 1951, he had made the telling comment:

5 August

... It is my own fault, but I do not feel that I have established with the new and younger Governors that feeling of close personal relationship that existed with their predecessors. Can it be that thirty years of getting along with people older then myself has left me without the ability to be friends with my own generation?

It was a comment he had made once before, and would repeat in future years. Evidently he was not far from the truth.

One of the causes of the anxiety to which Irene referred in her letter of September 1954, ("I know there is trouble, but further than that you won't tell me about it") was undoubtedly the organization of the administration of the university, a problem of long standing to which James had given considerable thought but without achieving much satisfaction. Although in 1947 he had taken great care with regard to the appointment of Sidney Dobell as comptroller and assistant to the principal, he had subsequently expressed from time to time his dissatisfaction with the way things were working out. Matters came to a head in 1951 when Dobell began to press for appointment as vice-principal. He spoke about the matter in May and then wrote James a long memorandum, arguing the case for this appointment. He particularly stressed what he called "extramural" relations:

As arranged in our brief conversation a day or two ago, I am giving you in this hurried memorandum my reasons for feeling most emphatically that I should be named a Vice-Principal. My reasons are summarized as follows:

I am quite convinced that it would help to promote goodwill for the University amongst the business community and other extramural friends of the University. I feel equally sure that it would react favourably upon the community in so far as you personally are concerned. Except for the Chancellor and Governors who, of course, are not full-time Officers of the University, there is virtually no member of the senior staff except myself who is known personally to very many of the community, upon whose goodwill we depend so much for financial and other support.

Furthermore, the Principal for many years past has not been a native Montrealer, or (except for Sir Arthur Currie) a native Canadian, and I am sure that because of the lack of a compensating factor, there has resulted on the part of the community a feeling of remoteness from the University as a whole.

I think that my appointment as Vice-Principal would be helpful in this respect, and would cause a great many people to feel that they had a closer and more personal interest in the University. While, of course, you personally are known to all, it is unfortunately but unavoidably the case that you are looked on by most people as a demi-god in an ivory tower, whom they see only from the spectators' side of a public platform. This naturally adds to the feeling of remoteness and I feel sure that if a person whom many of them know personally, and many others at secondhand, who moreover has been a member of their own community for 30 years was a Vice-Principal it would make for a closer link between town and gown.

Dobell then went on to remind James that at the time of his appointment he had been promised speedy promotion to the position of vice-principal, and that the promise had later been renewed with a time limit of two years, now long past. He finished with a request that James should submit "a favourable recommendation to the Governors" at their next meeting, and added in a postscript that he had sent a copy of his memorandum to Chancellor Orville Tyndale. This forced James to justify his personal decision to the chancellor, at the very least; if Tyndale saw fit, he could, of course, on his own initiative, place the matter before the board. A letter from the chancellor reached James before he had formulated his own response.

The Comptroller has sent me a copy of his memorandum to you of the 18th instant. He spoke to me about the matter last year, since when I have given it careful consideration; and I think the time has come to accept his proposal. You are, of course, more familiar with his work than I am; but I feel that we are most fortunate in having him on our staff, and my opinion is shared by many friends who have spoken to me about him. Apart from his professional ability, he has the great advantage of possessing an attractive personality and of being well known to and liked by many of the influential citizens of Montreal. He belongs to an old and respected family and is accepted by the "best" people as one of themselves. This may sound "snobbish", but, in my view, it is of some importance in the interests of the University. I know, of course, that Dobell does not possess a university degree; but he is a chartered accountant and can certainly be considered as of excellent intellectual calibre ...

Accordingly, I suggest that you put forward the proposal at the next meeting of the Executive Committee.

He then went on to chide James for working too hard and for never taking a real vacation.

This letter, kind as it was, was not at all to James' liking, and in reply he rebutted the arguments of Dobell's memorandum with great care. He disposed of the most dangerous one, implied by Dobell and explicitly stated by Tyndale, that Dobell belonged to the inner elite of Montreal as James did not, with a single short sentence: "all my experience of the family argument in Britain, the United States and Canada makes me regard it as a dangerous basis of appointment." Dobell's references to James' aloofness, to his living in an "ivory tower," and to his being seen only as "a demi-god" from the spectators' side of a public platform, Cyril ignored, because he would have been hard put to make an adequate reply. But the core of his response was in his second paragraph.

There is no way of *reducing* the tasks of University administration, since the central function is that of richly coordinating, within the limits of our financial resources, all the various phases of teaching and research in the fashion that facilitates as much as possible the rapid progress of those scientists and scholars who are able to move ahead. One person, aided by the advice and counsel of many, must be responsible for that task – and the Statutes of 1939, which were carefully debated for many months, have charged the Principal with that office. I accepted the job on that basis, not because it was easy but because it is both worthwhile and interesting. I will admit that it is a complex job, but there is compensation in the opinions of such people as the Rockefeller Foundation who, only a week ago, contrasted McGill most favourably with another famous University which is rapidly sliding downhill because a galaxy of able Vice-Presidents made it impossible for anybody to build up a true *studium generale.*

This was indeed the foundation on which James based his theory and practice of principalship: the principal's function is to co-ordinate; the power must be in one pair of hands; those hands are mine. Sidney Dobell must have been a man of some courage, since he could mount his attack on James' autocracy only from a non-academic base – and in a university that is a decided weakness. James' firm answer to both chancellor and comptroller was that he was not able to recommend Dobell to the position for which he had asked. To Tyndale he wrote:

Your aim and mine is to simplify the administration and to reduce its cost, while continuing to foster the greatness of McGill. That is not a question of titles or social connections, but of outstanding men who are willing and able to do a job.

Despite this rebuff, Dobell continued as comptroller until 1955, when he returned to the practice of accounting in Montreal. If he had been promised this promotion (a claim that was never denied), he had considerable grounds for grievance, but he does not appear to have borne a grudge; in a 1970s retrospect he contented himself with testimony to James' phenomenal ability to memorize a speech and to deal with correspondence at great speed.[4] But he had raised serious questions about James' style of principalship, and while those questions had been turned aside, they had not been fully answered. James knew this, and the matter rankled in his thoughts, and possibly in his conscience, all the time Dobell remained as comptroller and executive assistant. It was still a matter of concern to him as late as 1954, when Irene wrote her letter.

Publicly, however, affairs inside the university and out were proceeding so well on course that in 1955 Cyril planned for himself a further distraction of a different kind: a change of pace that would take him out of his normal environment – more thoroughly than perhaps he had bargained for. The jaunt began demurely enough. In early August, he was invited to join "a conference of the world's thinkers" who were gathering at Pugwash, NS as guests of Cyrus Eaton, the free-minded American industrialist, with whom he had already established a personal relationship. Among the other guests were Julian Huxley, the biologist, John Wilson, the Egyptologist, and Frederick Dunn, the jurist. The affair attracted much newspaper attention, and it enhanced James' public image to be included in the roster of invited guests, even though the annual Pugwash Conferences never produced any significant results. At least the one he attended provided a change of pace.

Rather more formal and proper was the ensuing visit to Scotland and Edinburgh. His reasons for crossing the Atlantic that summer, were, he wrote in a diary note, that "I had to represent McGill at the Edinburgh Festival, August 21–24", and also "at the Congress of the International Association of Universities, Sept. 16–24." He therefore "decided to take the intervening fortnight [three weeks?] as holiday in Greece." Although he had travelled widely, Cyril had seen very little of Europe; he had never had an opportunity to do "the Grand Tour." Now he was taking the chance while it offered. But the arrangements (which included a fair stretch of what he called "travelling rough") were clearly not designed to accommodate Irene: he was going off on his own. This may have been one of the reasons for the prevalent coolness between them.

James was one of a group of distinguished Commonwealth university heads invited to attend the Edinburgh Festival as guests of the city and to receive honorary degrees from the university. He arrived at Prestwick and crossed over to Edinburgh. There he telephoned twice to Barnet, asking Irene to come north to join him, but she refused. Her refusal, he recorded, was the only unpleasant aspect of the day.

Edinburgh is lovelier than I had dreamed. My window looks down on Princes Street and up to the Castle (around which I have already walked once by way of Castle Terrace, Lawnmarket, the Mound and Princes Street). I have also walked along the splendour of George Street. But even my room is pleasant with a great bouquet of flowers from the Lord Provost – and a private bathroom – and everything was in perfect order the moment I arrived at the hotel.

The weekend included formal dinners, government receptions, a university convocation, a lecture by Dr Gilbert Murray, the re-nowned interpreter of Classical Greece, and a white-tie-and-tails performance of the Gyndebourne production of *Il Barbiere de Siviglia*. It is clear that Irene, by her refusal to join Cyril, was foregoing a truly gala occasion – or she may simply have thought that she could not, on such short notice, dress up to such glamorous heights!

After his remarkable mixture of Scottish tradition, European culture, and establishmentarian splendour, James caught the train to London, and the great escape truly began. He made no attempt to go down to Barnet. He stayed the night in the United Services Club (the Athenaeum must have been closed) and the next day caught the train to Paris. The Southern Railway's "Golden Arrow Service" to the continent was uncomfortably crowded. James left his reserved seat and found one in the Pullman car; the others at the table were an Indian couple – who proved (are we surprised?) to be "the Indian Ambassador [High Commissioner?] and his lady of whom the train crew made much fuss." The ship from Dover to Calais "was far from deluxe – crowded to the gunnels and resembling nothing as much as a Southend steamer-excursion," which he remembered from his boyhood. But from Calais to Paris the *Train Bleu* was clean, fast, and comfortable, and revived his spirits. He slept that night in the Wagon-lits accommodation ("more chic than our bed-rooms") and alighted in Marseilles in time to find M. Pierre Mendès-France, economist, banker, and recent prime minister of France, leaving the next carriage; he greeted the prime minister politely. James was not, however, met in Marseilles by a courier as had been promised, and since he could not board his steamer until evening, he was left to his own devices for the day. He collected his steamer-tickets and

by that time Marseilles was hot, and I was sweating, so I ambled along to a café on the market square (which I was lucky to come across in my aimless wandering), took off my coat and settled down to enjoy a cold beer while I watched the hucksters setting up their stalls. It was lazy and pleasant – the kind of hours that have no importance but one remembers them with gratitude to fortune, as one of H.M. Tomlinson's "Gifts".[5]

His ship, when he found it, proved to be SS *Adana*, an old American "liberty" ship, one of those turned out at break-neck speed to help win the war, 5,600 tons gross, and now converted to passenger and cargo runs.

I have a little cabin to myself on the promenade deck, but in spite of "jalousies" and a fan, it is hot tonight. What I wanted most was a bath – but there is only one shower (no baths!) for the 40 male first-class passengers, and it is not working! Few of the Turkish crew speak French: one of them English, and so far I have not found any English-speaking passengers. At table for dinner (where, fortunately, there is no choice of food and one takes what one gets) there is a Turkish couple who have been on holiday in France (and speak French well), a Professor of Law from Paris – once an aide of [Marshal] Lyautey, old and charming – and three others who did not speak to any one of the four of us during the meal. I know nobody on board, except Mendès-France, and have not spoken to him since the station.

It must have been quite exciting to find the former resistance fighter, general, and prime minister not only on his train, but also on this little ship for the next few days. James was clearly intending this to be a mildly bohemian venture, an escape from his usual acquaintance of high-priced business men, high-ranking bureaucrats, high-level academics, and high-flight politicians – but even here, while roughing it on a Mediterranean coastal steamer, he still met some "very important persons." He was, however, determined to make a holiday of it.

Tuesday, August 30 – Genoa

No bath this morning; I shall now smell to high heaven! And breakfast was an experience: tea as strong as I have ever had it, together with dry toast and cheese.

But while I breakfasted the *Adana* tied up in Genoa, and I spent most of the day wandering around – the queer little alleys close to the harbour where vehicles should not go but motorcycles do; the great boulevard with flowered centres; the War Memorial and the Memorial to Christopher Columbus. I must have walked for nearly five hours – and I was glad to sit at a little restaurant in the old town where I had spaghetti, seafood (including *octopus* and mussels which I recognized from my visit to the Mercado de Pesche [Mercato del Pesce]) – and a big bowl of fruit, washed down with Chianti and "minerale"! A good lunch – that cost about a dollar. Prices are much cheaper here than in France, and I was tempted into the purchase of a pair of sandals for 2900 lira (about $5.50).

Tonight – after a day that has been, in the main, cloudy – the moon is shining clearly above a wine-dark sea, [James is trying, it seems to justify Homer] and the island of Elba loomed blacker than the sea to our right. I spent an hour talking to Mendès-France and his wife (also visiting Genoa for the first time) and our talk wandered over the yesterdays. (I find that I can *talk* French, but do not easily *think* French, so that my remarks became more banale [sic] than usual and his knowledge of English was an great help!)[6] The alleys in the older part of Genoa have heard the feet of seamen and carried the cargoes of merchants for two thousand years – and Napoleon at Elba is a modern interloper.

All the next day while the ship sailed down the Italian coast, James sat on deck watching the brown hillsides, the tightly clustered villages, the terraced vineyards, the grey-green olive groves, the occasional golden gleam of a tiny wheatfield, and the larger seaside towns with their busy little ports; he let them slip lazily past while he dreamed of Genoan galleys of five centuries ago, crammed with precious cargoes, or of even more ancient Greek and Phoenician ships "containing (like ours) a motley company of men and women speaking different languages and representing different walks of life."

At Naples, he drove with a party from the *Adana* "28 kilometres in an ancient Lancia with a driver who argued vociferously with the guide all the time," but Pompeii, he decided, was well worth it. He found it a delight to walk in the streets and to visit the houses in which Romans had followed the daily patterns of their lives two thousand years ago. The decorated wells, the elaborate baths, the little women's room with Priapus standing in the corner, and the frank sexual paintings, all caught and held his attention. "The Christian moralists might well say that the city was overwhelmed in punishment for its iniquity – but somehow I do not think that these people thought themselves wicked. I think that they enjoyed life more than we do – worked less and had less complicated lives." The other man's grass is always greener, even if it is two thousand years away.

Once the ship reached Athens, the bohemian lifestyle vanished, and James was quite happy with the relapse into gracious living. He was met at dockside by private car and whisked through customs to the Athenia hotel. His room was spacious and the attached bathroom positively luxurious; James emerged odorous no longer. Athens at first disappointed him as a very sleepy, shut-up sort of place – he had arrived at midday – but then he found that this was only because of the siesta; around five P.M. the stores began reopening, the cafés became alive, market stalls uncovered, the streets filled, and soon he realized he was in the throbbing heart of a great city. James revelled in it.

It quickly became apparent that his Montreal travel agency, Guy Tombs, had impressed their Greek counterparts with the importance of this visitor, for the tour arrangements made for him were not in the plebian style.

I had asked Guy Tombs to arrange a two-day trip to Corinth and Mycenae – but once again the Greeks rose higher than my wildest expectations. A big Buick car driven by a most interesting fellow (he *owns* a farm, as well as the taxi company, and his wife is one of the leading dressmakers in Athens), while the guide was Mary Komminis, daughter of one of the judges of the Supreme Court in Athens. The whole thing was more like a party of friends than the ordinary guided tour, such as I have experienced elsewhere.

Mary quickly became for James the delightful embodiment of the Hellenic spirit, both modern and ancient, and personified an experience of deep pleasure such as he had not known in years. The first stop was at Eleusis, where James supplemented his guide's information with memories of his own reading, and decided that he inclined to the view that the old mysteries had had "a close resemblance to Buddhism."

The hole through which Persephone returned from the underworld is close to Pluto's altar – and [to] the well beside which Ceres sat singing – so that as in modern India the religion must have embraced simple ritual at one end and philosophic abstraction at the other.

While he was brooding over Eleusis, rain began to fall, so they did not get out at their next stop, Corinth, but it was impressive even seen only from the car. They drove onto Mycenae to stay the night.

Awakened at dawn by the bustle of the inn, James tramped up the hill through the great Lions Gate and up to the top of the Mycenean acropolis. "That early morning glimpse, when I walked around entirely alone and dreamed of Agamemnon and Clytemnestra, as I looked into their graves and saw the great fortress they had built, was a rich joy." Later in the morning he returned with Mary, and learned a great deal more of the detail, and her personality and Hellenic accents brought the ancient days vividly close.

The party returned to Athens and James found himself free early the following morning to climb the Acropolis in the city centre, an experience challenging enough in itself, and then to spend the hours until a late lunch "taking pictures, walking, looking and thinking of all the people who trod those stones since Pericles began the restoration. This, like the Taj Mahal is better than all the descriptions of it." He experienced that sense of nostalgia richly satisfied, which visits all who have known the classical world only in studies, legends, and myths, and now behold it, clear and shining, for the first time. The day was completed when Mary took him to a performance of Gluck's *Orfeo ed Euridice*, given in the Odeon built by the Romanized Jew Herod Atticus. James was conscious of the extraordinary blend of Greek, Roman, eighteenth-century, and modern cultures in that memory-haunted setting.

After that we went out to the Kastella, on the Piraeus, and had dinner on the terrace while the moon made rippling patterns along the water, and listened to Greek folk songs sung by a quartet between the dances. The whole evening had a mad, unforgettable – and completely unexpected – quality, that was the spontaneous amalgam of music, moonlight, the water and Athens.

A second tour into the countryside around Athens had been arranged to take him by way of Thebes to visit Delphi. James found the setting of the tourist lodge, overlooking the great valley leading down to the sea, "quite heavenly." He tried, like any good tourist, to recapture the sense of the place, in the time of its greatness, but it was early the next morning that the visitation came.

This morning I woke early to hear, in the silence of dawn, the tinkle of sheep-bells on the mountain, and when I went out on the balcony the whole valley to the sea was an enchantment of blue sea, roseate hills and misty grey olives in the valley. It is as lovely as anything that I remember.

He slipped out early and wandered up the village street. An old shepherd and a rug merchant, some of his wares already over his shoulder, were in a doorway, drinking their first coffee of the day. Greetings were exchanged, a mug was generously found for the stranger, and a conversation of grins, signs, and goodwill happily continued while the hot, raw liquid went down. James went on his way warmed by something more than coffee. Greece was a wonderful country.

The next day, however, brought a return to reality. He read in the *Athens News* of serious riots in Istanbul, his final destination. He went to the Canadian Embassy to call on the ambassador, Terence MacDermot, a McGill graduate and an old acquaintance, and there he learned further grave news about Greek–Turkish tensions over Crete. In the evening there was a McGill reception at the Embassy – "a most successful party in which diplomatic chaps, Greek government and McGill graduates were mixed, so that I enjoyed it greatly." But the day could not have the same pleasure as before; in particular, one element was missing. "The day seems strange. This completes my first week in Athens and … this is the first day on which I have not seen Mary Komminis, who somehow has become intertwined with all my Greek experiences except those of today!" If James had been looking for a complete change of pace and a time away from official and domestic pressures, the days on the steamer and the excursions into ancient Greece had afforded that relaxation in full measure, and the companionship of Mary had obviously provided a great part of the charm.

He spent two more days in Athens and then moved on to Crete, which again produced some unforgettable memories.

… I am fascinated by the place. To describe the treasures would be impossible – and too many people have done it – but all the things I expected, and more, are here. It must be 35 years since I first read about

the Minoan civilisation – and here it is ... This evening I walked down
to the sea – across which the Minoan ships sailed to garner wealth –
and felt that Atlantis never disappeared. It was men who forgot what
[this island] had produced in that short four centuries from about 1900
to 1500 B.C. – when there was nothing on the Acropolis [in Athens] but
mud huts ... But much more important than any of the individual ruins
is the deepening impression of the whole island as a great center of
civilisation 3000 years ago ... Not only Zeus but the whole Greek civilisation was born on this island: I am sure of it!

James spent three more, thoroughly enjoyable days in Crete, but
when he returned to Athens it was to be plunged into the concerns
of contemporary affairs once more. The Turkish–Greek situation
had worsened rather than improved, and the "eastern end of the
Nato alliance was finished," according to the US chargé d'affaires.
He decided he should fly to Istanbul rather than continue his
journey by sea as planned. But the Hellenic experience had been
for him been something to remember with gratitude.

These two weeks have made me feel younger than I have felt for years.
It is an elixir compounded of dreams come true in my long desire to see
Greece, of long days in the open air, of walking on the stones where
great men walked long centuries ago, of the climate and landscape of
Greece, of the fact that Mary has treated me as though I were really
young – and, perhaps, of escape from routine, responsibilities and myself.
I am sorry that the chapter is ended.

The conference of the International Association of Universities
had long been planned for Istanbul, and the meeting was to
go ahead despite the recent anti-Greek riots. James stayed at the
newly opened Hilton Hotel, but when he stepped outside and
saw the wreckage of stores, markets, even houses, where Greeks
or Armenians had lived and worked, he was greatly depressed.
His former travelling-companion, Mendès-France, who had just left
the hotel, had told a mutual friend that he was present during
the riots and had seen nothing more terrible during the war.
James' own comment, not an informed or sober judgment, tells
us more about his mood than about the situation: "I must confess
that in all my travels, I have never been in a city which I found
myself liking less."

The conference itself did not prove interesting, and James was
constantly irritated by what he considered evidences of poor planning. In spite of his initial impressions, however, the physical

setting of the conference began to impress itself upon him more and more favourably, and this more positive attitude was further encouraged by his encounters with the city's inhabitants.

Monday, September 19th

This morning we had the plenary session to open the Congress. The speakers were dull, but the Sali Palace (built by Abdul Hamid to entertain Wilhelm II)[7] is admirable in its mixture of Versailles and Victoria! The gardens that surround it are lovely – and once again I am reminded of the many hills in Istanbul because this palace sits on the very top of one of them.

Had lunch at the Hilton snack-bar with Frank Bowker [of the College Entrance Examinations Board] and Earl McGrath (of Kansas City U) and we decided to "cut" the afternoon meeting. Using our passes we went down the tunnel and across the Galata Bridge to wander around the Spice Bazaar and explore the Rustum Pasha Mosque (simpler than the Blue Mosque, but impressive). Twice during the afternoon we lost our way and on both occasions the passing stranger whose aid we sought came out of his way to put us on the right track!

Tuesday, September 20

This morning's plenary session was a series of long speeches about what universities should do ... The more I see of it, the worse I think of the preliminary planning of this Conference – too many speeches, too little preliminary committee work.

At 5.30 we were taken out to Beyazit for a reception at the University of Istanbul – a magnificent building (once the Ministry of War) in the middle of a superb park! No University in North America could equal this splendour and Ataturk certainly turned swords into plowshares!

When Cyril James attended a conference well-intentioned but poorly conceived and ill-directed, his fingers itched to get at the controls and put matters right. The consequences were quite momentous, although the first moves were innocent enough.

Dined at the Park Hotel with the whole U.K. delegation – a delightful evening organised by Thompson (Medicine – Birmingham) who is a splendid organiser. Much talk of what we [should] do about the future of the Association and general agreement that both U.K. and U.S. will run Herman Wells and myself for the Administration Board. [8]

If this move proved successful, James would be placed in a position of world-wide academic influence. He was already a power in the Canadian Association of Universities, a strong influence (by virtue of McGill's membership in the American Association of Universities) in US academic circles, and a member and past chairman of the Executive Council of the AUBC. As James had once observed, with the American association covering North America and the AUBC covering the Commonwealth, the IAU could serve all other third-world counties developing in the Western tradition. But obviously they would need tutelage, and who more fitted to provide the guidance than experienced administrators such as Cyril James?

No doubt, the sense of power derived from being one of the movers and shakers of mankind played its part in James' motivation, but it is also legitimate to think his vocation to serve education, now not only in North America and the Commonwealth but also in the liberation of all mankind, was also a strongly motivating force. This was the great new vision of the postwar era, and James was one of the foremost of those who encouraged its emergence. Education is not the panacea of all human ills, but it is the only general prescription for the better ordering of human affairs that can be made. James had come to believe that more fundamental than economic prosperity or even than public-health provisions was the service of the need to know, the need to discover, to become informed and aware. Knowledge liberates not merely the body but the most human element in humanity – the mind. The modern university was in James' view the best instrument to procure and disseminate both knowledge and insight, and he was personally committed to furthering its interests throughout the inhabited world. Thoughts such as these, sometimes fully expressed in public speeches, often implied in minor decisions, but influencing the overall development of his activities and interests, were the guiding principles of his life. Education was his métier, and it is likely he sought nomination to the Administration Board of the IAU almost automatically, because that was where his greatest abilities could be used. Of course, there was also the bonus of exciting travel and opportunities to explore strange habitats of mankind, which interested him so hugely.

He continued attending sessions sporadically over the next two days, but also wandered off to see the tourist sights. On one of the later excursions he was given a disquieting glimpse of the tensions involved in university life under a military dictatorship. During a trip on a Bosphorus ferry boat, he received a rather mysterious invitation to leave it at "an unnamed dock," where he was

met by a young Turk and escorted along back alleys to a "door in the wall" which was opened by a servant in a fez[9] (the first I have seen in Turkey) who led us through splendid gardens down to a little palace, splendidly built and furnished, on the very shores of the Bosphorus. The party that greeted us comprised young teachers of economics and political sciences (one of them the nephew of the aristocratic owner of the palace) who wanted to talk about the difficult situation in which they find themselves. The Government is apparently using martial law to suppress the opposition – 4 newspapers have been suspended already and these young professors have been told that they must stop criticising the economic policies of the government. Since the Minister of Education seems to have the power to discharge any professor from the University – while martial law gives the government the power to arrest subversive persons – the situation may be serious, but the whole affair had an Arabian nights quality that was not dispelled by the breakneck ride back to Istanbul in a taxi that awaited me at the same garden gate.

It was a reminder that the quiet calm of a British or North American campus was not a luxury enjoyed by all and that the path of education in the larger world is often beset with real dangers. As for the conference, it did not improve.

The Plenary Session in the afternoon was a riot. Some of the people who have been dropped from the Administration Board started to attack both the Nominating Committee and its proposals – and Sarrailh was perfectly terrible as a presiding officer.[10] The constitution was amended, half a dozen motions were before the house on several occasions, and nobody knew what was happening. It was one of the worst performances that I have ever seen and when it was over and the new Administration Board met for a brief executive session, I think that all of us had a deep-seated feeling that if we cannot do better than this during the next five years the association might as well fold-up.

After he had returned to his own world, James could look back and survey the whole remarkable month: the urbane ceremonials of Edinburgh, the rich display of European culture in the festival, the holiday train-ride across France, the bohemian life on the Turkish ship, the fleeting friendship of Mary Komminis, the moving glimpses of Italy, Greece, Crete, and the fabulous, classical world from which the light of learning had first shone. Finally, there were those first contacts with the strange, exciting, potentially dangerous world he had glimpsed in Istanbul. He knew this month had been a time of profound and manifold enrichment.

When he arrived back in London on 24 September he stopped in at Barnet to see Irene before flying back to Montreal. He found his housekeeper waiting for him at 1200 Pine Avenue, "and the house looks very nice indeed." Settling in to clear up the arrears of work waiting for him in the office, he found no great problems had arisen in his absence. In fact, everything in his world at this the midpoint of his second decade at McGill was looking very encouraging – except when he let his thoughts turn toward his home.

Friday, September 30 [1955]

The first week of the session is nearly over. I have cleaned up the arrears at the office, held an Administration Meeting and a Dean's Meeting (everything seems to be under control) and had two long talks with Morrison[11] about the problem of Buster Brown's eligibility to play on the football team – so that the familiar round begins to follow its normal pattern.

But somehow I am disquieted. Bay sails from Liverpool today on the *Scotland* – and the memory of last Saturday, coupled with the memory of those earlier days at Barnet after Edinburgh, make me feel that the months that lie ahead of us are not going to be happy. I already seem to feel a little of the tension in the house – and it is impossible to get any real organisation into the running of it when I know that Bay will want it right back where it was last year as soon as she arrives.

Cyril James could grasp the problems of education on a global scale and contrive to get himself a place on the IAU Administrative Board, because he knew he had a valuable contribution to make, but solutions to the problems of his own hearth still eluded him.

CHAPTER TWELVE

Achievement for McGill

After his return from Greece and Istanbul, James found his relationships with the university once again subject to change. In the first part of the decade, his position on campus had been consolidated and his affections clarified, but in the second half he became aware that circumstances were still evolving, and he found himself entering a period of increasing uncertainty – no longer from merely his old insecurities but from strong forces external to himself.

The actual administration of the university was operating more smoothly than ever it had before. William Bentley retired as bursar, but George Grimson was competently taking increasing responsibility for the management of the university's financial business; T.H. Matthews had similarly retired as registrar and had been effectively replaced by C.M. McDougall, while J.H. Holton, who had proved his worth as the registrar at Macdonald College, had been brought in to serve as secretary to the Board of Governors. These dependable assistants (along with, of course, the indefatigable Mrs Mac) gave James solid backing in all the business affairs of the board: control of the budget, negotiations with the provincial bureaucracy, investment and real-estate management, dealings with the university solicitors, legal matters relating both to academic and non-academic appointments and to promotions, tenure, and pensions, and much more.

But he was aware of other developments – developments of which he heartily approved but that nevertheless made him feel that the university was beginning to pull away from him. The postwar knowledge explosion was being felt in all departments, Watson and Crick were unravelling DNA, Sputnik was taking to the skies. James was no longer needed in the same way as the intellectual leader, urging colleagues on to new adventures. They had already surged past him, leaving him in the role of the patient administrator, encouraging from behind. On the academic front, he found himself relying increasingly on the nine deans of the faculties. Nevertheless, he continued to make himself master of all administrative detail and to keep himself well-informed on academic matters; in the running of the university he was as decisive and competent as ever.

The major preoccupation of the years 1956–7 was a renewal of the political debates over federal grants to Canadian universities. After Duplessis had suddenly announced in February 1954 that Quebec universities would receive annual grants to make good the amounts lost to them by Quebec's refusal to permit its universities to accept direct-grant federal funds, McGill began to receive these provincial monies. It was a great step forward, but the provincial funds fells short of the federal aid in two ways – they were not statutory grants but needed to be voted each year (and with a premier as capricious as Duplessis, no one could rely on their appearance) and they were not as large. The Quebec universities' share of the federal grant was, however, being held in trust by the NCCU and, with interest being added, the amount was beginning to grow even more tantalizingly attractive – especially to McGill, with its low salaries and strict financial restraints.

For Cyril James, this situation had been frustrating enough, but now a new element began to increase his difficulties: its beginnings went back to 1950. At the meeting of the Canadian Learned Societies at Queen's University that year, a number of professors from different institutions had initiated discussion among themselves of the conditions and rewards of academic appointments. A particular irritant was that universities were run by boards of governors made up of wealthy businessmen for whom a seat on the board was a social accolade. Generally, these governors, who often had not themselves received a university education, were disposed to allow the executive head of the institution freedom to plot its academic course. Generally, also, they were expected and were prepared to be generous to the institution. But professors in Canada at large were beginning to feel that the intervention of the federal government into the universities' financial affairs had left the institutions less dependent on the benefactions of merchant princes, and that academics should have greater control of their institutions and of the circumstances of their personal careers.

Among those who joined in the initial discussions in Kingston were several McGill professors, particularly F.S. Howes of the Faculty of Engineering, a man motivated by social concerns that

CONVOCATION THURSDAY !

James, as involved in university detail as ever.

he had learned in the Student Christian Movement and had practised for many years in Adult Education programs. In April 1951, he and James Mallory of the Department of Political Science, along with some of their other colleagues, formed the McGill Association of University Teachers (MAUT). A month later, when the Learned Societies held their annual meeting at McGill, the Canadian Association of University Teachers was formed –

to consider what should be done to improve the lot of the University Teacher in Canada. The situation cried out for attention. Teachers were overworked and grossly underpaid; working conditions were incredibly bad; the universities were overcrowded with students and understaffed. Our administrators and Boards of Governors either could not, or would not, but in any case did not, do anything about it. It was high time therefore that we decided to do something for ourselves.[1]

Similar bodies to the McGill Association were formed in other universities – at least twelve in the first year of the movement – with the Canadian Association acting as a clearing-house for information and as a source of advice and support if any local association should find itself in trouble – as indeed, given the circumstances, some quickly did. At best, the local associations were regarded by governing boards as spurious imitations of legitimate professional bodies; at worst, they were regarded with deep suspicion as disguised trade unions.

At McGill, both views had their adherents, but in general the opinion prevailed that the aims and procedures of MAUT were consonant with the best interests of the university as an institution of higher education. The fact that respected individuals such as E.F. Beach, James' successor in the School of Commerce, R.F. Scott and Maxwell Cohen of the Faculty of Law, and D.L. Thomson of Biochemistry (and, from 1942, dean of graduate studies and research) played an active part in its program and activities gave MAUT prestige both on campus and with the administration. James' own attitude was, from the beginning, correct and proper; as a professor, he formally took out membership in MAUT and paid his dues, but as principal and vice-chancellor, his relationship with MAUT was never cordial.

In the second year of its existence, MAUT presented to the Executive and Finance Committee of the Board of Governors a cogently argued brief relating to university salaries. Seventy years earlier, McGill professors had written to the Board of Governors suggesting that a certain piece of university land be sold and the sale-price capitalized to provide an augmentation of academic salaries. The governors had replied that the letter was "unseemly, indecorous and an unwarrantable interference with the functions of the Governors" and that another such communication would be read as a letter of resignation.[2] For seventy years the professors had kept silence, but now they were speaking out again, and being heard with respect. The times were changing, and new relationships were being established. James, however, could not be unaware that the association was encroaching on his jealously guarded preserves and that its members were doing so not inadvertently but by intention. Politeness and the courtesies were preserved, but the writing was beginning to be legible on the wall: either Cyril James' autocratic conception of his role would have to change, or his time of usefulness to McGill would be seen as coming to an end.

It did not help matters that the principal's difficulties with Sidney Dobell had only recently reached a conclusion. Although Dobell and MAUT were influences working in isolation from each other, their effects tended to be cumulative. The principal's administrative assistant left the university in 1955, but MAUT would not similarly disappear. It gave every indication of being a new development that had come to stay. In November 1956, James recorded that "few weeks have been so tense and wearing ... I have had three ticklish meetings with MAUT Committees – one of them on the subject of Duplessis's attitude to the Federal grants."

This, then, was the internal situation when the political debate over federal grants to universities came to the boil once more. The initial move had been made in 1955 at the NCCU annual meeting, when E.F. Sheffield, a member of the Education Division of the Dominion Bureau of Statistics, gave a paper on Canadian students enrolment projections.[3] The effect was startling; "the graphic portrayal of an almost vertical climb in admissions from a figure of around 70,000 in 1954–55 to 140,000 in 64–65," wrote Pilkington, "was sufficient to convince even the most hardened skeptics in the Government and the universities that a crisis was upon them." As a first result, "a sense of buoyant energy was gradually built up and sustained by the continuing efforts of the NCCU publicity and finance committees, whose members were busily spreading the word from coast to coast."[4] This missionary fervour was similar to that which earlier had been inspired and led by Cyril James, but in this second wave of activity his own enthusiasm was somewhat dampened by the inability of McGill to benefit from any success in the campaign for more generous government funding.

The next development was that the Carnegie Corporation in New York, at all times a friend to Canadian education, was persuaded to make a $25,000 donation to the NCCU to permit the holding of a special conference in Ottawa the following November. The theme was to be "Canada's Crisis in Higher Education." The universities' needs were spelt out and tentative plans to provide for the necessary expansion were adumbrated. But where was the money to come from? Prime Minister Louis St Laurent, who had agreed to speak at the closing banquet, set the tone for the evening with his opening remark that this conference "may prove to be the most important in this field ever to be held in Canada." He then went on to say that the student per capitum grant, calculated at 50¢ per head of population, would be doubled and, further, that the money would no longer be paid directly to the universities but would go to the NCCU for distribution – a change intended to mollify provincial sensitivities. Finally, he announced that $100 million would be given to establish the long-awaited Canada Council, which would be expected to spend half of its funds over the next ten years in capital grants for the expansion of university facilities.

This was all that, and more than, Cyril James and his 1948–52 Finance Committee had organized and campaigned for; his dictum that only the federal government had resources large enough to meet the coming need had been more than substantiated; the November 1956 assembly was indeed "the most important conference" ever held in the field of Canadian higher education and, as a result of the federal government's continued commitment to the cause, has remained so.

For James personally it was an achievement of the highest order, both in that it was the culmination of his endeavours to involve the federal government in higher education and in that it permanently influenced the positive development of his chosen country. But the irony still remained that his own university, like the other Quebec institutions, could not benefit from the federal largesse. While the provincial grants were growing slowly year by year, they still fell far behind what other universities were receiving from their combined provincial and federal sources. And McGill would not be exempt from the coming pressure to expand; the university must be prepared to face another huge expansion, greater than any other in its history. When James heard Sheffield's paper in 1955, he saw at once that McGill would be besieged by admission-applications, like all other universities, but how could the university respond if the provincial premier had cut McGill off from the federal funding? The university was in a mood for great changes; he himself was as ready as ever to initiate great plans; among the academic staff there was no lethargy to be overcome, as there had been in 1944 – but this time his hands were tied. It was a maddening situation.

In discussion with his deans, James looked at one possible answer: that McGill should deliberately choose not to expand.[5] Let the other English-language institution in Montreal, Sir George Williams College, which had recently achieved university status, take in the swelling crowds while McGill would stay at its present 8–9,000 size, remain exclusive, charge high fees, and rely in the future as in the past on private benevolence for its capital needs. Someone around the table coined the phrase "McGill would become the Princeton of the North." It was a tempting prospect. But James' instinct and training warned him against the unreality of the plan. McGill, he said, would not become another Princeton but at best another Bishop's; there was not a sufficient economic base in Montreal, let alone a sufficient public will, to support with private funding a first-class, elite institution. Nor could McGill expect great generosity from elsewhere in Canada or the United States. This was a continent-wide crisis. Other cities would have their own local institutions to support. McGill had only lately come into the public domain, by means of Duplessis's grudging grants, but however difficult its present situation might be, that was where it must remain.

By the fall of 1956, another possibility began to come more sharply into focus. The federal government had deposited the total amount of the grants with the NCCU. McGill's cheque would come in the mail next March or April not from the government but from the NCCU secretariat. What if McGill should defy Duplessis and accept it? A young social commentator named Pierre Elliott Trudeau, writing in the Quebec magazine *Cité Libre*, argued that Duplessis was right to object to the federal government taxing Canadians in support of education – that it was not in the federal jurisdiction; but, he said, Ottawa had other funds which were not taxation-raised, such as profits from Crown corporations, which could legitimately be used to meet a national crisis in education. Further, he castigated the universities for capitulating to Duplessis and urged them to challenge him to give the universities what they need "to assume, untroubled by political manoeuvring, their cultural, scientific and financial obligations." It was an interesting illustration of the way in which even federally minded French-Canadians were loathe to surrender any point of provincial jurisdiction, even though they realized that James was right – only the federal purse was large enough to meet the national need.[6]

By the time Trudeau published his article early in 1957 the debate was being argued hotly throughout Quebec, but nowhere more vigorously than on the McGill campus. Professors' salaries were at stake, lack of new appointments had   forced them to acquiesce in large, unwieldy classes, buildings they taught in were inadequate, equipment was outdated, libraries were seriously underfunded, travel grants were few, sabbaticals were non-existent, pension funds were inadequate – the MAUT list of grievances was growing longer each month.

James had never been in such a difficult situation. On the one hand, the academic leaders on campus were looking to him to continue the logic of his previous arguments and activities by coming out boldly for acceptance of the federal funds; on the other hand, the majority of the members of the board favoured observance of the premier's prohibition. The strength of James' position at McGill had always been that he was the loyal servant of the Board of Governors and had carried out their policies – even if most of the time it was he who conceived and formulated those policies. But this time the board members, knowing their business interests were at stake, would not leave him to determine the course of action. This was particularly true of James' protector, benefactor, and friend, John Wilson McConnell, who was more vulnerable than most to Duplessis's vindictive retaliation. In the debates in the University Senate, James as chairman maintained a strictly neutral stance, but in the privacy of the board, he argued strenuously for defiance of Duplessis and acceptance of the federal cheque. As a result he lost favour in both bodies. In Senate the academics were disappointed by his apparent weakness, whereas board-members increasingly resented his truculence in advocating defiance. In particular, a deep rift developed between James and McConnell, which caused them both considerable hurt. James confided his unhappiness to his diary.

The arguments within the University on the subject of University grants have been bitter. I have shown to the Board of Governors my strong personal feeling that McGill should accept them – and as a result lost the confidence of McConnell (who is angry) and some of the other senior governors. With the academic staff I have felt that I should be neutral – since I cannot side openly with them against the Board – and some of them feel that I have not been enthusiastic enough about the idealistic independence of the University. On both sides, I have lost out ...

The matter moved ahead slowly. In early April 1957 the NCCU

distributed the cheques from the federal government. In a diary note that began with a comment on his health and drinking habits, James wrestled with the dilemma.

... I have decided to give up alcohol in all forms from now until Easter, as an experiment in self-control if nothing else. Yesterday, so far as I can remember, is the first day in more than five years, during the whole of which I did not have a drink!

Today I need a clear head. The cheque from Ottawa has arrived on my desk for the 1956–57 grant – $1,189,000 as against $750,000 offered by Quebec (but not yet received). This afternoon, the Joint Committee of Senate and the Governors will meet to make its recommendations to the Board and on Wednesday the Executive Committee must tackle the problem. The only new element in the problem is that Arthur Carter Q.C. (from whom we sought a legal opinion) is convinced that the Premier has a clear right to pass legislation prohibiting any university in Quebec from taking a federal grant. This is contrary to my expectation – but I find his reasoning convincing – and it means that if we did opt for the federal grant Duplessis (if he wanted to be nasty) could have us entirely at his mercy. He could cut off both Federal and Provincial grants!

Just how divided opinion was in the university, in the Senate, and even in the Board of Governors is revealed by an early draft of the press release, dated 21 June 1957, announcing the university's decision. In its final form, the sentences placed in square brackets were omitted, but James preserved the draft to record how narrowly the decision had been made.

The Board of Governors of McGill University, at its meeting yesterday, resolved [by a vote of 12 to 6] to return to the National Conference of Canadian Universities, to be held in trust, the cheque for $1,184,693.52, which represents the university's share of the grant of $16,000,000 made available by the Federal Government for the universities of Canada this year.

During the past three months the question of government grants has been under careful and intensive study by both the Senate and the Board of Governors, as well as by a Conference Committee made up of representatives appointed by both bodies. [At the last meeting of Senate, the final vote was 14 to 13 in favour of accepting the grant from the National Conference of Universities. At the last meeting of the Conference Committee the vote was 6 to 6].

The division of opinion within the University [which these votes reflect] is a reflection of wider uncertainties in regard to governmental policies in higher education in Canada, and to the role of private universities.

The statement goes on to say that at the national level greater clarification on the issues involved would have to be achieved before the university could make the decision "that will offer the greatest long-run advantage to McGill and enable it to continue to play with confidence its traditional role in the life of Canada."

This debate was important both for the evolution of McGill and for James personally. For the first time the university had resorted to a procedure for which the statutes provided, but which had not previously been used: a Joint Conference Committee of the Board of Governors and the Academic Senate. Little by little, led in great part by the McGill Association of University Teachers, academic members of staff were beginning to obtain a larger share in the direction of the institution, a step that James could not help but see was beginning to encroach on his direction of university affairs. One university wit, reading a notice posted by MAUT calling a meeting to discuss university salary policy, observed with a mock-languid air: "Ah, the natives are getting restless." Some junior staff (this being the period of guerilla warfare being waged in Kenya in order to gain independence from British rule) dubbed MAUT "the Mau-Mau." The banter was light-hearted, but it showed that the "winds of change," in Harold Macmillan's phrase, were beginning to blow not only in Africa but also on North American campuses. As yet at McGill they were still gentle breezes. Within the decade they would gather tempest-strength and finally blow the old Board of Governors completely away.

The decision not to accept the federal grant was made in June 1957. That summer, to a great many people's surprise, the federal Liberal Party, which had been in power for twenty-five years, lost an election to John Diefenbaker and the Conservative Party. What this implied for the universities of Canada could not be foretold, since Diefenbaker had taken no position in the educational debate. The NCCU lost no time in petitioning the new government for an increase in the federal funding: the numbers of students were continuing to increase and the operating funds currently available were proving inadequate. Diefenbaker replied that he could make no change until another election had given him a clear, comfortable majority. This came in March 1958, and Diefenbaker was given the freedom to plot his own course. As was to become characteristic of the Diefenbaker regime, the government avoided overt decision by not answering the NCCU brief, but in August, without prior con-sultation, the per capitum allotment was raised from $1.00 to $1.50.

This pleasing development did not, however, resolve the question of the Quebec universities. Other institutions across Canada were receiving the funds; the francophone universities in Quebec were receiving not too-inadequate provincial grants to support their (at that time) somewhat limited programs. It was only McGill that truly suffered, seeing its rivals for leadership, Toronto and UBC, steadily pulling ahead. As a stop-gap effort, James had already urged the governors to launch yet another financial campaign, and in 1956 the university had asked R.E. Powell, president of the Aluminum Company of Canada and a McGill Governor since 1950, to undertake its direction. With $6 million from 3,886 firms and corporations, $1.5 million from the Province of Quebec (to be spread over several years), and a special donation of $1.5 million from J.W. McConnell, the grand total declared in 1959 was $9 million, a most encouraging result. But its very success only emphasized the need for a more permanent solution, and that could come only with the resolution of the Quebec–Ottawa imbroglio.

In September 1959, came the dénouement – in an unexpected if not entirely unhoped for manner – for which the whole McGill community had been waiting: Maurice Duplessis died suddenly while visiting Northern Quebec. The Duplessis regime was over. His successor, Jean Sauvé, speedily approached the Diefenbaker government to work out an agreement between the federal and the provincial authorities regarding the federal education grants.

At first, the new arrangement seemed harmless enough. The federal government would take note of those provinces that increased the corporation tax by 1 per cent in order that the money so raised should be given to the universities in the form of statutory grants equivalent to the present federal grants; in those provinces, corporations would be allowed to deduct the increase in provincial tax from their federal tax payments. Only Quebec chose to avail itself of this option, and the NCCU continued to receive and distribute the federal funds intended for institutions in the nine other provinces.

As far as McGill was concerned, the 1959 agreement entered into by Sauvé brought Cyril James' achievements into full effect. In 1950, soon after James began his campaign for federal funding, McGill had received just over 4 per cent of total operating income from government sources. Now, ten years later, as a result of his endeavours, this had become 37.7 per cent of operating income. Nor was this simply a case of one source of funds taking the place of another; income continued from investment, fees, and private giving – from the last-named more than generously. The increased government funds received in 1960 represented truly new money. They were first used to allow a one-fifth decrease in student fees and a substantial raise in all salaries. The minimum for a full professor, for example, which had been only $6,800 per annum as recently as 1955, was raised in 1960 to $11,500, so that critical comments on McGill salaries were no longer as relevant as they had been in the past.

James' idea, conceived during the war, that the needs of Canadian universities were so large and so urgent that only federal funds could adequately provide for them, and that McGill was one of those universities and must have equal access to those resources, had been doggedly pursued for twenty years and was now brought to triumphant success. The restrained wording of the 1959–60 annual report only hints at what James must have been feeling.

It was, therefore, a happy occasion when, on March 7, 1960, McGill asked the Canadian Universities Foundation to hand over the $5,866,378 which represented the total of the federal grants that we had not been able to accept since 1952.

To complete this part of the story, it should be recorded that Cyril James expressed the opinion that the 1959 Sauvé–Diefenbaker accord could not provide a permanent solution to the Canadian dilemma and that this perception was substantiated within the decade. As the amount of funds grew, and the machinery for their distribution by the NCCU became necessarily more elaborate, the other provinces also became dissatisfied with this arrangement. At a federal–provincial conference convened in October 1966, Prime Minister Lester B. Pearson announced that in answer to provincial demands his government had agreed to turn responsibility for higher education over to the provinces. The federal government would still provide the money, but would give it to the provinces for distribution. James and his colleagues had fought hard and long to obtain statutory federal grants for Canadian universities; in so doing they had hammered out a national policy for the benefit of every province and all Canadians. In 1959, the opting-out arrangement had been for Quebec alone; in 1966, the clock was turned back, with the provinces being allowed to re-assume the direction of higher education in conformity with their local political interests. Pilkington comments: "Rather than fostering national unity, as Diefenbaker had envisaged, [the Ottawa–Quebec agreement of 1959] had the opposite effect of furthering the trend towards provincialism and parochialism"; she quotes W.L. Morton: "time was to reveal that it was an opening of flood-gates that could not be closed again."[7]

But if James and his committee were robbed by the politicians of the glory of being the architects of a national education policy serving truly Canadian ends, all was not lost. Federal resources had been permanently secured for higher education, even if the route they now had to follow was devious. In addition, the federal government reserved its right to continue to provide directly for university research, as well as for what was termed "adult education" – the training or upgrading of individuals who returned to school or university after at least three years in the work force. As Daniel Johnson, the Union National Premier of Quebec in office in 1966, sourly commented on the Pearson announcement:

The Ottawa government takes all kinds of precautions in its brief to persuade us that it wished to leave the education field an exclusive provincial responsibility. At the same time, however, it cautiously reserved indirect means to enter again in this field. In short, the federal government ... is resolved to use no more the front door, but gets ready to come back through four back doors: adult education, student aid, research and culture.[8]

Intervening years have justified this comment. Though the method of discharging the obligation has varied, the federal government, having once recognized a responsibility to higher education, has not failed to support if. Of course, the 1966 arrangements made no difference to McGill – the new procedures merely brought the rest of the country into line with Quebec. The gain to McGill had been permanent.

The other story needing completion is that of the relationship between James and his great benefactor, J.W. McConnell. A month after the close of the great debate in 1957, James wrote McConnell to explain the reasons for his strong advocacy for accepting the Ottawa cheque, an advocacy that he knew had hurt McConnell deeply. For James to have adopted a position opposed to McConnell's had seemed to the older man an act of disloyalty or of desertion. James' letter was, however, well received by McConnell, and he replied in terms that superficially at least, healed the breach between them.

July 10, 1957

Dear Dr. James,

Thank you for your very nice letter dated July 6th, only received yesterday at Dorval, telling me for the first time that you actually sponsored the Federal Grants, and had been urging them at Ottawa for several years past.

The Governors of McGill, I think, ought to have been told that, frankly, at the outset, which would have lessened the long arguments and debates, because I feel sure this was known to few, if any of the Governors.

It would have been more easily explained to the Committee at Ottawa, how impossible it was for the McGill Board to accept the Grants at once, because of Quebec's stand on the subject. After all – it is unlikely we shall lose anything by the final arrangement that the Federal Grants be held to McGill's credit under the terms set forth covering such cases "so that no University would be penalized for delay in acceptance" ...

Let us hope that we may never again be found on opposite sides of the fence ... I shall not soon forget the merry fight in a certain quarter with respect to the election of the late Morris Wilson as Chancellor, and the most disagreeable and spiteful speech delivered against you, resulting in a resignation. Nor the event later on where an inside man made the unbelievable declaration that 50% of the Governors would like to see you go. At your request, and upon your withdrawal from the meeting, I took the Chair and poled [sic] the Board one by one so that each member would express his views on the subject without persuasion, which resulted in 100% vote of confidence for you. I have no reason to believe that any of them have since changed their minds.

It is difficult to believe that McConnell did not know the extent of James' involvement in the fight for federal funds, but his assumed ignorance and his references to earlier battles when they had been on the same side (and the light he throws on the intensity of those struggles!) appear to be his way of saying that he continued, despite their disagreement, to have confidence in James. A year later, however, pleading advanced age, he resigned as senior governor and withdrew from the conduct of university affairs. He continued his generous benefactions to the university, but his relationship with James was never restored to its former intimacy.

As to the disposition of the funds that had accumulated in Ottawa in the later years of the Duplessis regime and were now released to the university by the 1959 agreement, everyone agreed that they should be used to provide the springboard for a program of university rehabilitation and expansion. The projected huge increase in the size of the student body and the daily demand for new disciplines and new inter-disciplinary centres and research groups gave urgency to the campus-wide demand for more space and for the radical rehabilitation of old accommodation. Expansion was in the air. But times had changed. No longer would Cyril

James single-handedly mastermind the whole scheme. That day was over. He had procured the resources, but the new planning would inevitably now be done in committee. In the late spring of 1960, the University Senate established a Building Priorities Committee, which a year later was recognized as a standing committee of Senate, to be known as the Senate Development Committee. The chairman of the committee, Carl Winkler of Chemistry, along with the other members, quickly demonstrated that McGill had professors possessing the intelligence, expertise, and experience necessary to make a significant contribution to the coming development of the university. All final decisions had, of course, to be made by the board, but the initiation and formulation of those decisions was now being done largely by academics. The significance of these developments for James was that for the first time during his principalship the initiation was not coming from his office. He was *ex officio* a member of the Senate Committee and its sub-committees, but the work went forward whether he was present or not. Nor did he seem to resist or resent this trespassing on what were once his preserves; on the contrary, in August 1961, after a long summer abroad, he commented in his diary:

The meeting of the Development Committee this morning indicates that a lot of work has been done while I have been away, and the whole pattern of the future campus is emerging as a result of the tremendous effort of Spence-Sales. I rather like the sense of it – and hope that Governors will adopt it without too much argument – but am sorry to lose my tall building on the Presbyterian College site, with its combination of Arts, Administration and Social Centre. Too many people – including D.L.T.[homson], G.A.G[rimson] and the Student Council – are opposed to it, and since I am anxious to get the other buildings going, I do not want to postpone the whole thing by a fight over it.

In addition to the important work of the Development Committee, the university had to prepare in 1961 a brief to present to a provincial royal commission to propose for Quebec a new, integrated educational system encompassing all levels from kindergarten through to university. For historical reasons, Quebec had functioned (except for a brief interlude from 1867–75) without a ministry of education in order to "keep politics out of education." In reality it had meant handing French-language education over to the Roman Church and English-language education over to the Protestant Committee of Education – on which James had served for many years. But in 1960 the Liberals under Jean Lesage regained power and ushered in "the Quiet Revolution," as part of which the Royal Commission of Education had been established. Clearly, the report of this body would redraw the educational map in the province, and McGill's interests were involved at every level. The significant development was that James entrusted the writing of the brief to hands other than his own; the major editor was Professor Kenneth Hare, with much input from colleagues and committees. Like the activities of the Development Committee, the production of this brief indicated a profound change in James' own attitude to his responsibilities. He no longer had the desire, or (he had to admit to himself) the energy, to accomplish all things unaided, as he had done during his first two decades. The demands being made upon the university were growing more complex; other able men and women were coming in to share the responsibilities of leadership, and he was content that it should be so.

But he was not ready to welcome any diminution of his formal powers. As principal he was also vice-chancellor, the only channel of access to the board by members or employees of the university. When the McGill Association of University Teachers addressed the issue of university reform in 1959, they expressed their dissatisfaction with this arrangement in a report on university administration presented to the Senate, of which James was chairman. In the ensuing discussion, Maxwell Cohen of the Faculty of Law referred pointedly to the role of the principal "as too narrow an isthmus of communication" between the academic community and the Board of Governors. James gave no appearance of recognizing this as an attack upon himself, and did not allow his usual calm to be ruffled, but merely observed that in North America it had generally been found desirable that, after due discussion at lower levels, decisions about academic concerns should be made in the Senate and then reported to the board by the one person charged by the board with their implementation, and that person at McGill was the principal; he then passed on to other aspects of the MAUT brief. Cohen, who, lawyer-like, had hoped to needle James into some display of resentment by his act of lèse-majesté, asked afterwards with reluctant admiration: "Does that man have blood or ice-water in his veins?" The truth was that while James had schooled himself to constant self-control in public and the appearance of being self-assured, it was appearance only. In private he often worried about the insecurity of his position, doubted his competence, and frequently deplored his lack of wisdom.

With part of his mind he sympathized with the MAUT aspirations, but he knew that the members of the board were not yet ready to relinquish their authority and that as long as McGill depended (as even after 1959, it still did) on their ability to raise the funds necessary for the university's well-being, their susceptibilities must be heeded. Moreover, he was always cognizant of the fact that his own appointment was in their gift. There might be tenure for professors, but there was none for principals. Nevertheless, he realized that the presentation of the MAUT brief on university government had marked a significant development in the evolution of the institution, and, because he was essentially a just man, he included mention of it in the 1959–60 annual report.

Early in 1959, a special committee of the McGill Association of University Teachers, under the chairmanship of Professor Maxwell Cohen, presented to the Senate a long and interesting report on administrative procedures. This report was debated at great length at a special session of the Senate meeting in Committee of the Whole and, when the Senate itself adopted the Report of the Committee of the Whole, a Joint Committee of members of the Board of Governors and of the Senate was created to deal with some of the recommendations.

Some changes in the Statutes have already been made, enlarging the size of the Board of Governors and providing for larger graduate representation, and other changes have been made in Senate procedure. This is not, however, a matter for sudden and spectacular innovation, but rather for gradual improvement where the possibility of such improvements becomes apparent.

In this way James gave the subject respectability, but in such cautious language that one had to read it twice to be sure of its meaning: "gradual improvement where the possibility of such improvements becomes apparent." Many small changes were indeed taking place in university patterns and procedures that went almost unnoticed, but they showed which way the winds were blowing.

CHAPTER THIRTEEN

Achievement Beyond McGill

Although in the middle and late 1950s James was performing in public with his usual air of competence, in his own mind he was continuing to doubt the wisdom of staying in his position of principal, and he welcomed activities outside the university to divert his thoughts and to provide him with interest and stimulation. In the late fall of 1955, he visited the Hebrew University in Jerusalem, briefly touring the Bible lands; in the winter of 1956–7 he led a team in a thorough review of the Wharton School of Business at the University of Pennsylvania. The invitation to undertake this responsibility was particularly welcome in showing that his friends there nursed no grudges for the events of 1953; he was also glad for the chance to renew old acquaintances. When he submitted his consultant's report to his friend Joe Willits, who was heading the review of the university at large, Willits wrote back to James with ebullient praise.

19 February, 1957

I have read your prospectus three times. Joseph Wharton lives again! Certainly this represents the greatest creative thinking in or about the Wharton School since 1881. I shall make certain suggestions as to modifications of emphasis and of detail; but the general scheme gives me the most profound satisfaction.

In every way, the Wharton Review Board was an exercise on which Cyril James himself could afterwards look back and echo Willits' words: "the memory gives me the most profound satisfaction."

He particularly welcomed opportunities for travel. In the summer of 1957, when Irene left for England, saying she was not going to return to Montreal, James commented in his diary, "it has been a quarrelsome year." He had found good reason to leave home twice that spring, to visit two of McGill's more unusual activities.

The first trip, in April, took him to the north on an invitation from the Arctic Institute of North America, the US–Canadian joint venture that James had provided with space on campus immediately after the war. By courtesy of the Royal Canadian Airforce, an itinerary was planned to include such places as Goose Bay, Frobisher, Thule, Lake Hazen and the Arctic Islands, so that James could see for himself some of the work being undertaken. The return was by way of Great Whale Inlet and Churchill, Manitoba, after which he spent a weekend at the Sub-Arctic Research Station that McGill had established at Knob Lake in Northern Quebec. When the Mc-Gill–Jacobsen expedition to Axel Heiberg Island was being organized a year or two later, the principal's understanding of the proposals and his ready support of them proved of great assistance to those involved in the business of gaining sponsors and funds.

The other journey undertaken that spring was to a more familiar destination. James, it will be recalled, had tried as early as 1944 to establish a link between McGill and the projected University of the West Indies, but had not been successful. He continued, however, to nurse the relationship, attending, as we have seen, the installation of Princess Alice, Countess of Athlone, as first chancellor of the new institution in 1950. His chance to achieve a McGill presence in the area arrived quite fortuitously the next year. As chairman of the Royal Commission on Arts, Letters and Sciences in Canada, Vincent Massey had received a letter, hand written by an apparently semi-literate person living in Barbados, who offered to leave his estate on that island for use by a Canadian university. Massey, not taking the offer too seriously, passed the letter on to James with, as the principal later recalled, "a semi-humorous remark that this kind of thing was likely to be of more interest to McGill than to Toronto" – a reference to the fact that Massey was at that time chancellor of the latter university. Characteristically James was interested enough to respond to the letter, and discovered that the writer was Commander Carlyon Wilfray Bellairs, late RN and formerly a Conservative member of the British House of Commons. The apparent lack of style in his letter proved to be a result of the writer's poor health and failing eyesight. James quickly flew down to the beautiful estate on the Barbados west coast and after some discussion, proposed that it become the home of a McGill marine biology research station. Later, the proposal was broadened to include geographical and sociological interests. Accordingly, the Bellairs Research Institute was established, a resident director appointed, and a cooperative relationship formed with the relevant departments of the University of the West Indies. In May 1957, shortly after his return from Knob Lake, James went down to Barbados again in order to attend the Second Annual Meeting of the Bellairs Research Institute Trust. On his return, he wrote a detailed account of the legal status of the venture and of the research prospects it provided. The link with the Caribbean that James had long sought to create had now been firmly established, and for more than thirty years the institute has proved itself a most valuable research-base.

A third major journey that year – to Indonesia in August – may have been even more welcome as an escape from pressures at home. James' brother Douglas, his wife Flo, and their two daughters, Pat and Judy, arrived in Canada to spend the summer in Montreal and were joined by James' sister Florrie for two weeks. But for the host the visit was not entirely pleasurable.

13 July 1957

Digs and Flo have been here three weeks; Florrie (who goes back to Vancouver this afternoon) for the past fortnight. I think they are all happy, and are enjoying the holiday – but even in that [situation] I somehow feel outside of the group rather than a member of it. A funny sort of way of living ...

When, five days later, the Indonesian embassy telephoned with the unexpected invitation to participate, in August, in Indonesia's independence celebration, James did not hesitate to accept, despite the short notice, even though it meant deserting the family in the middle of a tour of Nova Scotia.

11 August 1957

... I left [Digs, Flo, Pat and Judy] at Pugwash (much to Flo's annoyance!) to fly to Montreal and out here [Vancouver] on my way to Indonesia. Florrie (whom I hope to see this afternoon) spent the first two weeks of July with us in Montreal, so we have had the first family reunion since 1926, and enjoyed it.

I think, however, that short reunions are better than long ones – and two months of Flo is a little too much. It is also difficult to have a whole family camping for that long in one's house and rather taking it over, so that I am not really sorry (apart from the fact that it will be strenuous) to have received unexpectedly this invitation from Sukarno[1] to go out to Indonesia for a couple of weeks as his guest and participate in the celebrations of independence. [Professor] Wilfred Smith [Director of the McGill Islamic Institute], who arrives in Vancouver this afternoon, comes with me – and I am looking forward (my mind remembering H.M. Tomlinson's essays) to seeing the spice islands, whose names have always been a distant dream of bliss. I expect the reality will be different!

He was right; Sukarno, who had emerged after the collapse of the Japanese invasion of the islands as the strong man of the newly independent Republic of Indonesia, was determined to westernize his country as quickly as possible. His guests on this occasion were a mixed bag of VIP's, including two German academics, the McGill representatives (invited because of the growing reputation of the McGill Institute for Islamic Studies), a group from Tunisia, (invited for political reasons), and the vice-president of Yugoslavia. Their function, it soon became clear, was to add distinction to the Independence Day celebrations. On arrival in Djakarta, they were given red-carpet treatment by government officials, but with a noticeable lack of personal attention by their host. Sukarno, on the one occasion when James and the other Western guests saw him privately, apologized that he could give them so little of his time, but said he had to give precedence to the representative of the Yugoslav head of state (as he described the vice-president), who had apparently accepted the invitation only at the last moment. This circumstance had disrupted previous plans for the other guests' entertainment. Government or academic persons, hurriedly named to look after the Western guest, did so efficiently, and often graciously, but clearly as a matter of assigned duties.

At the one audience granted by Sukarno, James had no individual conversation with the president. He talked briefly with one of the leaders of the Masjumi opposition party but concluded that that party were no more realistic in their thinking than Sukarno and his supporters. At the Canadian embassy, the ambassador George Heaseman and the political secretary Paul Trottier discussed with James the role of the well-organized Communist party, the immense tactical problems in controlling the far-flung Indonesian archipelago (the outer islands were currently in revolt against Java and the central government), and also the contending policies and roles of China and Japan. They suggested that Sukarno was primarily engaged in a complex balancing act. All this James weighed in his mind and measured against the evidence of his own eyes.

My impressions are hurried: the harbour and the warehouses seem too big for their present use, and are not well cared-for – so that I should assume that the volume of trade is now much less than it was when Batavia was the great entrepot port of this area ... The men and women, bathing and washing clothes in the canal along one of Djakarta's main streets; the tired throngs in many different costumes walking home from work at the end of the day, and the primitive nature of the huts in many parts of both Djakarta and Tanjangpriok – all of these suggest a good deal of poverty and a fairly low standard of living. Yet I saw no signs of under-nourishment (such as are everywhere in India) among either the young or the old. The thousands of cycle-rickshaws (many of them delightfully decorated) and solid, prosperous appearances of many of the houses, as well as the large number of automobiles ... attest the fact that many folk are reasonably well-off ...

The country is, I think, more prosperous than India and the standard of living is higher – but I have the feeling that economic plans and political policies are not yet as clearly formulated. The general purpose seems to be to westernize the country ... I feel as I did in India, that there must, and should be, a middle road – a plan that enables these people to retain much of their tradition and social organisation, as well as their enjoyment of life, and yet to work together in the improvement of their lot. Education is important – but I do not think that western communities are so happy that Indonesia should slavishly copy them.

The bonus for James of this hurried jaunt across half the world was the opportunity to discover a very different and beautifully rich human culture. Although the visitors had been somewhat crudely manipulated as stage-properties to enhance Sukarno's show-day, they were paid handsomely for their services: car-drives and train-journeys up into the forested mountains of the interior, a visit to a plantation to view the elaborate processes of producing tea, and one evening, after dinner with the president of Gadjah Magda University in his home, a performance of Indonesian dance by students.

When the party crossed into the island of Bali they also crossed the boundary between the Muslim and Hindu cultures of Indonesia. One occasion was particularly memorable.

After a rather hurried dinner, we were driven a little further to the village of Peliatan where a village festival was to be held this evening; and, sitting in the torchlight among the villagers clustered in the square in front of the temple, we witnessed some of the most lovely and impressive dancing that I have ever seen. No words can describe the colour of the costumes or the precise muscular control of the dancers ... By this time we had fallen under the spell of Bali with its Hindu traditions reaching back more than a thousand years, and solidified after the Muslims had conquered the rest of Indonesia. There are temples everywhere, each village has at least one, many of them with statues exquisitely carved in stone that rest upon the red brick walls. There are little shrines outside many of the houses, and scattered through the rice fields. No man could count the total number ... Tuesday August 27th was my last day in Indonesia and, when I woke shortly after five o'clock, I found myself wishing that the trip had been twice as long, so that there were more opportunity to observe and reflect.

Why did James accept this unexpected invitation to visit Indonesia? In part, no doubt, as an excuse to disentangle himself from family involvement; in large part, also, to support Wilfred Smith and the McGill Institute of Islamic Studies in the effort to gain recognition in an important Muslim country – an effort that has proved highly profitable over the intervening years in fellowships and research opportunities. But the main reason was, we suggest, that Cyril James could not resist the challenge to learn a new subject; knowing practically nothing of Indonesia before he received Sukarno's invitation, he undoubtedly got in a good deal of reading in the three weeks before leaving, and by the time he returned on 5 September, after travelling over 20,000 miles, he had penetrated deeply into Muslim and Hindu culture. He had seen a new nation grappling with the problems of independence and gained a grasp of the Indonesian situation. On his return, he settled down to write his observations, experiences, and conclusions. His report is a carefully composed, often beautifully written document of forty pages, marked "Personal and Confidential"; probably he and Mrs McMurray were the only ones, while he lived, who ever saw it.

A break with the past was signalled in the spring of 1958 by the fact that his brother's daughter, Patricia, was graduating in May. She had spent five years in residence at Macdonald College, the subsidiary campus of McGill, but in his various diary-notes, James had made little mention of her. Since the notes were quite sporadic, that omission was quite fortuitous. She had, however, evidently been coming and going, on weekends and vacations, as opportunities and choice prompted her, and Cyril had been happy to play the detached but friendly role of the "useful uncle." Now he realized he was going to miss her very much.

Sunday, May 4, 1958
Pat comes home from Macdonald College today – probably for the last

time since I expect that she has passed her examinations, and will graduate this month. Her five years in Montreal (a quarter of the time I have been here) thus come to an end, and the place will seem a great deal lonelier.

When Patricia did graduate, he had the pleasure of "capping" her for her degree. She for her part later recalled both her shorter and her longer visits with genuine pleasure. "I was very fond of them both – probably slightly more of Irene because ... I could always have a laugh and a giggle with Irene, even when the atmosphere at 1200 Pine was strained, and I didn't know the reason why. Cyril on the other hand was always slightly reserved and shy, even with the members of his own family, although I remember vividly how relaxed he was the summer I spent with him in Montreal and all the crazy things we did together – something he never would have done had Irene been there."[2] This is welcome firsthand testimony that Irene could have a good giggle and that Cyril could relax and do crazy things. Both of them must have felt Patricia's departure very deeply.

Something else also came to an end that spring of 1958. All his life James had lived strenuously, assuming that his good health (apart from a cold or two) would continue uninterrupted. But in April he had a letter from his physician, Lorne Montgomery, telling him that recent tests showed his blood-pressure had been climbing and, more ominously, that sometime during the past year he had suffered "a so-called silent coronary thrombosis." "I do think you will have to go more easily," Montgomery wrote. He suggested a taxi home in the evenings, for the long climb up to 1200 Pine, and added in a postscript, "Would also suggest definite moderations with tobacco and alcohol."

All this set Cyril wondering again.

Somehow the past session has seen so much of change – the death of Dad and Mum [Leeper][3] emptying life of a long friendship, Monty's discovery of my own heart condition, which ends the complete reliability of my own health (on which perhaps I have relied too much) and now Pat's imminent departure for the U.K. – all of this adds up to so great a change in life that I am ending the session with the sort of feeling that each of the familiar end-of-term routines is the last occasion on which I shall perform the task at McGill. The mood is heightened by the persistent rumours on St. James Street that I am to become the Governor of the Bank of Canada – rumours that have no foundation, but have touched alive in me the memories of the days when central banking and monetary theory were my chief excitement. I have been wondering whether this is the time to resign from McGill and to undertake the history of the Federal Reserve System – about which I have thought fondly since I had to turn the offer down.

He had received the invitation to write the history of the American Federal Reserve System in 1953 from the Reserve City Bankers' Association but had decided it would be too much to take on in addition to his administrative responsibilities at McGill. However, he now heard that no candidate had yet been found and that the responsible committee was proposing to cancel the project and disband. In his unsettled mood he was ready to flirt with the idea of resignation, and to take up the committee's challenge, but it was only a flirtation. Something else intervened in June to re-whet his appetite for university affairs. "Strangely enough the NCCU meetings in Edmonton during the past four days ... have given me more of a feeling that I can still do something useful than anything that has happened for many months."

This "something useful" was the opportunity to exercise his old mastery of business-meeting procedures by steering through the unwieldy Edmonton conference a new structure for the NCCU. As a discussion-body, the NCCU needed no definite structure or powers, but once the association had been charged with distributing large sums of federal government money to the universities, the need for a legally constituted corporation became urgent. James was asked to chair a committee to find a solution to the problem. The committee's proposal (in reality, Cyril James' proposal, as everyone well knew) was to incorporate a body to be known as the Canadian Universities' Foundation, which would be able to receive the funds from the federal government and then, in accordance with governmental norms and its own enacted by-laws, distribute grants to the various universities. The NCCU would continue to meet annually for its traditional discussions, but it would be the CUF that would present to governments, both federal and provincial, the needs and opinions of the universities, as expressed in those conferences. The CUF would also administer the Rhodes Scholarships, the Commonwealth Scholarship Plan – which had become a considerable feature of the Canadian university scene – and a number of other scholarship programs, as well as the NATO visiting professorships. It would report on its activities each year to the NCCU, which would have the responsibility of electing the members of the CUF, as individuals and for a stated term of years. The president of the NCCU would be the chairman of the CUF and the two bodies would share one secretariat. The great advantage of the new arrangement would be the gain in continuity and the possibility of advance planning. The consideration of continuity was an extremely important item, for the NCCU was an amorphous and a constantly changing body: many participants attended only one or two meetings and had no knowledge of its history or long-term goals. Adoption of James' plan meant, however, that the universities, particularly the smaller ones, would be putting their trust, and indeed their financial welfare, into the hands of the elected members of the CUF. It was a great deal to ask, and it says much for James' persuasive powers that he was successful.

I thoroughly enjoyed the job of piloting the report of the Membership Committee through the sessions, and am happy at the almost complete unanimity (only D.C. Masters [of Bishop's] dissenting) with which the final version was accepted. I think that the structure of the Canadian Universities' Foundation really gives the kind of efficient university body that we have long needed, and [until now] found no way to create without hurting anybody's feelings. So that it was doubly pleasant to find so many people – especially from the smaller universities – enthusiastic about the final report.

The CUF was designed to meet an urgent need and in part succeeded well. By 1960, it was administering upwards of $30 million annually to the universities' general satisfaction, and it continued to do so for another five years, until Prime Minister Pearson's announcement in 1966, that the federal grant to universities would no longer be made through the CUF but through the provinces, robbed the foundation of a great deal of its *raison d'être*. Moreover, the late sixties became a time of mutual distrust in academic relationships, with students against staff, staff against governing boards and academics bitterly divided one against another. One of the early casualties was the Canadian Universities' Foundation. The NCCU itself, bereft of any great responsibilities, became a large, amorphous talkshop, with no sense of national purpose or presence, and faded into obscurity. James' scheme had one serious flaw: the cumbersome method of electing the CUF governors. But given goodwill, that part of the structure could have been amended and the great benefits of experience and continuity retained. In the confusion of the academic scene after 1966, however, there were no successors to such national figures as Sidney Smith of Toronto, Norman MacKenzie of UBC, W.A. Mackintosh of Queen's – or Cyril James of McGill. Instead, university presidents were each hastening off to his own provincial capital, and there was no longer a need of, or the vision for, a Canadian Universities' Foundation. But its eight years of effective existence remain as a testimony to James' managerial skills.

In 1958, however, the troubled days of the 1960s lay hidden in the future, and an air of optimism pervaded the campuses. The NCCU was to play host to the Association of British Commonwealth Universities, gathering for its quinquennial conference for the first time outside Britain. The preliminary meeting of the "executive heads" of the AUBC universities was to take place on the campus of the University of Toronto, with the main conference following in Montreal, where McGill and l'Université de Montréal would be the local hosts. In the pleasant academic fashion in which the Americans are accorded a style of honorary membership of the Commonwealth, some representatives of the American Association of Universities had attended the seventh Congress held in Cambridge in 1953. Their experience must have been agreeable, for in 1958 a considerably larger number of American presidents were planning to attend the Congress in Montreal, and had invited the executive heads attending the AUBC to pay them a reciprocal visit in Washington and Philadelphia at the end of the congress. While this visit was taking place, the remaining representatives of AUBC were scheduled to visit Quebec City, to be entertained by l'Université Laval and to attend a reception given by the governor-general in the citadel. After these excursions, everyone was to reassemble in Montreal in order to participate in one of eleven tours. As the AUBC *Proceedings* phrased it:

It was the wish of the Executive Council of the AUBC in planning its first large overseas Congress, that the delegates should thereby be given the opportunity of seeing not only the universities but also the physical environment of the country they were visiting, and in the fulfilment of this wish it was assisted by a generous gift from the Carnegie Corporation of New York which enabled it to offer to each delegate visiting Canada for the congress a planned tour of part of North America during the fortnight after its conclusion.

Seeing that so many academics were going to be gathered in one location, it also seemed sensible to organize a meeting of the Administrative Board of the International Association of Universities, of which James had been an assiduous member since the congress in Turkey in 1955. This proposal brought into the Montreal assembly the representatives of yet another dozen or so universities, including those of such renown as Brussels, Helsinki, Leyden, Istanbul, and Hiroshima. Altogether, the 1958 congress was as remarkable a gathering of the world's educational leaders as had ever been brought together in one place, and the one man who had intimate associations with all three rings of the *circus academicus* – Commonwealth, American, and international – was their gracious, competent, and ever-resourceful host, the principal and vice-chancellor of McGill, F. Cyril James.

At the more select gathering in Toronto over one hundred Commonwealth universities were represented by their executive heads, together with presidents of twelve American universities and seven national associations of universities. The following week the numbers of those attending the sessions in Montreal rose to above five hundred. The opening session in the Sir Arthur Currie Gymnasium, presided by the governor-general, was followed by receptions in the McGill principal's residence. A special convocation for the award of honorary degrees was staged in the sunshine of the lower campus, a McGill university dinner was offered under the great oak roof of the Redpath Hall, another reception and a dinner was given by l'Université de Montréal in the Centre Social, a state dinner was presided by the secretary of state for External Affairs in the Queen Elizabeth Hotel, and yet another dinner was given by the city of Montreal in the chalet atop Mount Royal. In all these grand occasions, James, as the chairman of the Canadian Organizing Committee and the chief local host, was deeply involved. He felt that if anything went wrong, it would reflect upon him personally, but if everything went well, McGill must compare at least equitably with Toronto. A great deal of the planning had been done by the NCCU secretariat, and still more by the local entertainment committee, and some of the burden was carried by l'Université de Montréal and its rector, Mgr Irénée Lussier, but the main responsibility lay squarely on James' shoulders.

There were some other subsidiary yet important events to take note of, satellite occasions, as it were, of the main events – a garden party in the Royal Victoria College for the Congress of University Women, a meeting of the General Assembly of World University Service at la Maison Montmorency outside Quebec City, and a very large "sideshow," the Tenth International Congress of Genetics, which proved to be "an outstanding success." But the real business was the Congress of the AUBC. The *Proceedings* record that

the sessions of the Congress were held in Moyse Hall in the Arts Building of McGill University for the first four days and in the University of

Montreal Auditorium on the fifth. The Congress was opened on Monday, 1st September, in the Sir Arthur Currie Memorial Gymnasium-Armoury by His Excellency the Rt. Hon. Vincent Massey, Governor-General of Canada, who had agreed to be the Patron of the Congress ... The working sessions of the Congress began the following morning and continued for the rest of the week. The principle set of topics were "Who should determine University Policy?", "Engineering Education and its Place in the University", "Medical Education and its Place in the University", and "The Establishment of new Universities" ... [On Friday] the executive heads of Commonwealth universities embarked as guests of the A.A.U. on a special train which took them first to Washington, where they were received by President Eisenhower at tea at the White House and where they were also addressed by Mr. Justice Frankfurter at the Supreme Court, and to Philadelphia where they were entertained by the University of Pennsylvania.

All this activity, including the visit to Washington and Pennsylvania, was passed over with no personal comment by James, but he must have had some anxious moments while the program unfolded at McGill and surely some moments of pride when he showed his friends from the Commonwealth the campus of his own alma mater, the stately University of Pennsylvania. What we do know is that the week at McGill was judged by all to have been a resounding success, and that James joined the party that took the special train down to Washington, Philadelphia, and back to Montreal. On his return, on 9 September, however, he left the eleven AUBC tours to begin their two weeks of wandering across Canada, while he boarded a chartered bus for Ste Marguerite in the Laurentian Mountains with the other members of the Administrative Board of the International Association of Universities. Here he first entertained the board to dinner at the Alpine Inn, and then joined in their discussions of the future of the IAU – it was time to give his attention to the third ring of his circus.

For him this was no mere side show: it was fully part of the main event; significantly, while he kept only the programs of the AUBC and the AAU activities, he retained a full, typewritten copy of the minutes of the IAU meeting at Ste Marguerite. James was chairman of the committee that had the oversight of publishing for the IAU, and one exchange of views recorded in the minutes shows the kind of importance he attached to the international body.

The Chairman thanked [Roger Keyes, the IAU Secretary] and said the members should discuss the suggestion made by Dr. James the previous day. [He had said] the time may have come for the Board to consider the question of future policy of the Association. The work of gathering reference manual material had established the IAU as important, but if this continues the Association could become merely a center of documentation. It should perhaps now enter into the study of broader educational problems.

Dr. James said that the proposed International Handbook of Universities, [placed alongside] the already existing "American Universities and Colleges" and "Commonwealth Universities Yearbook" would be Vol. III of the trilogy and would be a central reference work. Yesterday's question [was intended to highlight] the point of departure after this book is published in 1959.

James wanted this publication date to be the starting point of new developments for the IAU. He wanted to see the organization reaching out to the broader educational problems he had mentioned the previous day.

The rest of the conference concerned the qualification of various universities seeking membership, the delicate question of the circumstances in which institutions in Eastern Europe could be regarded as "independent institutions," and arrangements for the next IAU congress to be held in Mexico in 1960. At the end of it all, James wrote a summary note, the last paragraph of which shows that despite his remarkable tolerance for wordy, procedural discussions, he also retained a capacity for human reactions.

Thursday, September 11, 1958
The meetings of the Administration Board have gone very well during the past three days ... Looking back, I think that the whole thing has been a great success – Toronto, Montreal, Washington and Ste. Marguerite. More people attended from all parts of the world, and notably more of them brought wives. The business sessions were well attended, and the social events were a great success, so that more people met one another than at any previous university congress in which I have participated. In the long run, I suppose, that is the real purpose of these meetings.

Should I add a note about [the young woman who acted as secretary to the IAU Board]? It was on the spur of the moment, at the Mayor's banquet, a week ago, that I asked her to take on the job (since I had hoped that Mrs. McMurray would do it). During the past couple of days I have found myself thinking of her almost as much as about the IAU. She is the only person really worth looking at around the table!

Since the minutes give in detail the reports, comments and interjections (some of which were in French, which the young woman in question confessed she had followed only with difficulty), it appears that she at least must have kept her mind strictly on the task at hand. Probably in a roomful of mature academics, she found nothing to distract her.

The success of these meetings and of the tours that followed strengthened the bonds between the Canadian universities that had jointly hosted the congress and further consolidated James' position of leadership in Canada, where he was now one of the longest-serving executive heads in the NCCU. The members of his own university also took pride in the fact that their principal was accepted as a leader by academics from the world's oldest and most venerable institutions.

After the great strain of the congress, James needed rest and relaxation. He spent two weeks clearing up the backlog of work in his office and then flew to Vancouver. He had become so much a conference person that his idea of relaxation was to catch up with congress tour number eleven and join them in a series of visits to west-coast universities. At UBC, which laid on an "open house" program, he had the opportunity to see at first hand what his colleague Norman MacKenzie was making of that swiftly expanding institution and how he was coping with the same twin pressures as beset McGill – the need to build new facilities quickly and the need to establish new disciplines. Annoyingly, James makes no comment, either on the development of the institution or on MacKenzie's accomplishments as president. Although the two men were very different in personality and style, they had long served the same cause (MacKenzie from 1940–4 at the University of New Brunswick and since 1944 at UBC), and their work at the NCCU had been mutually complementary – MacKenzie as chairman of the Postwar Needs Committee and later a member of the Massey Commission, James as chairman of the Finance Committee and orchestrator of the drive for federal funding. But whereas much of MacKenzie's strength lay in his gregariousness, James found personal relationships difficult and uneasy. The two men worked well together,[4] but temperamentally they were too incompatible to become friends, and James passed over MacKenzie's successes on the new campus at Point Grey without mention.

On the other hand, he found much to interest him and to excite his envy south of the border on campuses at Washington, Stanford, Berkeley, Los Angeles (where the party attended the installation of Clark Kerr as the twelfth president of the University of California), and Albuquerque. It had been an informative, if not relaxing, tour. James found himself regretting it was ending.

This is the end of what has been a fascinating – and exhausting – experience. Ever since I took the train from Montreal to Toronto on August 24th I have been involved for most of the hours in each day in the affairs of the University congress – AAU, AUBC and IAU – so that I felt a real sadness yesterday afternoon when I said goodbye to the rest of the group and waved to them as their bus started off to Santa Fe. To my surprise, Baughniet[5] called me into the bus just before they left, and made a speech of thanks as he handed me a handsome book that all of the group had signed to "the inspirer of the trip". I suppose, as I look back, that I was, but I had forgotten the fact in realizing how many folk have worked to make it a success – but I enjoyed the words and the thoughts. After they had gone, I found that Felim Firat[6] had left me a package of real Turkish cigarettes from Ismir – which was equally touching.

  Somehow it is easier for me to do things than to accept thanks for doing them – but I have enjoyed this group and was sad at parting from them.

It was not, however, only the stimulation of his colleagues that had enriched this tour with pleasurable memories. In San Francisco he had written:

Sunday has not been a day of rest! The group decided to go sightseeing ... and I went along. We saw the usual sights in the city, and then drove out to Muir Woods to see the redwood trees, and that memory I cherish. Mrs. Merikoski [wife of the Rector of Helsinki] and I left the solid phalanx of the party, and its verbose guide, to wander among the trees by ourselves. In spite of the temperature of 95 Degrees it was cool in the heart of the woods and pleasant to walk: in spite of children playing, it was quiet.

Recalling that "cherished memory," we are a little intrigued by the ways James continues his comment on the departure of the other members of his tour group from Albuquerque.

To be truthful, *all* the group did not leave yesterday. Mrs. Merikoski stayed behind because she wanted to see the horses at the County Fair. Last night I took her to dinner and then we went out to the Rodeo – which she enjoyed for the horses and I because of the local colour of a part of the United States that I have not seen for a long time. This reminds me of Fort Worth, Bloomington, Topeka and a dozen other cities

– small cities of the Middle West and South West that are entirely different from Los Angeles or New York or Chicago. The clothes are different – the coats and dresses as well as the boots and wide-brimmed hats. The prices are lower and life is simpler. Here, too, the city has an air that is all its own because of the large number of Indians and of people of Spanish descent. One forgets that New Mexico was colonised by the Spaniards at the same time that Jacques Cartier was in the St. Lawrence – long before the Pilgrims landed in Massachusetts.

Horses, rodeo, local colour – and Mrs Merikoski – that was another "cherished memory" to bring pleasantly to a close what had been a most exciting summer.

While in Vancouver in September, James had made time to visit with his sister Florrie and her husband John Grull. She had told him then that she was due to retire at the end of the year after thirty-four years with the BC Telephone company. The retirement took place as planned, but only two months later James received a telegram informing him of John Grull's death. He flew out to comfort his sister in her bereavement and to attend the funeral. He enclosed a copy of the order of service in his private file, so he evidently thought well of John Grull. He also preserved a page of a BC Telephone Company magazine showing Florrie receiving the gift of a television set from her former colleagues at the time of her retirement. The photo shows a sharp featured, elderly lady, wearing a smile reminiscent of Cyril's own. Whoever John Grull was, he had made a home and a life for an immigrant girl from England, who apparently had no other support or friends in Canada. Her life had been very different from her brother's, but he must have been glad that in the midst of all his other preoccupations the previous September, he had found time to visit Florrie and her husband in their North Vancouver home.

In the year 1959, relations between the super-powers East and West had reached an uneasy stalemate. The Cold War had heated into an armed conflict in Korea in 1951, but this ended in an indecisive truce in 1954. In the United States, in the early 1950s, Senator Joseph R. McCarthy conducted a witch hunt against "crypto-communists" in high places, a program that besmirched the reputations of many persons in the government, the armed forces, and, particularly, the entertainment industry. McCarthy was finally censured in 1954 by his fellow senators for behaviour unbecoming to his office and was deprived of his influence, but his accusations and suspicions lingered long after his departure. Even in the middle 1980s, President Reagan could still refer to the Soviet Union as "that evil empire."

In Quebec an "Act Respecting Communist Propaganda" had been passed as early as 1937, by which those convicted of teaching communist ideas were liable to fine or imprisonment, and premises used for such purposes could be seized or closed for one year. Although the act had been declared unconstitutional by the Supreme Court of Canada in 1957, the man who had devised it, and who was the self-proclaimed enemy of all "socialist" thought, Maurice Duplessis, was still in complete control of the province.

The year 1959 was therefore not a good time for anyone in North America to be planning a visit to the USSR, and particularly not advisable for anyone in a prominent educational position in the Province of Quebec. Popular sentiment in Canada and the United States was still strongly anti-Marxist and anti-Soviet. Nevertheless, on 7 April 1959, James set out in good spirits for an extensive tour behind the Iron Curtain. He had private reason to be in a contented mood. The previous day the Executive Committee of the Board of Governors had raise his salary to $35,000 (about five times the salary of a full professor at that time)[7] and had agreed to supply him with a university car: "so," he recorded, "I left the University fairly happy."

How James came to be involved in this tour is not clear, but it is known that the president of the University of Michigan, Harlan Hatcher, had applied to the Ford Foundation for a grant to permit a small delegation from his university to visit the Soviet Union, primarily to investigate the teaching of literature, the humanities, and the arts in Soviet higher education institutions, with special emphasis on the teaching of foreign languages, as well as to explore the conditions, opportunities, and experiences of students in the Soviet system. Even on the premise "know thine enemy," that would have seemed a commendable exercise. James probably heard about the venture from his contacts with the Ford Foundation, which at this time were particularly close, and ever-anxious for a new experience, may himself have suggested that he be invited to join the party. In the event it comprised Dr and Mrs Hatcher, Dr and Mrs Norman Auburn (he was president of Akron University), William Dewey, a young Russian-speaking professor, Lyle Nelson, professor of journalism and director of public relations (the latter two both from the University of Michigan), William Pine, director of the scholarship program of the Ford Motor Company Fund, and Cyril James. He thought of the group as "the Ford Foundation party," and was a little annoyed when

Hatcher insisted on calling it a University of Michigan mission – "which makes it a little hard for me to place myself." Possibly Hatcher had already found it difficult to remain the number one person in a group containing Cyril James. Although no friendships emerged such as had developed in the group that undertook the west-coast odyssey, the party seems to have achieved and maintained congenial relationships in all their month-long journeyings.

The party was taken first to Moscow, Leningrad, Kiev, and Georgia, to visit the universities and also to see the tourist sights. James evidently took copious notes at interviews; on his return, he prepared not simply a detailed confidential document for his own satisfaction, as he usually did after these trips abroad, but also a small printed volume, *On Understanding Russia*, which sets out efficiently and succinctly a great deal of the information he gathered.[8] But it is his diary notes that provide the local colour and illuminate his personal experiences. Unfortunately, these were infrequent and for some reason ended after his visit to Tbilisi in the Georgian Republic.

Sunday, April 26 – Palm Sunday (Greek Orthodox) Tibilisi [*sic*] This is an attractive town, set in the basin of the surrounding hills, and in spite of the fact that it has been drizzling all the morning the loveliness of spring enfolds it. The new green leaves – of a dozen different shades – the lilacs, and the hundreds of trees that I do not know, with small red blossoms the shape of a pea-flower are delightful. Every street is lined with trees, and the lilacs are in bloom – I find myself liking it immensely and – as so often – wishing that I understood Russian so that I could talk with the people and understand something of their minds.

Last night we saw a Georgian Ballet – with what I suppose are historic Georgian costumes – and it was delightful. More and more I begin to think that we must refine our definition of the humanities if this group is to fulfil this mission. Ballet, opera, theatre and symphony concerts – these are all splendidly available in every town that we have visited, and New York could not improve the stagery. All that we call culture is here in abundance – and the facilities available for the training of youngsters are excellent. Knowledge of foreign languages is more widespread than with us – and the facilities for having specialists, once again, are better than anything that we have to offer. People read more – and read more widely. All this is evidence of the vitality of the humanities – a vitality greater than what we have in North America.

The other half of the question is less clear. What would happen to Socrates, Descartes or any other rebellious questioning mind in this society? Athens condemned Socrates. I am not sure how long he would survive

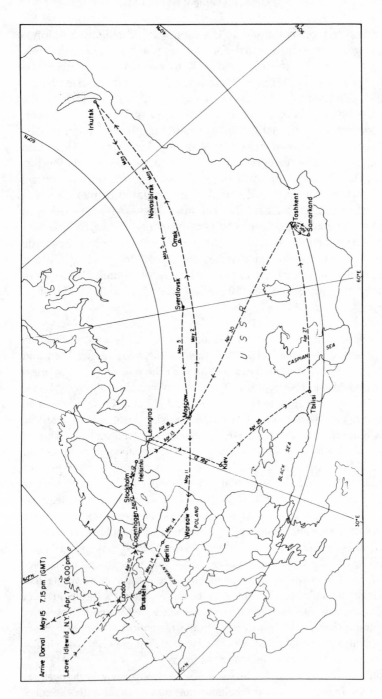

James' Soviet tour, 1959.

in North America – but I think his opportunity to corrupt youth would be shorter here.

Seeing the Soviet Union when he did, in the dark chill of the Cold War, James' readiness to appreciate the positive achievements of Soviet exploration of the humanities testifies to the breadth of his judgments.

After Tbilisi he scribbled the occasional remark on some itinerary sheets, but that is the only remaining record of his personal impressions, and it remains unknown what he thought as he experienced the splendours and the tragedy of the Central Asian republics and visited the markets and great mosques of Tashkent, Samarkand, and Bokara, or what he thought on the huge flight from Moscow to Irkutsk and back (as far as from Montreal to Moscow), all to see some wooden cottages, an onion-domed church or two, and a lake – or was it rather to glimpse the resurgent vitality of Russian culture, which not even 3,000 miles of *taiga* could suppress? Again, what went through his mind as he stood in Red Square in Moscow on May Day and saw the might of the Soviet armed forces paraded before the Soviet commanders? Unfortunately, these thoughts are not recorded. On 8 May he had an interview in the Kremlin with Anastasias Mikoyan, at that time first vice-chairman of the Council of Ministers, but James' private papers record that Henry Heald, president of the Ford Foundation, and his colleague Shephard Stone were also present. A week later, James lectured on Canada to the Moscow Institute of World Economics – but the only diary comment is "two hours of discussion!" This at least suggests the lecture was stimulating.

A visit by car to two of the Soviet Union's oldest cities rounded off the journey. The party left Moscow on 10 May, driving 130 miles north-west to Vladimir, second in age only to Kiev and, like that city, an important staging-post for the early Viking traders. After visiting with great appreciation the old city gates and the Cathedral of St Vladimir, the party continued another sixty miles, in bright sunshine, through rolling pasture land dotted with dairy herds, to Susdaal, "a small village of log houses, with fourteen great monasteries and churches – pure middle ages, as unique as Samarkand."

Some last-minute diary notes written on his return to Moscow sum up James' personal comments.

Sunday, May 10, 1959

Tomorrow we shall leave Russia – via Warsaw – and I shall have completed a most interesting month. There have been frustrations – some of them inherent in the membership of the party, some arising from a language that I do not know and an alphabet that I can scarcely read, some from the Russian way of doing things ...

If one wants to be captious there is enough to criticize – but the frustrations are small compared to the very real pleasure of being here. I like the people that I have had a chance to sit down and talk with – all the way from Leningrad to Samarkand and Irkutsk. I am delighted by what remains of old Russia (and happy that so much has been preserved not only in the Kremlin and the Hermitage but in the form of old buildings) and I have the greatest admiration for what this generation of Russians is trying to do in the fields of economics and education. I shall leave with reluctance – because I should genuinely like to stay and learn more, as well as to enjoy the ballet and the opera, and I hope very much that I shall come back!

These are clearly the comments of an open-minded man, ready to appreciate what is good in a culture markedly different from his own. He was by no means a convert to Communism, nor was he strongly antagonistic – he was ready to be critical, but also to appreciate. But like all travellers from the West on exiting from the Iron Curtain countries, his appreciative comment on arriving in Brussels was "What a contrast!"

When he returned to Montreal, James wrote six long articles for *The Montreal Star*, which he then furnished with a brief introduction and published that same year as the small book, *On Understanding Russia*. This volume, depending in large measure as it did on the author's own notes and experiences, was balanced and reliable. Tables of statistics illustrated the text. A great deal of the material is, of course, now dated, but for a snapshot impression of what the USSR was like in the Khrushchev years, it is still an important and trustworthy source.

One or two paragraphs are particularly worth quoting. In the introduction, James tried to help his readers understand the depth and sincerity of the prevalent Soviet belief in the validity of Communism as a political philosophy – indeed, *the* political philosophy – by reporting on his interview with Anastasias Mikoyan.

Communism is a new force in the world, and Russia believes in Communism. There is no doubt about that. Mr. Anastasias Mikoyan, when he received us in the Kremlin shortly before our departure from Moscow, opened the discussion by pointing out that Russia differed from western countries in believing that Karl Marx had formulated the philosophy which would, in the long run, appeal to the minds of all men throughout the world. This ultimate victory of Communism, he emphasized, was not a matter of military conquest but of intellectual conviction. Many generations might pass before all men became convinced, but ultimate conversion, in his opinion, and that of most Russians, is inevitable. Mr. Mikoyan was merely stating briefly, and cogently, the idea that seems to lie at the back of the minds of all the people we met in the U.S.S.R. ...[9]

After this introduction, James selects for each of his seven chapters an instance of the way in which the system of belief affects and shapes the life of the Soviet people and their institutions. Naturally, with his interest in educational patterns and institutions, most of his material relates to those subjects, but in the process he ranges widely over Soviet intentions and activities. His seven chapters are "Universities, Colleges and Research Institutes," "The University Student," "The Relation of Education to Life," "The Cultural Pleasures of Life," "The Embers of Religion," and "Freedom of Thought?" Obviously, in sixty pages he cannot provide a comprehensive survey, but he does give the reactions and judgements of a highly intelligent and widely experienced observer. The importance of the book lay in its acceptance of the fact that by 1959 the Communist way of life was an established order, and that, as far as anyone could then see, changes of top-ranking office-holders would not alter the fundamental convictions. In James' words, "We must recognize this fact and live with it."[10] This was certainly the way things looked then and continued to look for another twenty-five years. But James also wrote:

One of the significant things about Russia is that there is more freedom of thought today than there was ten years ago ... Whether conditions will return to the dark night of oppression and regimentation, or continue to develop toward still greater freedom, I do not know. I have no gift of prophecy. It is my own opinion that the present educational effort of Russia, which encourages millions of able young men and women to think, to ask questions, to discuss ideas, will make it harder and harder as the years go by for any future government to impose upon human thought the regimentation that Stalin imposed during the later years of his life. Only the passage of time can show whether that hypothesis is sound.[11]

The passage of thirty years has amply justified Cyril James in this faith in education. Mikoyan's dictum that the ultimate victory or defeat of Communism would be a matter not of military conquest but of intellectual conviction has been stunningly vindicated (if not in the way he or anyone else then expected) by the popular

Cyrille James, retour d'URSS

La Presse, 11 June 1959

rejection of Communism in Eastern Europe and its ongoing modification in the Soviet Union itself. James recognized the truth of
the dictum and put his views forth boldly, at a time when such
thoughts were not popular. Although the book was not substantial
enough to create a great stir, as a "tract for the times" it provided
a much-needed contribution to a debate in which the level tones
of reason were not often heard; as a voice from the past it records
a rare tolerance and an uncommon foresight.

Maurice Duplessis, of course, was enraged by the book, and
said many foolish things – and since he was still the powerful
premier of the province, these could not be dismissed with the
amused disregard they warrant now. But if the premier was angered
by James' boldness in reporting on his trip, at least the principal
had some support from the cartoonist of *La Presse*. On the other
hand, when the public relations officer of the university Al Tunis,
read *The Montreal Star* articles and warmly proposed to the principal
that the Board of Governors be asked to print them up as a
pamphlet for distribution to McGill's many graduates, James replied
that he did not think "the members of the Board would be very
enthusiastic." James knew that his readiness to appreciate what
was good in the Soviet system would not increase his popularity

with the business men who constituted the McGill governing body; but that risk he was prepared to take.

In April of the following year, 1960, James travelled to Jerusalem again, this time to participate in a survey of the progress of the Hebrew University. Most of his follow-up report concerned itself with the broader questions of Israel's future, rather than the university matters; those items he had presumably dealt with in the committee sessions. His written report perceptively analyzed how Israel had come to the present stage of development; it finished by stating there were three possible ways the young nation could hope to survive and, in comparative terms, to prosper: a slowing down if not elimination of the rise in the standard of living, a reduction in the rate of capital investment (which would ultimately have the same effect), or an increase in the aid received from sympathetic outside sources. James did not believe the first two options would prove acceptable; the real question facing Israel, he concluded, was whether the Jewish leaders in the homeland and abroad could generate sufficient concern to make the third option practical and achievable.

His report evoked a warm response from the Jewish authorities, especially President Mazar and George Wise, chairman of the Hebrew University Board of Governors. Here was another national enterprise to which Cyril James had devoted time and concern and personal effort, in order that he might understand its pattern of living and, if possible, encourage and assist it. He was more and more beginning to see eduction not in national or even Western terms, but as a global concern.

These international experiences of 1958, 1959, and the spring of 1960 proved to be the prelude to the main event, the Quinquennial Congress of the International Association of Universities, held in Mexico in September 1960. The declared purpose of the IAU – a creation of the United Nations Educational, Scientific and Cultural Organization in 1947 – was "to promote academic cooperation at the practical level, and in this way to provide useful services to university institutions around the world, as well as to other bodies concerned with higher education and scientific research." It sounded both straightforward and pragmatic, and by 1960 those intentions were being fulfilled. Another equally commendable purpose was to serve as a meeting place, where university administrators and teachers could gather to exchange information and opinions and renew the *consensus academicus*. This opportunity was well provided for Western universities by such organizations as the NCCU in Canada, or the AAU in the United States, or the AUBC in the British Commonwealth, but in many Third-World countries university administrators were trying to raise standards, create values, and defend their own integrity without the understanding of their own society or encouragement from abroad. For such men and women, the IAU provided an invaluable service, simply by its existence and its witness to academic ideals. Through its permanent secretariat in Paris, it also performed many useful clearing-house and publishing functions. James had recognized the potential of the association in 1955, when he saw it trying to put its house in order in Istanbul. Having secured election to the Administrative Board, he had then worked hard at improving the organization's performance – among other things bringing, as he did, the board members to Montreal in 1958, so they could see for themselves the AUBC's vitality and achievements. It was a practical homily on the text, "Go thou and do likewise." James' visit to the Soviet Union and his perception of the serious regard for education in the socialist countries had strengthened his commitment to international encouragement of higher education world wide. It is difficult to think of any university administrator among the three hundred or so attending the 1960 conference in Mexico City who had more knowledge of or zeal for international cooperation at the university level than Cyril James of Canada.

The conference opened on 6 September, with the Mexican president welcoming the delegates from more than sixty countries. The sessions were devoted to the three themes of the conference: "University Education and Public Service," "The Interplay of Scientific and Cultural Values in Higher Education Today," and "The Expansion of Higher Education." No one expected anything startlingly new to be said in these sessions, and the subjects themselves were hardly original; but like a folksong, they provided a familiar theme around which various speakers could weave a set of variations, which, when taken together, re-stated and re-expressed their common academic ideals.

Other delegates have referred to the psychological pressures of which they were aware (or which they fancied) in the high-altitude city. "Everywhere there was the pervading gloom of Aztec sacrificial crimson; the acres-wide murals of Revolution; the blood and sand of bull fights; the rain that fell every afternoon regularly at four; the 'melancholia' that Graham Greene claims afflicts all visitors."[12] But James had a more realistic and personal problem to wrestle with: he was being pressed to accept nomination for the presidency of the association. The arguments against taking on such a position were strong: Irene wanted him to work less and to be more available for her, certainly not to increase his responsibilities; the Board of Governors would not welcome the news of further distraction from what they saw as his main job; and he himself was beginning to wonder if he was attempting to carry too great a load. But if the position were offered him, how could he possibly refuse what would be the culmination of two decades of commitment to international university cooperation? It was something he had believed in, worked for, and sacrificed for; the opportunities to do good in the world would be so great; and his sense of personal achievement would be complete.

James explained his dilemma and ultimate decision in a letter to his niece Doreen.

... fundamentally, I suppose that my sense of irritation ... arises from the fact that throughout the past week a variety of delegations – U.K., France, U.S., Sudan, Japan, German (and even Russian!) – have been buttonholing me to urge me to take on the Presidency of the International Association of Universities! I had thought about this in a random way a couple of years ago and then rejected the idea. It is too big a job – tremendous opportunities in the present world, but demanding lots of work and infinite patience if any of those opportunities are to be realised – and I had come to the conclusion that I wanted a little more rest and leisure in which to write; not a chance to work even harder than I have these past 5 years. I am irritable and lonely – because everybody talks about a job and nobody thinks about me! Childish? Yes, I agree, but I know in my heart that the work is important and that I cannot refuse if they decide on Monday that they want me to do it ...

And so, when nominations were called for Cyril James allowed his name to stand.

Colin McDougall, an accomplished writer and novelist, who was also one of the McGill delegates at the Congress, has provided a lively account of the circumstances of the election process.[13] His narrative, somewhat tongue-in-cheek and preserved in a draft heavily scored with crossings-out (some of which have been restored, because the embellishments were too good to omit), conveys the excitement and drama of what must have been a most unusual academic conference.

The congress was to last for six days, from Tuesday, 6 September to Monday, 12 September. Nominations for the presidency had to be entered by mid-week, with the election to be held on the last day. One other candidate was nominated: Nabor Carillo, rector of the host university, the National Autonomous University of Mexico. The plotting and political in-fighting that followed the nominations seemed incredible to the staid American and British Commonwealth delegates. But this was Mexico, where "the Revolution" was till in progress. The Mexicans had nominated their man; it now became a matter of national pride to get him elected.

Their candidate was indeed an interesting one. On arrival each delegate had received an envelope containing a brochure published by a group of students that bitterly attacked Dr Carillo. The writers alleged that he misappropriated university funds in order to maintain a harem in Paris to which he travelled by aircraft several times a week. After reading the brochure, the delegates naturally looked forward to meeting a man who could generate such interesting rumours, especially since he was now nominated to run against James for the presidency.

The conference proved to be a week of lavish entertainment, with the government, the various embassies, and the host university trying to outdo one another in fulsome hospitality; the sessions, receptions, banquets, dances, and excursions flowed continually one after the other. But the intervals between conferencing and dancing were spent by delegates in assiduous political lobbying for one or the other presidential candidate.

In addition to the Canadians, the American, British, and other Commonwealth delegates were solidly behind James. He also had strong support from European and Far-eastern countries. But the congress was taking place in Latin America; that bloc of countries was almost solidly for Carillo. Each university with a delegate present on election day would have one vote; unfortunately the Latin-American universities were present in much greater proportional force, so that while, for instance, Canada was represented by ten universities, Chile alone could muster the same number.

The foreign embassies were, of course, located in the conference city, and their diplomats were caught up in the frenzy of activity. The lobbying led to some strange alliances. Toward the end of the week, word was leaked that both East and West Germany, at the urging of their ambassadors, had pledged their votes to the Latin-American candidate. Apparently non-academic considerations such as undertakings on international trade agreements had been brought into play. As for the Credentials Committee of the IAU, it assumed an importance it had never known before, its chairman – the rector of an Italian university – working tirelessly to issue legally assigned proxy votes. McDougall himself was armed by some strange logic with the proxy vote of the University of Pennsylvania. "The odd thing was," he wrote, "Dr. James himself had never anticipated a contest of this kind. He had accepted the nomination as a public duty at the urging of others, and with misgivings because he knew full well the demands the presidency would make on his time and energy. Naturally, he took no part in the lobbying and he remained the most urbane and dignified delegate at the Congress; in justice, [it has to be recorded that] Dr. Carillo conveyed some of the same imperturbability."

When McDougall came to the story of the election morning itself he gave himself full licence to capture the drama of the event.

On the morning of Monday, September 12th, every seat in the largest amphitheatre of the University of Mexico was filled. A wave of electric anticipation crackled through the audience. The roll call by nation and university began. Each delegate, as the name of his institution was called, stepped forward to the electoral urn at the front of the hall and, having been duly identified, placed his ballot into the urn. A Canadian, Dr. Walter Johns, President of the University of Alberta, presided at the urn, and flanking him, two steely-eyed Mexicans scrutinised every move.

In his turn, this delegate went forward and cast his vote for McGill University. When, however, the name of the University of Pennsylvania was called, he rose with more diffidence. At his reappearance at the urn the looks of the two Mexicans became cold and hostile. Indeed, they followed him back to his seat, studied his name-badge, made notes, and departed muttering.

While the votes were being counted the routine business of the meeting droned on. The delegates waited impatiently. Finally, the result of the election was announced. Dr. James was declared the winner by a large margin. There were seconds of silence, then a thunder of applause. For some of us present it felt as though Canada had just won the World Hockey championship. But after the first rejoicing the tension was dissolved at once. Dr. Carillo was among the first to congratulate Dr. James. The I.A.U. had elected its president, and could now resume its normal role of dealing with the affairs of the universities of the world.

The importance accorded to this election by a great many people world wide – and by their governments – is the measure of Frank Cyril James' achievement. The man who had accomplished so much for his own university, and through its national conference for his country, had now been voted the highest honour his profession had to offer. But he himself characteristically saw it as an opportunity to serve.

CHAPTER FOURTEEN

Resignation and Retirement

After the excitement of the IAU Conference in Mexico, James returned to McGill, and life reassumed its more normal patterns. But two events during the academic year gave him great pleasure, and echoed, as it were, the plaudits of Mexico City. In November he received a letter asking if he would allow his name to be placed in nomination as an Honorary Fellow of the London School of Economics; in March he was asked if he would be willing to receive an honorary degree from Harvard.

The latter distinction speaks for itself. At Harvard the custom is to eschew long laudatory speeches and to produce in a single sentence an epigrammatic summary of the graduand's career and character. For James the convention served particularly well.

Frank Cyril James: political economist, scholar-leader of a distinguished university, protagonist of higher learning throughout the world.

In his lifetime, there were many other political economists; there were not a few distinguished scholars directing universities; but there was no one described more justly than he as "protagonist of higher learning throughout the world." Yet it was the fellowship of LSE that meant most to James himself. It recalled the days when he had only poverty, native wit, and great expectations to spur him on, and now as he looked at the select company into which he had been invited he had good reason to flush with pride. In London, he had enjoyed only one year of student life, another struggling year of night-school, and an examination. For that effort he received what he himself described as "that rather despised degree, the B Comm." Now he was being invited to join Clement Attlee, William Beveridge, Hugh Dalton, Louis Rasminski, R.H.

Tawney, and a scant score of others, truly the pick of LSE teachers and students. The letter of invitation informed him that

no duties are attached to the status of Honorary Fellow. The School hopes, however, to enjoy the company of its Honorary Fellows on some at least of its formal public occasions, and they are invited to dine together and with representatives of the School once a year.

Honour, ceremonial dining, and an absence of duties – a very civilized invitation, rejoicing the heart because it came from the place where the whole adventure began.

But while these and other lesser distractions enlivened the slow progress of the months, from lovely fall through challenging winter to the misery of March and the bright, false promise of April, in James' mind another slow struggle was taking place. For many years, he had flirted on and off with the idea of resignation from McGill, but this academic year 1960–1, he contemplated the possibility seriously. He corresponded frequently with the Ford Foundation, discussing an appointment as educational adviser to their representative in India and Pakistan, a man described in the correspondence only as the "elusive Sharif" – simply, one gathers, because he was difficult to get hold of. The officers of the Ford Foundation were prepared to offer $20,000 a year tax free and a car if James took up residence in Pakistan for an initial two-year term, with the added assurance that thereafter he "would no doubt fit into the Foundation organisation somewhere." At the end of December James reflected on the possibility of retiring.

It was a very pleasant [Christmas] day – and had that bitter-sweet quality inherent in wondering if it will be the last such Christmas ... the last in this house (where we have lived longer than any other), the last at McGill, the last with Bay?

All of these possibilities have been raised during the past few months – and I feel utterly uncertain and indecisive. The election as President of the I.A.U. at Mexico last September brings things into sharp focus, but I do not think it changes the weight of the arguments half as much as the victory of the [Provincial] Liberals last June, which means that I have been on the inside of government planning for the past six months and therefore find McGill and Montreal much more exciting than they seemed a year ago. The decision is also complicated by the fact that, fundamentally, Bay does not only want me to give up the Principalship of McGill – which I could do by accepting the Ford Foundation offer (about which we are still talking) – but to leave Montreal and go to live in England.

Les 50 professeurs de McGill

Mon cher John,
Cette lettre ne reflète aucunement l'opinion de l'Université
Cyril James

Le Devoir was not impressed by Principal James' attempt to dissociate
the university from professors' criticism of Lesage government policy, 1961

"James can't control the professors."

"Fifty concerned professors" at McGill published a letter critical of government policy.
James felt obliged to send a telegram assuring Prime Minister Deifenbaker that the
letter did not represent official university opinion. *Le Devoir* 21 December 1961

I'm far from sure that I could negotiate a pension that would finance
this, afraid that I shall find nothing active to do …
   Basically, I feel that this is the time to leave my job at McGill – the
financial pattern of support [for the university] and of relationships to
Government is as nearly settled as it is ever likely to be and even the
present Government is apt to grow more critical and demanding when
it has been longer in office. It is a good time for a younger man to come
in and take over the next ten years of building and development –
physical, [and] in terms of staff and in terms of long range policies.

The reference to the Provincial Liberals refers to the fact that
in 1960 the Duplessis party, shattered by the loss of its leader,
had been ousted in a provincial election by Jean Lesage and the

Liberal Party. This was the beginning of the "Quiet Revolution" in Quebec, which broke the power of the Conservative–Church coalition and brought the province abruptly into the twentieth century. James was invited to serve on a committee to advise on the reform of the economy, and it was this experience that was tempting him to stay on at McGill and in Montreal. But this, as later events proved, was not a dependable augury. The wave of French-Canadian nationalism that was about to be released would have ensured that as an anglophone his role in the new Quebec would have been, if anything, a minor one.

It was not, however, the developments in the province that were to determine his future but the developments on the campus, or, perhaps one should say, in the mind of the chancellor, R.E. Powell. A little further in the same diary entry, James wrote: "The Chancellor has an idea he can run the university better than I can." Powell had also been heard to say, "James is losing control of the professors," a reference to the activities of MAUT. A few lines later, the diary records: "Both Powell and Bay insist that I am neglecting the University." One has to ask if this were true. Certainly, given the number of references in this biographical account to travels and conferences and to national and international associations, the charge might seem justified. But what has not been emphasized is that these activities took place between long bouts of close attention to university affairs. Since he had little home-life, no hobbies, and no relaxation other than reading, James was able to give the university's business its due attention and more, and still have considerable time for travel and extramural activities. Sidney Dobell, James' personal assistant for eight years, has testified that "there can be no doubt that Cyril James did the work not merely of one average man, but of two or even three";[1] Mrs McMurray strongly supported this judgment. Irene had her own quite personal reasons for saying that Cyril was "neglecting the university" when she really meant "neglecting me," and the chancellor also had personal reasons for being critical of James.

Ray Edwin Powell had become chancellor of McGill after an outstanding business career. Born in Illinois in 1887 he had been forced to drop out of university from lack of financing, and had joined the Aluminum Company of America. In 1929 he was sent north to Canada to head up a new enterprise, the Aluminum Company of Canada, "Alcan." For the next twenty-eight years, Powell devoted tremendous energies to the organization, taking full advantage of the challenge of the war-years; in doing so he built up both an immense industry and a tough personal reputation.

His initials, R.E.P., and his uncompromising patterns of management earned him the nickname "Rip" Powell. He had been dedicated to Alcan as tenaciously as James had been dedicated to
McGill, but in the competitive world of business there had been
little opportunity for Powell to become aware of wider horizons
or of larger purposes than those of his company. When he retired
in 1957 at age seventy from the presidency of Alcan, he still had
great abilities but little occupation, and he accepted the chancellorship the same year, expecting no doubt to find in the university
some outlet for his formidable energies. But the vice-chancellor
was not the kind of man to allow the chancellor much room in
which to operate. Both were masterful men, and while superficially
relations were cordial, the two personalities were too alike to be
wholly compatible. It is not surprising, then, that if fault was to
be found with James' conduct as principal, Powell would be the
man to find it. Indeed, given his experience in industry as a tough
boss, he would argue that it was his job to look for shortcomings
in his subordinates before they became apparent to others.[2]

From the annual reports of the university for the years 1959–62,
the last ones James wrote, it is evident that never had McGill
been in such splendid and promising health, and that James was
aware of, and supportive of, growth in every department. This
does not mean every department and every faculty was fully
satisfied – no healthy department ever is; nor does it mean that
no individuals remained disgruntled. But, by and large, the last
years of James' administration were years of greatly increased
budgets, higher salaries, new appointments, better equipment, and
new or restored buildings. Such times do not breed a spirit of
rebelliousness, but rather a spirit of expansion and hope.

In the annual report for 1960–1 (after honouring priorities by
mentioning the McGill football team's triumph in the Eastern
Intercollegiate Championship for the first time in twenty-two years),
James detailed the financial results after the new policies had come
into operation.

The spectacular improvement in the financial situation of the University
did not attract as wide attention as the football championship, but to the
members of the teaching and administrative staffs – as well as to the
students who benefited from a substantial reduction in tuition fees – the
advantages were very real.

The figures in Table I show that, in spite of a reduction of approximately
half a million dollars in the income from tuition fees ... the total operating

revenues of the University increased [by approximately 20%] ... This substantial increase in financial aid to McGill, and to the other universities in the Province, is but one of the many indications of the revolutionary change in the attitude of the Quebec Government to education.

This was indeed a new day for education in the province, and a major part of the credit has to be accorded to James, who had encouraged in Canada and (despite Duplessis) in Quebec, a climate of public opinion ready to acknowledge the community's responsibility for the costs of education at all levels.

In his final annual report, that for 1961–2, James was also able to draw attention to the improvement of the university's physical facilities. Three new student residences, Gardner Hall, McConnell Hall, and Molson Hall, and the central refectory-facility, Bishop Mountain Hall, represented the first-fruits of the building program, along with Peterson Hall, a newly acquired centre for modern languages, and, at Macdonald College, the extensive rehabilitation of the Main and Biology Buildings. In addition, the Senate Development Committee had, James reported, identified nineteen further projects, requiring some $46 million for their realization.

Consideration of these major building projects, each of them costing millions of dollars, should not lead us to overlook the hundreds of less spectacular – but most important – ways in which the facilities for teaching and research are improved each year. It would be tiresome to offer a complete catalogue of the hundreds of rooms – offices, classrooms, and laboratories – that have been improved by the Department of Buildings and Grounds through the installation of new seats and benches, new lighting fixtures, better blackboards, and other equipment.

Even at this early date, he reported that the university computer had proven inadequate for the demands made upon it and had been replaced with a larger machine. Finally, he mentioned developments at the university's research centres at Bellairs in Barbados, and, at the other extreme, at the survey camp established by the McGill–Jacobsen Expedition on Axel Heiberg Island in the Arctic. In sum, the annual reports for these last years of James' principalship give solid evidence that he was as involved in the university's manifold activities as he ever was.

In his penultimate report, that for 1960–1, James took up a particularly significant question – that of the role of the university. The removal of financial worries as a main item from the university's agenda had, he wrote, facilitated an active intellectual ferment in all parts of the university, as "is apparent in the reports from the Deans of Faculties which are appended to this report."

This intellectual ferment within the University – matched by that in other institutions of higher education throughout the world – is a reflection of the basic challenge that confronts us in this decade of the nineteen-sixties. What is the role of the university in modern society?

A century ago, the answer was clear. The university was of no more than marginal importance to society. If students wanted to go to college, and could afford to, the community did not hinder them but it certainly did very little to encourage them. Neither government nor business recognized that it had any real need for university graduates, outside of the professions of law and medicine, and even in these fields a man could often qualify himself for practice without attending any university ...

But now that view was no longer acceptable. In newspapers, in the organs of public opinion generally, and in parliaments and legislatures, the view prevailed that government money should be available to support the institutions of education at all levels. "The technological and scientific revolution, which is continuing at an accelerating rate, confronts the community with an urgent need for larger numbers of highly trained men and women." But James looked at these matters not merely from the McGill point of view; he recognized them as instances of an immense change of understanding worldwide.

The focus of power in world affairs is no longer in Western Europe and North America. Russia has developed her natural and human resources with a speed that would have been thought impossible a quarter of a century ago, and has underlined the role of universities and research institutes in the process. China is moving along the same road, and dozens of newly independent states in Africa and Asia are now free to choose between the social patterns, the economic policies and the political ideals of the Western world and the Communist bloc. If we of the West are to attract, and hold, their friendship we must be able to understand them and to work with them. We need large numbers of men and women who can speak their languages, who are familiar with their customs, and who understand their religions. Where, but in our universities, can such men and women be educated?

This coming of age of the university in the new "global village" coincided with the election of James as president of the IAU. The two events were by no means unrelated; as a result of his world-ranging travels and his participation in university associations, James could see, and could help others to see, the work done in their own universities in an international context. So far from having lost out because of his extramural interest, McGill had gained immeasurably. Constant preoccupation with administrative detail narrows the mind of any man or woman involved in it, as James well knew. Because he had from time to time lifted up his eyes to wider horizons, he retained more than most academic administrators a lively intellectual curiosity and, to the end of his tenure, a professional enthusiasm.

Although Chancellor Powell was, then, misguided in thinking James had been neglecting the university, he was undoubtedly right in believing the time had come for James to resign. James was finding his stimulation not in McGill and its future but in these broader interests of education. In January 1961, he embarked on a series of conferences for the AUBC and the IAU that took him to Hong Kong and Kuala Lumpur. On his way home, he reached Paris, where, in the words of a laconic notation in his private papers, "FCJ had a slight heart attack on January 27 and had to go to bed for the rest of the week." On his return to Montreal, he spent a week in the Montreal General Hospital undergoing a thorough medical examination, after which he asked the governors to grant him sick leave until the end of March. He and Irene went to Bermuda for two weeks. Early in April he resumed his duties, but that same month his appointment as consultant in higher education, South and Southeast Asia, based in Karachi, Pakistan, was confirmed privately to him by the Ford Foundation, to commence at a date to suit his convenience after 1 June 1961. He was keeping his options open.

In August he and Irene took another vacation, this time in Troon, Scotland, where he decided that yes, the time had come for him to resign. But when he returned to Montreal his opinion wavered.

Now that I am here I must really decide the problem that we debated at Troon – and rather more querulously while we were at Barnet during the past ten days – but the arguments do not help me to a clear and simple decision. Perhaps there is no simple decision!

One can sympathize with Irene's exasperation. James knew the time had come for him to resign, and yet could not bring himself to face that fact. In September he was speculating that perhaps he should, after all, stay until the academic year 1964–5. He would then have completed twenty-five years – he does not add, although it must have been in his mind, that he would still be only sixty-one, an early age for retirement. He knew Powell would not welcome this delay, but then Powell himself would come up for re-election in the following summer; "there is the chance of helping to elect a new (and I hope different kind of) Chancellor," someone who would presumably be glad to have the principal remain for a year or two, while the new chancellor accustomed himself to his role. In December 1961, James discussed at the Board of Governors meeting ("with appropriate reticences") his pension position if he should retire before the age of sixty-five, and the board appointed a committee to consider the matter. They also agreed to appoint new administrative staff to lighten the principal's burden and to look for or build a principal's residence "easier to live in than 1200 Pine Avenue – all of which does not sound like enthusiastic argument that I should retire in a couple of years! We shall see how things march!"

But things did not "march" as James expected. Powell astutely took the opportunity of the committee appointed to discuss the principal's pension, *if* he should decide to retire, to produce from it a decision that the principal *should* retire – immediately. He wrote James on 24 February 1962, to inform him that assuming his date of retirement to be 30 June 1962, he would receive a further year's salary and thereafter a yearly pension of $15,000. The letter added:

If I correctly interpret the views of the Governors, they would like to have the resignation presented to them during the next meeting of the Board, now scheduled for 16 April 1962. That should provide the Board with time to consult its Senate and to do the other things that are necessary to prepare for the succession. There has been no opportunity to seek the Board's formal approval of the foregoing but I have reasons to believe that such approval will be forthcoming.

Like a man on the edge of a pool, James had been hesitating a long time, trying to make up his mind to dive. Powell had now given him a firm shove.

There is no doubt the chancellor had acted on his own responsibility. The members of the small pension committee may have known what was in Powell's mind, but the other members of the board had not been consulted or even informed. Many came to a rescheduled meeting in March quite unprepared for the turn of events and were left to believe that the initiative in the matter had been the principal's. The Board of Governors minutes record that when a vote was called for on a motion to accept the proffered resignation, majority approval was given, but the minutes cannot record the confusion in the minds of many of those who voted. One member, seeking an explanation, asked one of the academic deans a day or two later if he knew what was going on, and voiced his own suspicion: "Has the principal," he asked, "been railroaded?" But few in the academic community had any knowledge of the situation or any presentiment of what was about to happen. Powell had single-handedly engineered a coup d'état.

One person, at least, had the courage to protest. The former chancellor, Bertie Gardner, now an emeritus governor, had been present at the meeting. He observed what took place and termed it a "dismissal." Afterwards he wrote to his successor what can best be described as a gentlemanly but severe rebuke.

21 March, 1962

Dear Rip,

Since the meeting yesterday I have given serious thought to the proceedings and to the conclusion reached and I should like to put some views before you.

The meeting started with the suggestion that all was not well at McGill and it was suggested that Dr. James should either resign his post or withdraw from his extra mural activities. As the discussion developed it was suggested that he might continue his connection with McGill by creating a new office of some kind from which he could continue to do his outside work. As the discussion proceeded it was clear that this proposal did not appeal to the majority of the members, and the view was then advanced that a clear-cut break must be made, that Dr. James must sever his connection completely so that the newcomer would not be hampered by his predecessor.

Having got so far as this, a show of hands was asked for Dr. James's dismissal, which was easily carried. I think you noticed that I did not vote, as I had no right to do so as a Governor Emeritus. You were authorized to inform the Principal that his services were no longer required.

I took exception to the wordlywise view that Dr. James's illness was a fortuitous incident, creating circumstances which facilitated getting rid of Dr. James. Now I wish to back a little. At the beginning of the meeting you told us that when you last spoke to Dr. James about his absences he had replied that he would discuss the matter on his return. This has not been done and you are now to confront him with a notice of dismissal. Is this a proper or courteous procedure? I think not, and I reached the conclusion that an hour's discussion did not give the Governors sufficient time to consider this very serious and important matter. Certainly in my case I find my ideas clarified by a few hours' contemplation.

In my view the meeting might well have been adjourned to an early date in order to give the members of the Board time for reflection ... From what I have written you may gather that I am particularly interested in the procedure and in doing justice to a distinguished educationalist who has served the University to the best of his ability for twenty years. In my view an order of dismissal would react most unfavourably on McGill.

It seems to me that you and the Principal should have a preliminary talk which should then be followed by the calling of a second meeting of the Governors to receive your report of the conversation with Dr. James.

If you wish to show this letter to any of your colleagues on the Board this will be quite agreeable to me.

Yours sincerely,
Bertie

But Powell was not to be deterred. No such second meeting of the board took place.

As for the academic community in general, the degree to which it was unprepared for James' termination is well illustrated by a letter written by the dean of engineering to the principal as late as 13 April, just three days before the next meeting of the board, which was formally to endorse acceptance of the enforced resignation.

Dear Dr. James,

I was quite flabbergasted and, for once, almost speechless when I heard today of recent developments.

I would have thought that, of all the people who have ever served this University, there was no one who has done so much, or deserved so well, as yourself.

I understand that there are some who wish you to leave your position with what I can only describe as indecent haste. I am sure that it is unnecessary for me to assure you of my strongest support ...

With my most sincere best wishes,
Donald Mordell

James' response to Powell's intimation of dismissal was written on 6 March, two weeks after he had received the chancellor's letter; it had taken him that long to make up his mind. But having reached a conclusion, he stayed with it.

Dear R.E.P.

If the Board of Governors agrees with your proposal for a year's leave of absence and with the subsequent proposals set forth in your letter of February 24th, I should be very happy to vacate the office of Principal and Vice-Chancellor on December 1, 1962, or at any date thereafter on which my successor has been appointed and is ready to take office.

I suggest this date, rather than the June date in your letter, because McGill must in any case begin the 1962–63 session with a new Vice-Principal, a new Dean of Arts and Science and a new Warden of the R.V.C. I should not want to complicate matters for my colleagues by resigning at the same period ...

If the Board of Governors accepts these proposals, I agree with you that a public announcement should be made after the April meeting of the Board – but suggest that it be postponed for a few days so that the Senate, which meets on Wednesday, April 18, might receive the announcement before it reads it in the newspapers ...

James' words that he "would be very happy to vacate the office of principal" were more than just a graceful phrase. After spending so much time agonizing over the decision himself, to have someone else make his mind up for him, brought him an undoubted sense of relief. The matter had been settled. But mingled with the relief was also a deep resentment at the manner of his termination. In public, he was allowed to say he had decided to retire, but in private he knew, and the governors knew, that he had been summarily dismissed. "Rip" Powell had lived up to his business reputation; when the opportunity presented itself, he had acted swiftly and decisively.

When Stalin's body had been removed a few months earlier from its resting place in Red Square, Moscow, James had written a mocking comment on the downfall of the once-great dictator.

When a body meets a body
Coming through the Square,
Someone that was in, is out,
And someone here is there.

When a body meets a body,
Either quick or dead,

Someone that was up is down,
And nobody's ahead.

Now at the moment of his own downfall, his mind went back to
those verses, and he began his diary note for 16 April 1962 with
the last two lines.

Someone that was up, is down,
And nobody's ahead!
I wonder! All of the incidents forecast in the preceding documents came
to a head this afternoon! The Board of Governors with solid and stone-
faced unanimity decided that F.C.J. should retire on December 1st – with
a good pension of course – and at the end of the meeting (from the
greater part of which I had been absent, of course) refused to admit
that the actual retirement should await the coming into office of a
successor!
We did, at the same time, appoint a Committee to nominate a successor
to R.E.P. as Chancellor – under the chair of J.D. Johnson. Is it unreasonable
to insist that it must be a *successor!*[3]

This last comment is the one gesture of resentment James permitted
himself to record of his feelings toward the chancellor, but in fact
he was no longer in a position to insist on anything. But in the
confusion of his feelings, he retained an intellectual awareness that
the governors were acting within their rights. He had based his
whole McGill career on the premise that the board was the master,
and he, however cleverly he had at times manipulated its members,
only the servant. But for all that, 16 April 1962 remained a traumatic
experience for Frank Cyril James, the deepest-hurting of his life.
Irene tried to help. Unable to penetrate his emotional barriers
with spoken words, she wrote him a note, characteristically strongly
in his support.

Dearest,
What could be said, and what should be said, is not possible when
we are under strain. But I do love you – and I do understand – more,
believe me, than you can realize when you go into a shell. I understand
that, too.
But it is not every man who has still so much to give the world, when
they have already given so much. Yes, we've got what it takes, darling.
I believe that with all my heart – and there is still so much to do. Many
more people need you.
Bay.

This was a wifely attempt at consolation and appreciated as such. He kept the note with his private papers. But it could not touch the spot. At home, he retreated, as Irene put it, into his shell, letting the turmoil of his inner feelings smoulder.

In public he continued in his customary unruffled, omnicompetent role. In that persona, he had one last major occasion on which to play his accustomed part – the general staff meeting of the entire university, coincidentally to take place just two days after his dismissal. He would take full advantage of this coincidence to make a public announcement of his resignation. Many on campus were beginning to sense something unusual was in the wind, but few had any notion what it was; almost everyone who was not lecturing that Wednesday at noon crowded into Moyse Hall for the meeting. At fifty-eight, his tall figure slim and vigorous, his hair only touched with grey, James still possessed an impressive platform presence. His pleasant, rather high voice, with its distinct articulation and musical tones, reached clearly to the back of the hall, without the benefit in those days of microphones, and he had no difficulty catching the interest of his listeners.

I talked to you a year ago about our hopes in the matter of academic salaries. You may remember that at the time I had to report – what each of you personally knew – that our salaries were below those at other leading Canadian universities ... I am very happy indeed in the fact that it has been substantially remedied. In the last report of the Alberta Survey which has just come to hand for 1961–62 McGill is ... in first place in regard to the average salary of full professors; it is in the first place in the average salary of Assistant Professors across Canada; and it is in second place in regard to Associate Professors ... We have substantially improved the situation in regard to the matter that is of vital concern to each one of us and I hope will be able to maintain that position in the coming session.

The promise implicit in the last words was to be spelled out a little later, but the main fact was already clear: McGill, which traditionally had been proud but poor, was now on a par with the best in Canada, not merely in salaries, but in all those other things that comparative affluence permits and poverty inhibits: facilities, equipment, new staff, and, most important, new hope. James was sounding an upbeat note that had not been heard at McGill since the years before World War I.

Having thus brought his audience into a mood of gratification for achievements already consolidated and for further benefits yet to come, he turned to the university's future, to strengthen still further the mood of expectancy. He reminded them that the university must be prepared for a further large expansion in enrolment. The Committee of Deans, with the assistance of the heads of departments, schools, and institutes, had been carefully exploring the maximum capacity of McGill that might be expected over the next decade. The graduate faculty was expected to increase to 2,300. But the principal and the deans had been sensitive to the criticism that McGill should not become a top-heavy graduate school. Consideration must also be given to the needs of the undergraduate faculties, future enrolment in which was projected as 12,300. These numbers would necessitate a considerable expansion in physical facilities. James then went on to speak of the projects already accomplished and those still in the planning. After reminding his audience of the exhibition modelling the planned expansion of the university to be opened in the Redpath Library the following week, he continued.

In summary then what I am trying to convey to you is a programme of planning which has taken shape much more quickly, much more clearly and much more useful for the University than I anticipated last year – a programme in which a substantial number of members of the University are involved and one which I am confident is going to be carried out.

Everyone present recognized this was an historic moment; under Cyril James' leadership, the university had achieved unparalleled accomplishments; now he was pointing them forward to greater heights and instilling a strong confidence that under his continuing guidance those goals would be reached. But then came the dramatic denouement.

As a last statement today I want to tell you that in view of these developments and of the smoothness with which they are moving forward, I have been discussing with the Board of Governors the appropriate time at which I should vacate my present office and let a younger person come in and carry these plans through to completion, and as a result of all the discussions over the last two weeks I shall be vacating that office somewhere around the end of this calendar year: as soon as a successor is appointed. Although we may have another staff meeting in the autumn I should like, in view of that, to express to each one of you my whole-hearted appreciation of the support you have given me: some of you over a period of 23 years; all of you since you joined the University staff. The older ones of you have lived through a period of difficulties and frustrations when we felt we were not getting anywhere and this was painful. All of us have realised that when you get rid of frustrations and start extensive programmes of development it may be exciting but it is certainly a great deal of more work. I want to thank you for taking on these extra burdens and, as I said a moment ago – to express to each of you my very sincere appreciation. Thank you very much.

Although he was to make many more public appearances, they were in the nature of curtain-calls; the last dramatic scene of Cyril James' principalship was played out on the Moyse Hall stage on 18 April 1962. The role accepted on that same stage at his installation on 12 January 1940 had been played for over twenty-two years with mounting success and authority, and now he had crowned his performance with a dazzling display of targets achieved and successes to come. He had also provided himself with an unbeatable exit-line.

But where to exit to? What was he to do? The next seven months were spent in a strange mixture of unruffled public appearances, innumerable farewell receptions and dinners, a flood of personal letters and good wishes, and an agony of private indecision. He had to tell the Ford Foundation that his health would not permit two years' residence in the Indian sub-continent; the Reserve City Bankers had lost their enthusiasm for a history of reserve banking; his old friend Joe Willits had retired from his posts of influence for the final time; Hector Hetherington had retired from Glasgow. James was still president of the IAU but these were only part-time duties. He found himself in the position of the man whom everybody delights to honour and no one wishes to employ. He had devoted himself to one cause only; now he had been dismissed from its service, and the future appeared an empty blank.

During this period of confused emotions and even more confused orientation, James tried to turn back to the practices of the religion that he had learned in his youth.

Monday, August 6
Each morning now I come up to the study before breakfast – to read a little of the Bible and to pray that God will show me his will, and give me the strength and the humility to obey it. So many alternatives loom ahead that I need guidance – but it is hard for me to feel the presence of God and to know his will. Paul says the gospel is the power of salvation to every one who has faith. I can only keep trying and praying.

But the efforts and the prayers did not gain any notable results. Later, when he had settled in England, religion does not seem to have played any large part in his life. In October 1963, when he met with an old schoolfriend who had moved from banking to the pastorate, James commented,

Fred [Harding], retired from the bank that never enthralled him, is now the full-time minister of the Congregational Church at St. Alban's – and thoroughly enjoying the splendid work he is doing. He is no scholar. He insists that my own small theological collection is larger than his, yet he is a real Christian and I am not sure that I am, even though I try to be.

James had "the will to believe," but it is clear that to the end, in matters of religion, he was left with more questions than answers.

Meanwhile there were farewell appearances to be made and to be endured. To his surprise, James found them enjoyable rather than painful, although strongly emotional. The first occasion was that of the fall convocation, the day before James McGill's birthday, Saturday, 6 October.

Yesterday – the Founder's Day programme – was tiring, and I had been worried about it! But it went off splendidly and I feel deeply moved and happy. Not many Governors came along (the Friday before Thanksgiving weekend is always difficult), but the Senate turned out in full force for the luncheon and the honorary graduates all spoke well. To my surprise – complete surprise – Rip recalled that I have a birthday on Monday [8 October, my fifty-ninth] and proposed that all the company should drink to my health, which they did.

Convocation was also well attended and there were very few empty seats. It is hard to say a public "good-bye" simply and without dreary reminiscence – but I tried, and had taken my seat for a second or two, glad that the speech was over, before I realised that the whole audience was on its feet applauding. At that moment I had a hard time to keep the tears out of my eyes – and again when Edgar Collard in his convocation address talked in a crisp sentence about what has been achieved during the past 23 years.

Edgar Andrew Collard, at that time editor of *The Gazette* newspaper, was already widely known for his interest in the history of Montreal and Quebec. It was a happy coincidence that he had been invited to be the convocation speaker; his theme, "faith in tomorrow," could not have been more appropriate.

One of the grandest chapters in McGill's creative history of faith in tomorrow is the history of the last twenty-three years. When our Vice-Chancellor entered upon his duties in 1939 the world was under the encircling gloom of war and no man might know what the future would bring forth. In his inaugural address on a wintry day in 1940 our Vice-Chancellor said, "As we stand on the threshold of another decade we see many question marks and few sign posts".

Though he entered upon his duties when there were few sign posts, he may look back upon these twenty-three years and see many milestones. And as it is the lot and purpose of those with faith in tomorrow to sow that others may reap, the full measure of his wisdom and foresight will be revealed only in the long tomorrow of the coming years.

The public ceremony was followed by a more private one, the traditional principal's reception for senior members of the academic staff. Friday evening before Thanksgiving weekend though it was, James' colleagues and their friends attended the reception in great numbers. The Redpath Hall was particularly welcoming in the fall evening, with its subdued lighting, its great hammer-beam roof dim in the shadows above, and the long central table generously offering refreshments; from the walls the many portraits of distinguished men and women looked down on the long line of well-wishers waiting to pay respects to the principal and his wife, and on the lively conversation, and animated groups that came together, grew, broke, and reformed elsewhere, as colleagues and friends visited and were visited across the crowded floor. In the midst of the renewal of old acquaintance and the good fellowship everywhere, James was heard to observe in true amazement: "I never knew I had so many friends!" He was not mistaken; that large crowd of colleagues, graduates, and many members of the board were indeed gathered to show their respect and affection for the man who had served them and their university so long and so well.

But when the crowds filtered away, and the bright lights dimmed, and Cyril was left alone with his own thoughts, the scene of the approaching loss weighed even more heavily.

Saturday, November 10th

The rest of the farewell parties has taken place ... and (since we have agreed on terms) the transfer of Piper's Croft is now in the hands of the solicitors[4] I begin to feel that the McGill chapter of my life is really drawing to a close, and relish every hour that I can spend up here in my study. Whatever happens (and I don't really expect much) I shall never again have a room like this, from which I can look out over the world, or sit quietly in silence.

When the time came for the announcement of his successor's name, and Rip Powell telephoned to say that James must vacate his office by 30 November, so that he new man could begin cleanly, with no encumbrances, the dreadful end became real and final.

Wednesday, November 21, 1962

Last Monday the Board of Governors voted to appoint Rocke Robertson as Principal, effective Dec. 1st. Today I announced it to the Senate – and afterwards we had a press conference to tell the public.

It is all over, all my travelling
In clanging, curious time, and I
Of every lovely thing that life can bring
Have only left to die.[5]

I don't expect that I shall die in the near future – but that is the thought that comes to mind. Rocke is a grand person, and I am delighted that he succeeds, since (I think) I was the first to suggest him. But I do feel that the thing I gave my life to is broken (more poetry!) and do not look forward to the future with any confident enthusiasm, in spite of the house at Amersham and all my public statements (and Rip's) about the I.A.U. Maybe the change is a good thing for McGill. At the moment I do not know, and I am tired!

The inevitability of time proved itself once more. Saturday the first day of December dawned, and Frank Cyril James was no longer principal and vice-chancellor of McGill University.

Departure for flight around the world, June 1950

Irene's Coronation dress, 1953

Visit to Professor Max Dunbar and his Arctic research vessel
M.V. Calamus, 1955. Centre: S.G. Dobson, McGill governor

Caribbean visit, 1956

Indonesian dining, 1957

Doreen's wedding, 1959

Visiting a museum in the Soviet Union, 1959

The principal and Professor Muriel Roscoe
visit the Physics department, 1960

Surplus achieved, 1961

Mrs Dorothy McMurray at the time of her retirement,
1962, with Alexander McMurray and the principal.

A Fall Convocation Reception, October 1961(?)

Professor Muriel Roscoe retired
as warden of RVC, 1962

Japanese hospitality, 1965

The study, Piper's Croft. In the background, the Cleve Horne
portrait, now in the Board Room, F. Cyril James
Administration Building, McGill University.

CHAPTER FIFTEEN

The After Years

The show was over, but the farewells continued. A grand occasion was provided at the beginning of November when the celebrated pianist, Ellen Ballon, gave a white-tie dinner at the Ritz-Carlton Hotel at which the socially elite of Montreal, the "best people" as Orville Tyndale had once called them, gathered to salute the departure of one whom they recognized as a great man. When he had first arrived in Montreal, some of them had tended to think of him as an upstart and an interloper, but now they realized that he had done much for their city, for their university, and for them; they had the grace to want to say thank you, and they said it grandly.

At the student banquet, Gordon Echenberg, the union president, had thoughtfully arranged that all his predecessors who had served during the "James Era" should be present. The evening was filled with reminiscences and not a little laughter. James endeared himself to his hosts by telling a story against himself. During the war, when the draft caught in its net the young and popular Professor Culliton, there was a student campaign to retain him, and the engineers hung a banner from their window: "Keep Culliton, Draft James." Cyril could afford to tell the tale; had not the students, only three years earlier, spontaneously given him their coveted Gold Award? This night they renewed that award for the year 1962 and added a plethora of other gifts.

In addition to all this, the *McGill Daily* yesterday published a special edition to honour of what they called *The James Era* – to rival the slide-show produced by the McGill Associates and the special issue of the *McGill News* that is to appear next week.

No man could have more. No other Principal at McGill has had as much – and there is no question but that R.E.P. by forcing my early retirement has erected the occasion for this. If I had stayed on (as I wanted) for longer, the community might have tired of me (as seems to have happened with Larry MacKenzie,[1] who sounds bitter in his letters) or I might ultimately have fallen ill.

The special convocation, held in the Sir Arthur Currie Memorial Gymnasium, was a truly memorable occasion. Seating was provided for 3,000, and the hall was crowded. James was presented for his degree by the vice-principal, Noel Fieldhouse, and formally invested as principal emeritus by the Chancellor, R.E. Powell. James gave the convocation address. After having addressed the university community so often over so many years, it was, as he himself said, difficult to say anything strikingly new, nor would he want to. Rather, he returned to an old theme, reiterating it with renewed conviction. First, he spoke of McGill's intellectual achievements and of the university's pre-eminent commitment to excellence in all things academic, and then he continued:

Some years ago, [Prime Minister] Mackenzie King suggested that during the years immediately preceding Confederation McGill University played a significant role in the unification of Canada. Under the leadership of Sir William Dawson, it was a bridge between the Maritime Provinces and the English-speaking Canadians et les Canadiens de la langue française.
... The importance of such bridges is even greater today. We need bridges to link Canada to the rest of the world, we also need bridges that surmount the Iron Curtain and the Bamboo Curtain – bridges that will permit the kind of intellectual traffic that creates a peaceful world ... McGill has never been an ivory tower. I like to think of it as one of those fascinating medieval bridges at the crossroads of human wanderings, a bridge lined with houses in which the traveller might find rest and refreshment. Those houses were important, sometimes splendid, but their significance was fundamentally dependent on the roads that radiated out from the bridge to the uttermost ends of the earth. McGill is such a bridge. May its contribution to understanding among men grow steadily greater.

No theme could have been more expressive of his vision of the university in society. He never thought of himself as a man in an ivory tower; he thought of himself as standing on a bridge from which the roads ran out into the world and were constantly alive with two-way traffic.

James' final comments on his departure were expressed in a

diary note written on Christmas Day in the study of the principal's residence, where so many of his self-communing had been scribbled, late at night, or, like this one, early in the morning.

The red sun is just coming up over the horizon into a pink sky – and starting to throw pink and purple shadows along the snow. It is a "white Christmas" alright, and a cold one. It is the last Christmas here at 1200 Pine – where the pink reflections of the window frames pattern the opposite wall of the study.

Yesterday Doreen gave birth to a daughter – and both are doing well – so that a new era *is* beginning. This is an additional reason to make England attractive to Bay – and to me as well – an additional reason for happiness today.

James had almost fully come to terms with the fact that he was no longer principal and that his McGill chapter had ended.

The McGill Governors had been generous in the matter of pension, as James remarked once or twice in his diary notes. He received full salary, $35,000, for a year (1963), $15,000 per annum thereafter (with half-rate reversion to Irene, if she should survive him), and the interest on the Cyril James Retirement Fund, plus access to the capital during his lifetime. It was this last clause that had made it possible for James to acquire Piper's Croft, a delightful residence in Amersham, England. The weeks of rearranging the house and garden to their liking were interrupted only by James' visit to Paris, to speak as IAU president at the French-language universities' congress being held at the Sorbonne. He found the experience challenging – but also a delightful escape from too much domesticity.

According to René Maheu[2] and Roger Keyes, the speech went well – but I found it a bit of an ordeal to speak French in the large amphitheatre of the Sorbonne with the Rectors of all the French universities (in full regalia) massed on the platform, especially in view of the fact that I have done little public speaking of any kind even in English during the past four months!

For the rest, these days have been a real luxury. A room to myself at the hotel and a private bath (I miss these luxuries that I enjoyed in Montreal!) and, during the day, the activities at the Congress and the I.A.U. business at the office. I feel that I have accomplished something and have enjoyed doing it – so that I am almost sorry that I fly back to England tomorrow.

A little later in the year, James was invited, as a fellow of the London School of Economics, to attend the dinner for B Com graduates, and to propose the toast to the school; from the detailed notes he wrote out for the occasion, it is evident he took the occasion seriously. Performances that had at one time occurred frequently and become routine were now special events requiring careful preparation. Correspondence, university publications, and occasional visitors – former colleagues on leave in England or passing through London on their way across the world – kept him informed on major events in Montreal, and he paused, in his preoccupation with making Piper's Croft into a home in which he could take both pleasure and pride, to think occasionally of what for twenty-three years had been his constant preoccupation. But already the fascination had begun to fade.

June 18, 1963

McGill seems to be having its problems. There was a $2.0 million deficit on the budget, and tuition fees are to be prised, since the Province cannot increase its grant adequately ... I do not really know whether I am glad or sorry that I no longer have to wrestle with all these problems – but I am sad that so many of our leading lights are all departing! The University will be a different place, but Robertson may be able to find replacements that are as good. I hope so, and do not envy him that task, because talent is scarce in the senior brackets nowadays.

The pleasures of home and garden and the rewards of leisureful activities were beginning to weave their spell. Only a week after commenting on affairs at McGill, James was back from a joint UNESCO–IAU committee on research in higher education, and he had no regrets at leaving that world behind.

Tuesday, June 25

Last week I was in Paris – for I.A.U. business and a meeting of the Joint Steering Committee – and it was a delight to come back to Piper's Croft! In spite of the pleasant Square Louvois beneath the window at my Paris hotel, this is a vivid and delightful contrast [here at Piper's Croft] and Saturday evening, when I arrived, was as lovely as June evenings can be, with a glorious light on the lawns, the brickwork, the roses and (especially) the trees! I must admit, too, that the peace and leisure of Piper's Croft is a pleasant contrast to working in Paris!

In July, when the Commonwealth Universities Congress met in London James, as president of the IAU, was invited to be present.

He enjoyed the celebrations a great deal, but recognized that this was one more stage in the process of being weaned from his former life.

The Commonwealth Universities Congress last week was a great occasion – superbly organized by Jock Logan [Principal of London University] and his committees and providing a galaxy of social occasions that could not be equalled anywhere else in the world. But it was nice to hear so many of the delegates recall with pleasure our simpler congress in Montreal four years ago ...

But I have come to realise during these talks – for the first time – that I am quite happy to be out of my old job, and have no desire at all to go back to it!

In August he travelled to Kuala Lumpur for a joint UNESCO–IAU conference on the development of institutions of higher learning in Southeast Asia, but the experience did not, as formerly, provoke personal comments and diary notes.

In September, he left home again to fly to Washington, DC, where he made a major speech to the conference of the International Federation of Catholic Universities. His address on this occasion was vintage-James: arresting, informative, at times scintillating, and, at the end, strongly advocatory. In it, James was pleading for what he truly believed and for what he had consistently laboured.

I have talked of technological and scientific education, but, in this company, the words of that great Encyclical of Pope John XXIII – *Pacem in Terris* – must be deeply embedded in the minds of each one of you. "Scientific competence, technical capacity and professional experience ... are not of themselves sufficient to elevate society to an order that is genuinely human ..." Do not those words echo the injunction two thousand years ago that "Men shall not live by bread alone, but by every word which proceedeth out of the mouth of God"?

What I have to say has been better, and more clearly said by Wilfred Smith [in his recent book] entitled *"The Meaning and End of Religion"*: "Unless a Christian can contrive intelligently and spiritually to be a Christian not merely in a Christian society or a secular society, but in the world; unless a Muslim can be a Muslim in the world; unless a Buddhist can carve a satisfactory place for himself as Buddhist in a world in which other intelligent, sensitive, educated men are Christians and Muslims – then I do not see how man is to be a Christian or a Muslim or a Buddhist at all." That is the most fundamental challenge to the international understanding of men's thoughts and ideals of a global scale ... This, if I may again quote *Pacem in Terris*, "is an immense task incumbent on all men of good will – the task of restoring the relations of the human family in justice, in love, in freedom."

Although James enjoyed that visit and making that speech, he recognized that the former will to work at his old interests had gone. It had to be a very special event that could blow the old fires into a flame.

The last major excursion James made from his quiet retreat was to the Fourth General Conference of the International Association of Universities, held in Tokyo in September 1965. Appropriately, for his last appearance in his old position centre-stage, the occasion was one of unusual magnificence. The report of the conference, a style of document not usually given to descriptive phrasing, recorded the setting.

No university has ever seen within its precincts so large a concourse of Rectors, Presidents and Vice-Chancellors as the University of Tokyo during the Association's Fourth General Conference – As the inaugural ceremony began, in the crowded Yasuda Amphitheatre, introduced by Japanese music of subtle and mysterious power, this impressive newcomer among academic occasions of the world seemed both heir and herald, appropriately charged with memories and hope.

When Cyril James rose to express a brief welcome to the members of the conference, he was flanked by the Crown Prince and Princess of Japan, Eisaku Sato, the Japanese prime minister, Umekichi Nakamura, the minister of education, and René Maheu, the director-general of UNESCO. Before him were gathered the leaders of education from all the Western countries, many of the Eastern-bloc countries, and a great many, too, of the so-called "Third-World" developing countries. The roll-call of institutions evoked a recollection of the most famous place-names in the history of learning – Bologna, Rome, Paris, Brussels, Oxford, Harvard, Moscow, Leningrad, Prague, Berlin. Also present were representatives of Mexico and Latin America: of Delhi, Lahore and the sub-continent; of Southeast Asia, Africa and the Islamic schools; of Australia and the islands of the South-west Pacific; even China was represented by Taipeh. From these great centres of learning, old and very new, men and women had come to join their Japanese colleagues in the discussion and investigation of their common interest, and it was to this great company that, after the greetings of the dignitaries, Cyril James rose again to give his presidential address.

This was not the time for expansiveness, flights of fancy, or reminiscence. It is interesting to compare the address to this conference with the more leisurely, more allusive, more entertaining address to the Federation of Catholic Universities in Washington, two years earlier. This time the speech was designed to set a tone of hard-headed thinking, to encourage business-like discussion, and to remind the assembly of the serious nature of the conference business.

Universities in Europe came to birth almost a thousand years ago. If we trace the origins of our academic institutions still further back – the great Islamic universities, the academies of classical Greece and the ancient Buddhist foundations in Asia – their history lengthens to twenty-five centuries.

That is a long period, half the history of civilization on this planet, but I venture to suggest that never before has there assembled in one place so ecumenical a group of university men and women. Every continent is represented, every race, every religion and every major academic discipline. We are met to renew old friendships and to make new friends. We have come together to exchange ideas and to find solutions to our own problems from the experience of others. Most important of all, we demonstrate by this meeting that universities in all parts of the world share a common heritage and recognize a common purpose, to which the three major themes of this Conference are related.

Let me address myself to that common purpose, in the attempt to offer a framework for our discussions. I do so humbly before my peers in this audience. Many able men, from Plato to Ibn Kaldun to Cardinal Newman and President Clark Kerr, have tried to formulate the ideal of the perfect university. There are sharp contrasts among the patterns they have formulated! All of you are familiar with the vast body of literature on the subject. Most of you have formulated clearly your individual working hypothesis.

My task is one of selection rather than of creative originality. I suggest to you that at this moment in human history, when knowledge is exploding at an unprecedented rate to endow mankind with opportunities undreamed of in earlier generations, *the purpose of the university is to educate men and women who will promote the development of society to the highest attainable level.*

This role of the university in the development of the community is one of our major themes for discussion, and the working papers relating to the Unesco-I.A.U. study of South-East Asia are intended to throw light on a world-wide problem by the analysis of conditions in nine countries. If you accept the working hypothesis of that study, and the implications of my definition of the purpose of the university, we can at once eliminate from consideration a lot of things that have been said about universities in the past. They are *not* ivory towers, or cloistered oases of peace providing escape from the problems and frustrations of the contemporary world. They are the battlefields (often of fiercely contending forces) on which the victories will largely determine the future pattern of our society.

This was, from first to last, James' estimate of the university, and possibly no one has ever ranked its importance in society so highly or given himself so wholeheartedly to its service. James set out to serve McGill, but through McGill he reached out to that other, ideal university, which is the *mater alma atque inspirans* of the human race. He was indeed "protagonist of higher learning throughout the world."

But what he had to give he had given, and after steering the Tokyo conference through efficient and profitable sessions (in great contrast to the inefficiency of Istanbul in 1955 and the politicizing of Mexico in 1960), he had to leave the implementation of its decisions, and the realization of its visions, to others. He returned to Piper's Croft, to his garden, and to the small concerns of everyday life. He allowed himself to be initiated as a Mason, not because the rituals or the organization particularly appealed to him, but because his friend Bertie Challoner, and some of the other men whom he appreciated among his neighbours, were also members. But the craft never became a great enthusiasm of his. More to his taste was the expanding work of Oxfam, the organization seeking to relieve hunger, whether in the next street or across the world. He served conscientiously and effectively for several years on its executive committee.

It is clear in retrospect that James had burned himself out at McGill, at the early age of fifty-nine. Had he continued the other two years he had wanted, he would no doubt have flogged himself to execute his duties conscientiously, and would have performed his role to general satisfaction, possibly with some lessened enthusiasm and energy for extramural activities. The university had become the addiction necessary to keep his nervous powers fully charged. But when he was deprived of that stimulus, the fires died down quickly. For occasions such as the visit to Washington in 1963 or the final performance in Tokyo in 1965, they could be briefly rekindled, but as time passed he found increasingly at Piper's Croft a deeply satisfying way of life. It was here that his love of nature, especially of its flowers, and his quick response to the beauty of a landscape could find expression. His last love-affair was with Piper's Croft, where he could not only cherish beauty but tend and enhance it. The house and garden were the great satisfaction of his retirement.

But the question that had begun to haunt him long before his resignation from McGill became a reality still remained: What should he do? What worthwhile task within his competence and circumstance could he undertake? The idea of writing an autobiography which he had been urged to undertake by more than one of his friends and visitors, did not initially appeal to him. As he looked back over the years, he realized what a daunting task it would be. Nevertheless, he began to gather papers together and commenced the writing about 1970, five years after the Tokyo conference.

The work proceeded slowly, but, from the style of reminiscence, it seems the author derived a good deal of pleasure from it. However, his work on it was sporadic; probably his own sense of weakened powers and Irene's increasing dependence on him made it easier for him to forget the task for considerable periods. He had reached only the early years of his Pennsylvania days when on 3 May 1973, at his beloved home, he suffered a heart-attack and before help could be called, died.

Wordsworth speaks of "that best part of a good man's life, the little nameless, unremembered acts of kindness and of love." There were many such actions in Cyril James' life, generally known only to the recipient, for he had a shy way of doing kindness by stealth. A get-well card, a note of condolence to a bereaved friend, a small grant from the Principal's Discretionary Fund (the capital provided by another man who did much good covertly, J.W. McConnell) these were small things that found their way into no record. Mrs McMurray, who worked closely with James, was foremost in saying she had over the years received many of his kindnesses, and certainly she knew more of the "nameless, unremembered acts" than anyone other than himself.

In his will James left most of his personal fortune to his family, the children of his brother and of Irene's sister. But his precious books, the Cleve Horn portrait of himself given him by the medical faculty, the original Rodin cast of "The Thinker," and his academic gowns and hoods he gave to McGill. He also gave one-eighth of his own fortune to the Faculty of Religious Studies, that part of the academic enterprise he had done much personally to secure for McGill. As for Piper's Croft, if and when he or Irene could enjoy it no longer, it was to be sold, and the proceeds, together with the rest of the capital of the Cyril James Retirement Fund, were to be returned to the university, to be used as the Board of Governors saw fit.[3] Cyril James truly loved McGill.

His funeral took place in a simple service at the Chilterns Crematorium, Amersham. The service used the plain unadorned liturgy of the Church of England he had loved as a boy. The priest appeared to have no personal knowledge of the man he was burying: no eulogy was offered, no reference was made to the deceased by name. He had become simply "our dear brother here departed." The chapel was well-filled with Amersham neighbours, Masonic brethren, and representatives of the Oxfam Executive Committee. By good fortune, the author of this biography was passing through London on his way to the Middle East and was able to be present and to represent McGill University. James had asked that his ashes might rest at McGill in the Osler Library, which had been rebuilt in the Medical Sciences Building on the old site of 1200 Pine Avenue. Some difficulties, however, presented themselves regarding this arrangement, and the university chose instead to place the ashes in the wall of the University Chapel, the lovely place of worship in the faculty that James had evidently regarded as peculiarly his own. He had attended services there and had preached, more than once, the baccalaureate sermon at spring convocation. On a campus much changed since his own days, this would undoubtedly remain for him a recognized and beloved place. The memorial plate on the wall says only: "In Memoriam Frank Cyril James 1903–1973 Principal of this University 1939–1962" – a modest end to a career the influence of which subsists strongly in his university, and indeed throughout the world, wherever students gather around professors who discover new truths, or wrestle with old truths and make them fresh again.

Irene remained attached all her life to the young man she had chosen while a schoolgirl at St Mary's Church, Stoke Newington, though he led her to unforeseen experiences, through some good days, and some that for her were not so good. But finally he came home with her, and she had ten years of domestic quiet, until he died, and then again she followed him, not many days later.

Notes

CHAPTER 1: EARLY INFLUENCES

1 This quotation and all those that follow in this chapter, unless identified as from another source, are taken from the unpublished James autobiography.

2 i.e., per thousand pupils in attendance at LCC elementary schools. See Flann Campbell, *Eleven Plus and All That* (London: Watts Company 1956), 88.

3 The Good Templars was a church-oriented social organization for young and old of both sexes; the Alliance of Honour was a movement organized among young men in Anglican parishes.

4 Janet Beveridge, *An Epic of Clare Market* (London: G. Bell 1960), 6.

CHAPTER 2: YOUNG PHILADELPHIAN

1 In 1929 the authorities decided that his 1923 entry had been verified in 1925 as legal for a non-quota resident alien visa – which sounds very cumbersome but apparently satisfied all concerned. Letter of American Consul in London, dated 10 August 1929; James Scrapbook I.

2 Quotations in the following pages unidentified as to source are taken from the unpublished James autobiography.

3 He could not receive the degree at this time, however, because he had not received his undergraduate degree, the London B Com. These matters were not completed until June 1925 when he returned briefly to England and passed the B Com final examinations. Presumably to save complicated explanations later, he listed his degrees as B Com (1924) and MA (1925); the reverse would have been nearer the truth. In fact he receive both his MA and Ph D degrees in 1926.

4 W. Herbert Burk. *The Valley Forge Guide.* North Wales, PA: N.B. Nuss 1908; seventh edition, 1928.
5 Carl F. Barchfield (Wharton 1935), letter to author, 4 May 1985.
6 Charles T. Zelter (Wharton 1936), letter to author, n.d., 1985.
7 Thomas P. Townsend (Wharton 1939), letter to author, 29 April 1985.
8 Memorandum of Deposit, James Papers, McGill Archives, 28 September 1970.
9 Memorandum of Deposit.
10 A copy of the text of the lecture is in History of McGill Project File 2.4.11.

CHAPTER 3: RISING STAR

1 Denis Brogan, *The Era of Franklin D. Roosevelt* (New Haven and Oxford: Yale University Press 1950), 53.
2 Brogan, *The Era of Franklin D. Roosevelt*, 42.
3 The maximum figure was originally set at $5,000.
4 *Philadelphia Record*, 30 October 1929.
5 *American Economic Review* 21, No. 1 (March 1931): 155–6.
6 James Scrapbook I, 9 October 1931.
7 *Public Ledger*, Philadelphia, 3 October 1931.
8 *The Times Literary Supplement*, London, 3 October, 1932.
9 *Journal of Business*, Chicago (October 1932): 400.
10 *Annals of the American Academy* 165 (1933): 231.
11 Letter, 3 January 1933; James Scrapbook I.
12 James Scrapbook I, 26 February 1933.
13 *Public Ledger, Philadelphia, 23 November 1933.*
14 The list was published 26 December 1933 by, *inter alia, the Wall Street Journal*, New York, *The New York Times*, and the Philadelphia papers.
15 *The Inquirer*, Philadelphia, 15 May 1935.
16 See for example, the editorial in the *Philadelphia Inquirer*, 15 March 1936; also the *Public Evening Ledger*, Philadelphia, 7 May 1936.
17 *The Bulletin*, Philadelphia, 12 June 1936.
18 Diary comment, 24 June 1936; from 1 June of this year James began hand written diary comments on broad sheets of looseleaf unlined paper, on which other materials could be pasted or whole items interleaved. The comments are intermittent and sometimes break off for several weeks or months. They continue until two years after his retirement.
19 *The Southern Banker* (Atlanta, GA), August 1936.
20 Diary, 9 July 1936.
21 Diary, 29 June 1936.
22 Diary, 11 July 1936.
23 Diary, 15 July 1936.

24 Diary, 28 June 1936.
25 Florrie seems to have immigrated to Canada a year or two before Cyril left for Philadelphia.
26 Report to the Reserve City Bankers' Association, August 1936.
27 Diary, 21 August 1936. In the family Irene was known by the nick-name Bay.
28 Diary, 22 September 1936.
29 Diary, 16 and 21 February 1936.
30 F. Cyril James. *The Growth of the Chicago Banks*. 2 vols. New York and London: Harper and Brothers 1938. Reprinted in the Allan Nevin's "Reprints in American Economic History" series (New York: Harper and Row 1969). Foreword by Fritz Edlich, Emeritus Professor, Harvard University.
31 *Chicago American*, 24 October 1938.
32 *New York Daily News*, 18 November 1938.
33 Diary, 23 December 1936.
34 *American Economic Review*, 29 (1939): 398–400.
35 *Journal of Political Economy*, 47 (1939): 421–3.
36 James, *The Growth of Chicago Banks*, Vol. 1 (Allan Nevin's Reprint Series, New York: Harper and Row 1969), xiii.

CHAPTER 4: NORTH TO CANADA

1 Diary, 11 March 1939.
2 See S.B. Frost *For the Advancement of Learning, Vol. 2: McGill University 1893–1971* (Montreal and Kingston: McGill-Queen's University Press 1980) 206–8.
3 Ibid. 151–3.
4 Diary, 6 April 1939.
5 This quotation and others following that are not otherwise designated as to source are from the James diaries.
6 The salary was finally agreed at an even higher figure – $15,000 plus a tax-free $3,500 entertainment allowance.
7 E.A. Collard, Ed., *The McGill You Knew: An Anthology of Memories, 1920–60* (Don Mills, ON: Longman 1975), 251.
8 Frost, *Advancement*, Vol. 2, 217–19.
9 This is the legal name of what is generally known as McGill University.
10 Diary, 8 February 1940.
11 The Installation Address, 12 January 1940.
12 Charles Hendel was leaving McGill to accept an appointment at Yale – James was losing another trusted adviser. The new dean of arts and science was Professor Cyrus Macmillan.

13 The Hon. Victor Doré, superintendent of education for the Province of Quebec. At this time there was no minister or ministry of education in the province.

14 Oskar Holecki, Polish refugee historian; founder of McGill Polish Institute and Library.

15 Principal's Agenda. Executive and Finance Committee, 28 March 1941. But some of the students did not give up so easily; there were further protests, which apparently died away during the summer vacation – see Diary 5, May 1941. For the drunken party, see Diary, 22 and 23 April 1941.

16 J.S. Thomson, *Yesteryears at the University of Saskatchewan, 1937–1949* (Saskatoon: University of Saskatchewan Press 1969), 37.

17 J.L. Ralston, minister of national defence; J.G. Gardiner, minister of agriculture and also, 1940–1, minister of national war services.

18 H.J. Cody was president of the University of Toronto, 1932–44.

CHAPTER 5: COMMITTEE ON
RECONSTRUCTION

1 It is possible that the suggestion of the need for such a committee came from James in the first place. It was after he proposed to Arnold Heeney, clerk of the Privy Council, that a small committee of university presidents would be very helpful in the matter of governmental–academic relations that such a committee was established, with James as one of the members. A similar suggestion, made either to Heeney or to Ian Mackenzie, minister of pensions and national health (1939–44), may well have been the genesis of the Committee on Postwar Reconstruction.

2 R.A. Young, "Reining in James: The limits of the Task Force," *Canadian Public Administration* 24, No. 4 (1981): 596–611.

3 Quoted in Young, "Reining in James," 598.

4 Ibid.

5 James Office Files, "Committee on Reconstruction," *Basic Memorandum* (First Draft), 1. McGill University Archives, Administrative Records 1940–62 (Restricted). Some of these papers are available also at Public Archives of Canada, R.G. 19, Vol. 3583, "Committee on Reconstruction."

6 *Basic memorandum*, Fourth Draft, 5.

7 Young, "Reining in James," 599.

8 See p. 53.

9 Geoffrey Shakespeare was MP for Norwich, 1929–45, parliamentary secretary to the Board of Overseas Trade, and chairman, 1940–2, of the Children's Overseas Reception Board. Ivison MacAdam was secretary and director-general of the Royal Institute of International Affairs, 1929–55.

10 A former Conservative member of parliament, active in the House of Lords.

11 Arthur Greenwood, long-time socialist politician, formerly minister of health in Ramsay MacDonald's second Labour government (1929–31), was currently in the War Cabinet as minister without portfolio. Sir John Reith, later Lord Reith, had made his name as the high-minded director of the British Broadcasting Corporation (1922–38) and was in 1941 minister of works and buildings.

12 J.W. Pickersgill, *The Mackenzie King Record, Vol. 1: 1939–44* (Toronto: University of Toronto Press 1960) 317.

13 Mackintosh was later to become principal of Queen's University, 1951–61, and a close collaborator with James in the work of the National Conference of Canadian Universities.

14 Vincent Massey, Canadian high commissioner in London, later governor-general of Canada (1952–9).

15 D.H. Miller-Barstow, *Beatty and the CPR* (Toronto: McClelland and Stewart 1951), 151–2.

16 The phrase is taken from the Roosevelt-Churchill "Atlantic Charter."

17 Waldorf Astor, second viscount, married Nancy Witcher Langhorne of Virginia, USA; he was MP, 1910–19, when she succeeded to his constituency and became the first woman MP in Britain. He was chairman of the Royal Institute of International Affairs; she was a prominent political hostess.

18 William Maxwell Aitken, first Lord Beaverbrook, was the Canadian-born newspaper magnate who served in the War Cabinet, 1940–1, as minister of aircraft production and in 1942 as lend-lease administrator in the US.

19 Sir Richard Stafford Cripps, socialist politician, ambassador to USSR, 1940–2; returned to England to enter War Cabinet and succeed Beaverbrook as minister of aircraft production.

20 Sir Alfred Zimmern was a prominent lawyer who specialized in international law.

21 British colonial administrator who nurtured the concept of a federal world order; one of the founders of the Royal Institute of International Affairs.

22 *The Times*, London, 25 February 1942.

23 Ibid.

24 Brittain was a former vice-president of the Royal Commonwealth Society and although not a McGill graduate he was co-founder and honorary president of the McGill Society of Great Britain.

25 Archdeacon F.G. Scott was an outstanding wartime chaplain and a minor poet in his own right. He was the father of Frank Scott, the jurist and poet, and of Chief Justice W.B. Scott of the Quebec Superior Court.

26 See Miller-Barstow, *Beatty*, 169–72.
27 Young, "Reining in James," 600.
28 Ibid., 601.
29 Ibid.
30 Leonard Marsh, *Report of Social Security for Canada* (Ottawa: The King's Printer, 1943), Prefatory Note.
31 *Saturday Night*, 27 March 1943.
32 Brigitte Kitchen, *Journal of Canadian Studies* 21 No. 2 (1986): 47.
33 Young, "Reining in James," 597.
34 Ibid., 604.
35 Ibid., 605.
36 *Report of the Advisory Committee on Reconstruction*, submitted October 1943, tabled in the House of Commons January 1944, and published by the King's Printer, Ottawa, 1944. The citation is from p. 2. Attached were six sub-committee reports on Agricultural Policy, Publicly Financed Construction Projects, Housing and Community Planning, Postwar Unemployment Opportunities, and (rather remarkably) Postwar Problems of Women.

CHAPTER 6: CONTRIBUTING TO WAR

1 At this time James began dictating lengthy daily journal entries, and this and the following citation are typical excerpts. Mrs McMurray typed out the entries until 1948 when the practice petered out. The occasional hand-written diary notes continued throughout the period and are of course much more frank and revealing. All subsequent references unidentified as to source are from these journal entries and diary notes.
2 The Arts Building caretaker Bill Gentleman was generally held to be infallible in his knowledge of student or faculty opinion with regard to campus-pump politics.
3 In 1943 there were again 155 summer registrations, in 1944 only 93, and in 1945, 114.
4 The information that follows relating to "the 1943 Manpower Crisis" is largely drawn from Gwendoline Pilkington, *Speaking with One Voice: Universities in Dialogue with Government*, (Montreal: History of McGill Project 1983), 28–34.
5 Pilkington, *Speaking with One Voice*, 29.
6 *Globe and Mail*, Toronto, 24 December 1942.
7 President of Manitoba 1934–44, of Toronto 1945–57. He served as secretary of state for external affairs, 1957–9.
8 English-speaking Canada voted 80 per cent in favour of conscription, while Quebec voted 72 per cent against.

9 Pilkington, *Speaking with One Voice*, 28–33.

10 Watson Kirkconnell, *A Slice of Canada, Memoirs* (Toronto: University of Toronto Press 1967), 235. Kirkconnell became president of Acadia University in 1948.

11 F.W. Gibson, *To Serve and Yet Be Free, Queen's University. Vol II: 1917– 1961.* (Montreal and Kingston: McGill-Queen's University Press 1983) 207. Wallace had earlier appeared to be less concerned, but evidently had subsequently changed his mind.

12 Gibson, *To Serve and Yet Be Free*, 212.

13 F.J. Hatch, *The Aerodrome of Democracy: Canada and the Commonwealth Air Training Plan, 1939–45* (Ottawa: Directorate of History, Department of National Defence 1983), 181.

14 As Kirkconnell gladly acknowledges, Toronto and McGill were the strongest supporters financially of the newly-founded HRCC. (Kirkconnell, *A Slice of Canada*, 246).

CHAPTER 7: PREPARING FOR PEACE

1 D.H. Miller-Barstow, *Beatty and the CPR* (Toronto: McClelland and Stewart 1951), 170–2.

2 See S.B. Frost, *For the Advancement of Learning. Vol. 2: McGill University 1893–1971* (Montreal and Kingston: McGill-Queen's University Press 1980), 187–209.

3 See Roger Magnuson, *A Brief History of Quebec Education,* (Montreal: Harvest House Montreal 1980), 38–101.

4 He had agreed to write a speech for the governor-general, who was to open the proceedings. The other two were the presentations of Roosevelt and Churchill for their degrees.

5 Eden was the British foreign secretary and Leathers the minister of transport.

6 This and the Churchill citation are taken from a typed account of the convocation written by the university registrar T.H. Matthews and included in the James Private Papers. There are pencilled annotations and slight corrections in James' handwriting. The reference in the second citation to "students of our sweet English tongue" is a quotation from James Elroy Flecker's poem "To a poet of a thousand years hence," but "sweet" does not sound well in the context; James should also have avoided a pretentious word such as "climacteric"; but both citations, produced at less than twenty-four hours' notice, deserve high marks.

7 James McGill in his rank of Lt Colonel had been the first commanding officer of the First Battalion of the Montreal Militia, which was later incorporated into the Canadian Grenadier Guards.

8 M. Howe, ed. *The Correspondence of Mr. Justice [Oliver Wendell] Holmes and Sir Frederick Pollock.* Cambridge, MA: Harvard University Press 1941.

9 James had received a letter from the chairman of the Canadian National Committee of the International Geographical Union, in September 1943, urging the establishment of a department of geography at McGill. This may have been one of the contributing influences. See J. Brian Bird, "Geography at McGill," History of McGill Project files.

10 Raleigh Parkin was a business executive (Sun Life Assurance Co.), author, and member of the Canadian Institute of International Affairs. He served as governor of the Arctic Institute of North America, 1945–6.

11 Harold Adams Innis, professor of political economy, Toronto, 1920–1952, best-known as author of *The Fur Trade of Canada.* Toronto: University of Toronto 1930; rev. ed. 1956.

12 Despite the unfavourable judgment on Trevor Lloyd at this stage, he became a leading figure in northern research in the United States and Canada, and came to McGill in 1959 as a full professor in the Department of Geography to direct the university's vigorous program in the Arctic.

13 F.K. Hare later became chairman of the department, and in 1962–4 served as dean of the Faculty of Arts and Science before leaving McGill to become, after a term as Master of Birkbeck Hall in London and president of the University of British Columbia, professor of geography and physics at Toronto in 1969.

14 Sir James Irvine, long-time principal of St Andrew's University, Scotland, had recently been appointed chairman of the Committee of Higher Education in the West Indies.

15 The committee chairman was N.A.M. MacKenzie of UBC; for his major role in these matters see P.B. Waite, *Lord of Point Grey, Larry Mac-Kenzie of U.B.C.,* (Vancouver: University of British Columbia Press 1987) 102–3.

16 J.S. Thomson, *Yesteryears at Saskatchewan, 1937–1949,* (Saskatoon: University of Saskatchewan Press 1969), 77–8.

17 Cyrus Eaton was a steel-maker, financier, and, in his later years, philanthropist.

CHAPTER 8: INSTANT COLLEGE

1 N.A.M. MacKenzie at UBC was facing the same challenge of numbers, and he turned to the army huts being vacated all over the province; he carted, hauled, even floated huts to his Point Grey site.

Both solutions had advantages, but on the whole, McGill came out ahead. See P.B. Waite, *Lord of Point Grey, Larry MacKenzie of U.B.C.* (Vancouver: University of British Columbia Press 1988), 124.

2 A town twenty-five miles southeast of Montreal on the Richelieu River.

3 Gillson, professor of mathematics, was the first vice-principal of the college. He left McGill in 1948 to become president of the University of Manitoba.

4 *McGill Reporter*, "Dawson College," 13, No. 11, 19 November 1980.

5 V.M. Jolivet and D.H. Kennedy, "Dawson College, 1945–1950." Engineering class term paper, March 1950, History of McGill Project, File B 10.

6 E.A. Collard, ed., *The McGill You Knew, An Anthology of Memories, 1920–60* (Don Mills, ON: Longman 1975), 258.

7 Craig Carleton, professor of civil engineering, was assistant to the vice-principal at Dawson College.

8 Hector Hetherington, principal of Glasgow University, who became increasingly one of Cyril's friends and admirers. Typically of his friends, Hetherington was some twenty years older than James.

9 Principal, 1855–93, thirty-eight years; James would have had to stay in office until 1978 when he would have been 75!

10 The ideals of the socialist political party, the Cooperative Commonwealth Federation.

11 Pall Mall, the avenue leading up to Buckingham Palace.

12 In the event, there was yet another reconciliation, which fortunately proved permanent.

13 The illness required much longer treatment than the prognosis at that time suggested but finally reached a happy conclusion.

CHAPTER 9: WIDER HORIZONS

1 H. Keith Markell, *The Faculty of Religious Studies 1948–1978* (published by the faculty, 1979), 17.

2 Probably M. Abdul Basir Kahn, Ph D 1949 (Parasitology).

3 Transcript of press interview, 9 January 1950; included in James' papers.

CHAPTER 10: IRRESISTIBLE LOGIC

1 P.B. Waite, *Lord of Point Grey: Larry MacKenzie of U.B.C.* (Vancouver: University of British Columbia Press 1987), 145. Waite cites N.A.M. MacKenzie and D.C. Rowat, "Federal Government and Higher Education in Canada," *Canadian Journal of Economics and Political Science*, 16, No. 3 (August 1950): 354.

2 The benefit of this fine effort was offset by the need in 1951 to build the Physical Sciences Centre (now named the Frank Dawson Adams Building) and in 1952 to build the new Redpath Library. Together, the two buildings cost approximately $3 million.

3 *Proceedings*, NCCU (Ottawa 1949), 76.

4 Gwendoline Pilkington, *Speaking with One Voice: Universities in Dialogue with Government* (Montreal: History of McGill Project 1983), 54–6.

5 For an incisive sketch of Vincent Massey and for an engaging account of the work of the commission and of N.A.M. MacKenzie's part in its deliberations (he was then president of UBC) see Waite, *Lord of Point Grey*, 146–56. The other members were Arthur Surveyeur, a civil engineer from Montreal, Georges-Henri Lévesque, dean of social sciences at Laval, and Hilda Neatby, professor of history in the University of Saskatchewan. The commission was obviously stacked in favour of the universities.

6 See *Proceedings*, NCCU, 1950, 10–14. Gwendoline Pilkington gives a detailed account of these developments in her doctoral thesis, *A History of the National Conference of Canadian Universities 1911–1961* (Toronto 1974), 508–40.

7 Pilkington, *Speaking with One Voice*, 64.

8 *Annual Report*, (McGill University 1949–50), 19.

9 Sir George Williams College had only recently (1948) received degree-granting status.

CHAPTER 11: MANY DISTRACTIONS

1 This must allude to some belligerent memorandum on the subject from Mrs Mac, who never hesitated to express her opinion on any subject.

2 Presumably McConnell had prepared notes for what he was going to say and James asked for a copy of them, which he stored with his diary notes. The style is very characteristic of McConnell.

3 Backus, for many years president of the McGill Graduates' Society of Great Britain, was a prominent London psychiatrist.

4 See E.A. Collard, ed., *The McGill You Knew, An Anthology of Memories, 1920–60* (Don Mills, ON: Longman 1975), 261–2.

5 H.M. Tomlinson, essayist and novelist, was one of James' early and favourite authors. *Gifts of Fortune, With Some Hints for Those About to Travel* (New York: Harper 1926) prompted critic F.P. Mayer to write: "Tomlinson has never sought eternal youth – he is the eternal youth." Tomlinson was in no small measure responsible for James' love of travel.

6 "Although he spoke French fluently, he usually spoke in English when among his French-speaking colleagues, like other English-

speaking colleagues in the 1950s; and Monseigneur Parent, who was rector of Université Laval, once told me that having heard Dr. James speak only in English on so many occasions, he was taken by surprise when he heard the Principal speak excellent French to the Ambassador from Paris." David Munroe, director of the Macdonald School for teachers, in Collard, *The McGill You Knew*, 257.

7 Abdul Hamid II of the Ottoman Empire (1842–1918); Kaiser Wilhelm II of Germany (1859–1941).

8 A.P.D. Thompson, executive dean, Faculty of Medicine and Dentistry, Birmingham, UK; Herman B. Wells, president, Indiana State University, US.

9 Kemal Ataturk banned the wearing of the fez in 1925 as a gesture of liberation from Turkey's Islamic past.

10 Jean Sarrailh, rector, University of Paris; president, IAU, 1950–5.

11 R.G.K. Morrison, an engineering professor greatly interested in sports.

CHAPTER 12: ACHIEVEMENT FOR McGILL

1 "The McGill Association of University Teachers" – from an historical review prepared by Professor Fred Howes in December 1962 (issued, n.d., by MAUT). See also J.R. Mallory, "Teachers' Union," *Queen's Quarterly* LXI, No. 1 (Spring 1954): 53–62.

2 S.B. Frost, *For the Advancement of Learning: McGill University 1801–1893* (Montreal and Kingston: McGill-Queen's University Press 1980), 212–13.

3 E.F. Sheffield, "Canadian University and College Enrolment Projected to 1965," *Proceedings of the NCCU*, 1955.

4 Gwendoline Pilkington, *Speaking with One Voice: Universities in Dialogue with Government* (Montreal: History of McGill Project 1983), 70.

5 The author of this biography was one of the deans present at the discussion.

6 Pierre Trudeau, "Federal Grants to Universities," *Cité Libre* (February 1957). Trudeau republished the article in *Federalism and the French Canadians* (Toronto: Macmillan 1968), 79–102. He became prime minister of Canada that same year (1968).

7 Pilkington, *Speaking with One Voice*, 92–3.

8 Cited in Pilkington, *Speaking with One Voice*, 136. Johnson made his remark at the Federal–Provincial Conference, 1966.

CHAPTER 13: ACHIEVEMENT BEYOND McGILL

1 President of Indonesia from the proclamation of independence from Dutch rule in 1945 until 1968.

2 Correspondence with author, 16 November 1989.

3 Thomas Leeper died in October 1957 and Louise Leeper in March 1958.
4 See P.B. Waite, *Lord of Point Grey,* (Vancouver: University of British Columbia Press 1987), 149.
5 Rector, University of Brussels.
6 Rector, University of Istanbul.
7 This, it will be noticed, was before the Sauvé-Diefenbaker accord of late 1959, which permitted the salary increases of 1960.
8 F. Cyril James, *On Understanding Russia,* Toronto: University of Toronto Press 1959.
9 Ibid., 4.
10 In the uncertainty of the present (1990) Gorbachev period, it may be even more important to remember that perception, and to judge Gorbachev's probabilities of success in its light.
11 James, *On Understanding Russia,* 63.
12 C.M. McDougall, McGill registrar and secretary of Senate, who also attended the congress.
13 A copy of McDougall's account of the presidential election is to be found in the History of McGill Project's file 2.4.11, item 44, entitled "Victory in Mexico."

CHAPTER 14: RESIGNATION

1 E.A. Collard, ed., *The McGill You Knew: An Anthology of Memories, 1920–60* (Don Mills, ON: Longman 1975), 262; D. McMurray, *Four Principals of McGill,* (Montreal: History of McGill Project 1974), 51–2.
2 In Collard, *The McGill You Knew,* 257, David Munroe, director of the Macdonald School for Teachers, 1949–63, refers to "some restlessness and criticism among his colleagues" because of the principal's absences. He cites instances of deans also being chairmen of departments and refers to a "doubling-up" of offices; but that practice was traditional at McGill and would have continued whether James travelled or not. Most academics knew of the principal's presence or absence only from what they read in the newspapers, and, it has to be said, were little affected one way or the other.
3 Powell was nominated for re-election as chancellor and served until 1964.
4 Piper's Croft was the home he was negotiating to buy in England.
5 We have not been able to identify the source of these lines; they may be of James' own composing.

CHAPTER 15: AFTER YEARS

1 MacKenzie, the president of UBC, had been pushed out of his position rather messily only nine months before James was dropped from

McGill; see P.B. Waite, *Lord of Point Grey*, (Vancouver: University of British Columbia Press 1987), 190–3.

2 Director-general of UNESCO.

3 The Cyril James Retirement Fund has, since 1975, sustained, not the academic salaries, but the research and secretarial expenses of the History of McGill Project – a subject that interested James greatly.

Index